USING FABRICS FOR FUN

Books by the same author

New Manual of Sewing, *E. J. Arnold*
Making Stage Costume for Amateurs, *Routledge & Kegan Paul*
Soft Furnishing: A Practical Manual for the Home Upholsterer, *Routledge & Kegan Paul*
Needlecraft for Juniors, *Routledge & Kegan Paul*
Making and Dressing Figures, *Routledge & Kegan Paul*
Primary Embroidery Stitches and Designs, *Routledge & Kegan Paul*
Knitting for Pleasure, *Collins*
Blackwork Embroidery, *Mills & Boon*
Weaving is Fun, *Mills & Boon*
Performing Toys, *Mills & Boon*

Teaching aids

Look and Stitch, *E. J. Arnold*
Sewing for Pleasure: Gifts, *E. J. Arnold*
Creative Needlecraft Cards, *Macmillan*
Set 1: Things to make
Set 2: Things to make
Set 3: Basic Processes
Set 4: Stitchery

USING FABRICS FOR FUN
ALICE WHITE

MILLS & BOON LTD London

First published in Great Britain 1971 by Mills & Boon Limited
17–19 Foley Street, London W1A 1DR
Reprinted 1972

© Alice V. White 1971

All rights reserved. No part of this publication may be reproduced, stored in a retrieval system, or transmitted in any form or by any means, electronic, mechanical, photocopying, recording or otherwise, without the prior permission of the copyright owner.

ISBN 0 263.51595.8

Printed in Great Britain by
Fletcher & Son Ltd, Norwich

ACKNOWLEDGEMENTS

I wish to thank all the teachers who have attended my refresher courses and who have encouraged me to go ahead and write this introductory book on textile crafts. I am once again grateful to Christopher Roberts for helping me by doing many of the illustrations in this book.

CONTENTS

Introduction 1

Fabrics 2

Tools and equipment 4

Flat and cone figures 5

Collage 10

Toying with fabrics and threads 24

3-D patchwork 31

Things you can do with a circle 34

Things you can do with a triangle 42

Binca canvas 45

Tie-and-dye 55

Fabric printing 78

Embroidery 98

Flat maths 110

Making up of fabrics 120

General information on stitches and processes 130

Index 135

Introduction

It can be great fun to destroy fabrics, for instance to fray them and pile up the threads in certain colours, and then use them again on a collage; or to use part of the fabric which remains after a lot of the threads have been removed. I have only touched lightly on this area, both in the use of frayed fabrics, e.g. 3-D Yo-Yo panel, and animal heads and insect bodies.

Not sufficient use is made of puppets, the clothes of which can be great fun to design, either with fabric printing or tie-and-dye, or even by designing puppets made solely from tied-and-dyed fabrics.

Age is unimportant as far as doing tie-and-dye is concerned because you can use clothes-pegs to hold the tie-and-dye fabric firm even when you cannot tie fabrics securely. Your early examples may be used for collage and later on you can plan designs for toys or puppet clothes, etc. The same applies to fabric printing. The first prints may be made with a cork on a plain piece of fabric, and then this could be used for a puppet dress.

Although this is emphatically not a needlework book, I have included a small section on the making up of simple articles so that the work carried out in the creative design of textiles may be used for a specific purpose. I know it can be great fun just to print material, but it is equally enjoyable to realize how you can make an apron or beach-bag with your own design printed upon it.

There are times when certain pieces of fabric must be sewn together. I have included a section on basic stitches because if you try to do some items of sewing without any knowledge at all, the finished results may be poor. It is no use pretending that you do not need to learn how to fasten off a thread, when you discover that a piece of sewing has fallen apart.

Endless pleasure can be found in making full use of the materials available. I have tried to give an introduction to the use you can make of a wide range of textiles. Much use is made of adhesives today, but when stitchery is appropriate, it is used. It is not often fully realised what a wide range of designs can be produced from very few stitches.

Fabrics

WOVEN FABRICS

There are woven fabrics, i.e. materials made up from threads which go down the length of the fabric and threads which are threaded (woven) across the width. These fabrics may be closely woven, such as fine cotton, or loosely woven like tweed. When wool is woven with the threads close together and then treated in such a way that the threads shrink and mass together, the fabric is really felted. Great use is made of felted fabric in creative work when a piece of fabric which does not fray is required. Materials which do fray, however, can be used to great advantage in creative designs. Sometimes complete lengths of thread are removed and then applied to a background fabric with adhesive; or the fabric may be cut into shapes and small areas of the threads removed to give a lighter edge to a fabric.

Some fabrics have a pile, i.e. a depth of thickness which is soft to the touch, such as fur fabric, velvet, plush, etc. These fabrics can be incorporated into designs.

Canvas, Linden Beach or Binca can be purchased in a few colours. Its name may vary according to the manufacturer. Canvas is a woven fabric with holes evenly placed in the fabric.

Java canvas is a more finely woven fabric.

Gingham is a cotton fabric woven to produce a check design, usually in one colour with white.

Printed cotton; this should be closely woven, soft to handle and clearly printed. It need not be expensive, especially if purchased from a reputable firm. Beware of some sale bargains and fabrics which contain dressing. These usually feel very firm.

Plain fabrics. Choose a closely woven fabric but free from dressing. The cost will be slightly more than the printed fabrics.

Note: R.S. equals right side of material;
W.S. equals wrong side of material.

KNITTED FABRICS

A great many of the clothes we wear are knitted. A cardigan or jumper may be hand-knitted (this is most likely if the garment is thick). Most knitting is carried out on machines and perhaps you will have seen a knitting-machine in someone's home. The knitting carried out on machines is often much finer than hand-knitting and the garments we wear are usually made up from very finely knitted fabrics which are produced on very large machines. Jersey fabric is the name given to ordinary knitted fabrics from which underwear is often made and thicker jersey fabric may be used for outer garments. These fabrics do not fray but when a stitch is not secured at a seam, or a thread is broken, a stitch will run down and form a ladder. Stockings and tights can be good examples of this.

Double Jersey is knitted in such a way that the fabric will not ladder and this is therefore useful for some toys. It is, however, inclined to stretch and for this reason it may be backed with iron-on Vilene to keep the fabric firm. The seams of toys may be stitched on the outside as with felt.

Bonded Jersey is a jersey fabric backed with a firm fabric which will prevent stretching. These fabrics are ideal for toys and designs where a firm edge is required. There are various weights, e.g. very thick, medium or light weight but the thick would not be easy to sew or manipulate into small shapes. The thin fabric would be ideal for cone figures, toy designs, and even for some fabric printing. The printing inks suggested in this book, however, are only suitable for cottons if the fabric is to be washed. Other fabrics will not really be fast-dyed for washing.

NON-FRAY FABRICS

In the book the words "non-fray fabrics" are meant to include firm knitted fabrics or even woven fabrics which have been backed with iron-on Vilene.

SCRAP MATERIALS

A good range of scrap materials is essential and should include:

Thick loosely woven tweeds.
Smooth fabrics (perhaps shiny knitted jersey or woven material).
Thin transparent materials which may include nets and jersey fabrics of man-made fibres.
Plain and patterned fabrics. These may be woven or knitted, i.e. jersey fabrics. The patterned effect may be obtained from printing a design on a plain fabric, or

woven to give a raised design, or from colour and pattern introduced into the weave. All of these should show a wide range of colour.

Pile fabrics. These may be fur fabric, knitted or woven. Velvet, brushed nylon (this gives a raised effect), or any brushed fabric which has been in vogue.

Braids and Lace. These can be stored on cards as in a shop.

Beads. These can be stored in transparent containers, with buttons and sequins.

Some of these items may be obtained by purchasing decorated garments at a rummage sale.

Feathers. Some are very colourful and these can be collected from aviaries; feather-trimmed hats may be found at rummage sales. Feather dusters also often have colourful feathers.

Paper and Card. Sugar-paper is thin and cheap and usually obtainable in dull colours. Manilla card is a stiff card obtainable in a wide range of colours.

Threads. Embroidery cottons, thick and thin; knitting yarns, raffia (real and plastic); string of various thicknesses; unravelled threads, perhaps from fabrics or knitting.

Paste. Polycell paste made thick and kept in a screw-top jar. Apply with a brush or paste spreader.

Adhesive. Copydex or Bostik.

Tools and equipment

Very few tools are necessary for creative textile craft, but they should be of good quality.

1. Pair of sharp scissors with good points, total length to be 6 in. (15 cm).
2. A 12-in. (30-cm) ruler.
3. A selection of mercerised cottons.
4. Tailors' chalk, useful for marking on fabrics, especially felt.
5. Pins made of steel. Make a pincushion to wear on the wrist of the left hand. This makes it easy to pick up a pin when required.
6. Needles (Tapestry). These are thick with blunt ends, used for working on canvas.
   Needles (Crewel), Size 7, are used for most stitching.
7. Paste spreader (plastic).

Flat and cone figures

TEXTURE AND COLOUR

When you first look at fabrics you may be unaware of the wide range of texture. Some fabrics are smooth, like those we wear for underclothes; or may be thick with pile like sheep skin or fur, yet both may be man-made. Try using the variety of the texture of the fabrics to dress a figure.

FLAT FIGURES

The simplest form of figure is that in Fig. 1, which can be cut out from a piece of cardboard, maybe from a box which has contained a breakfast cereal. The figure is about 10 in. (25 cm) high and the arms can be cut out easily by cutting up from the skirt to the waist of the figure, and continuing until the arm shape can be clearly seen.

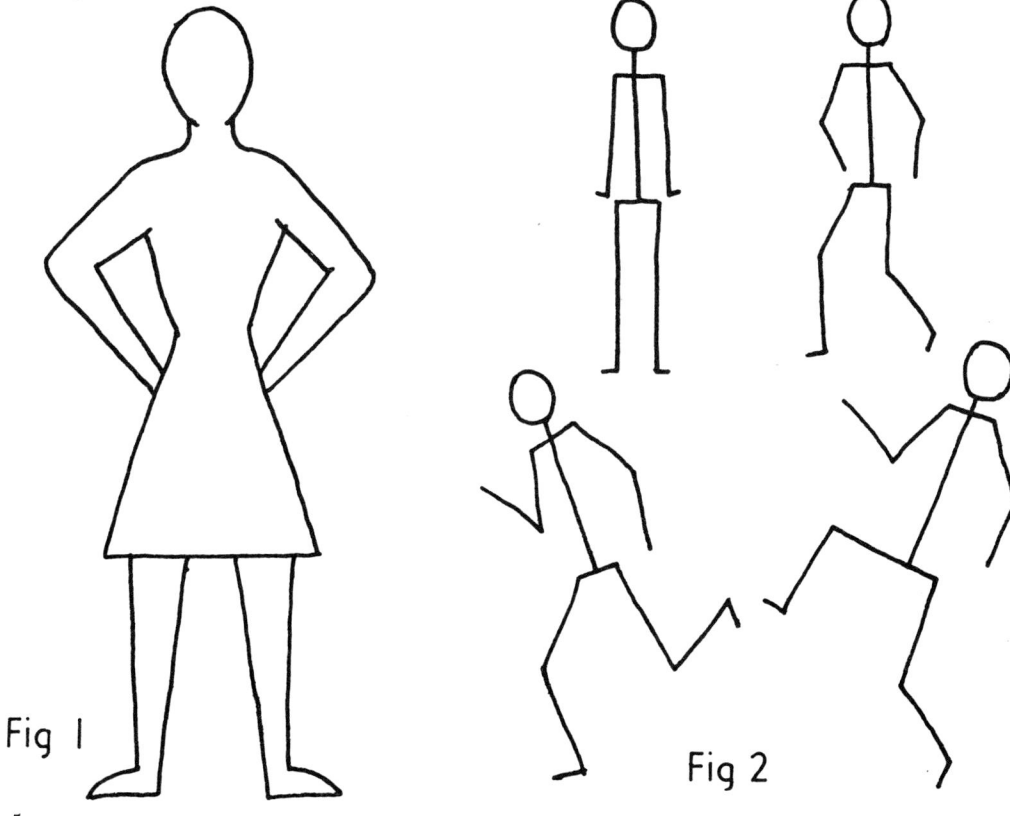

Fig 1

Fig 2

Draw in the features using felt-tip pens, and dress the figure by covering the cardboard with paste and sticking on fabrics to represent clothes.

These figures can be used on a frieze. For a 3-D effect stick a match-box at the back so that the figure stands out.

The figures can illustrate action, as in Fig. 2. These simple match-stick figures can be easily drawn and the lines made thicker to represent the body and limbs. Cut out in stiff card and dress with fabrics. Scenes such as a football-match; winter sports; playing in a park or road safety can be quickly created.

Why not plan a wardrobe of clothes suitable for a holiday, or maybe clothes one would like to have? For this one would require a sheet of stiff paper for the background and a cardboard figure. Draw round the figure and cut out pieces of fabric to represent clothes of all styles. Arrange these on to the paper, plus the cardboard figure, which should also be dressed with fabric, Figs. 3 and 4. Some boys may like to plan clothes for a football team to wear when they are going away to play a match, or for a winter sport.

Fig. 3   Flat-figure collage. A cardboard figure of a girl is cut out and pasted on a piece of background paper. Around the figure are pasted pieces of a variety of fabrics to represent a holiday wardrobe.

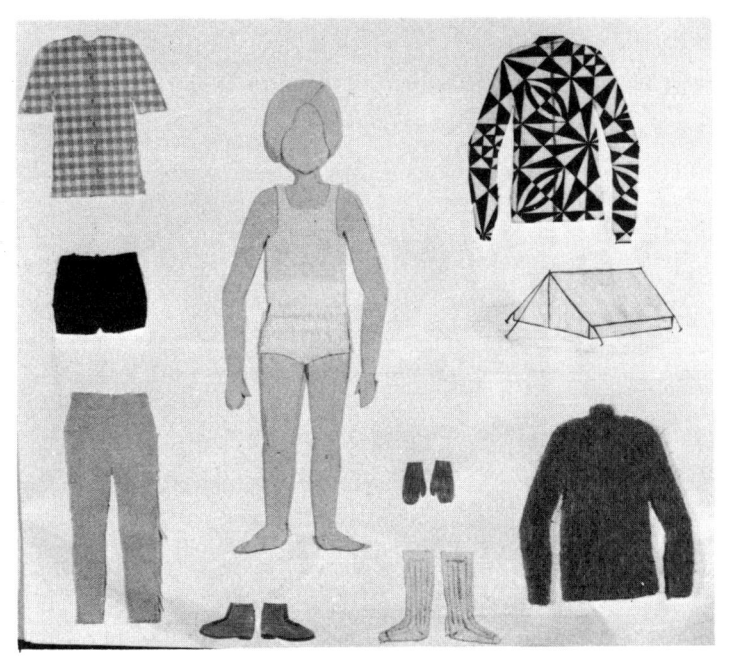

Fig. 4 This is the same idea as in Fig. 3. In this case the figure is that of a boy with an assortment of camping clothes.

CONE FIGURES

Materials required

Two pipe-cleaners.
Piece of stiff paper 5 × 10 in. (13 × 25 cm).
Scraps of fabric or paper for dressing.

To make

Cut out half a circle using the stiff paper, and curl round to form a cone, Fig. 5. Pin with a paper-clip or plain pin, Fig. 6.

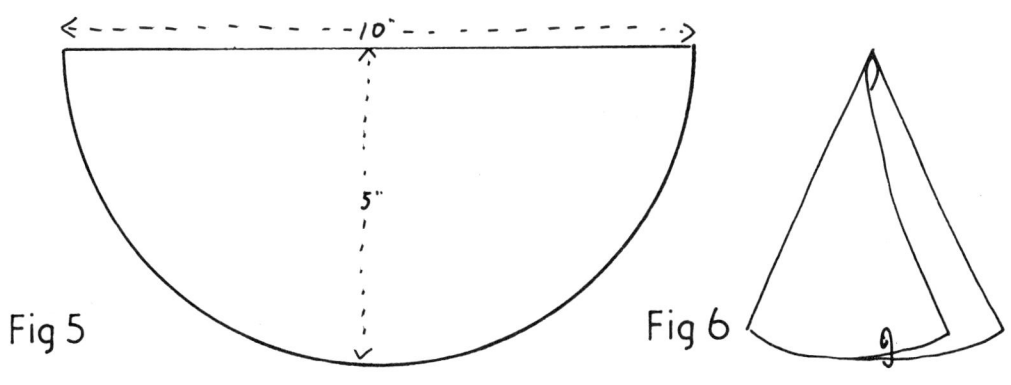

Fig 5

Fig 6

Thread bead on to pipe-cleaner and bend over at top, Fig. 7(a). Thread pipe-cleaner down centre of cone, Fig. 7(b). Secure pipe-cleaner to cone with Sellotape, Fig. 7(c).

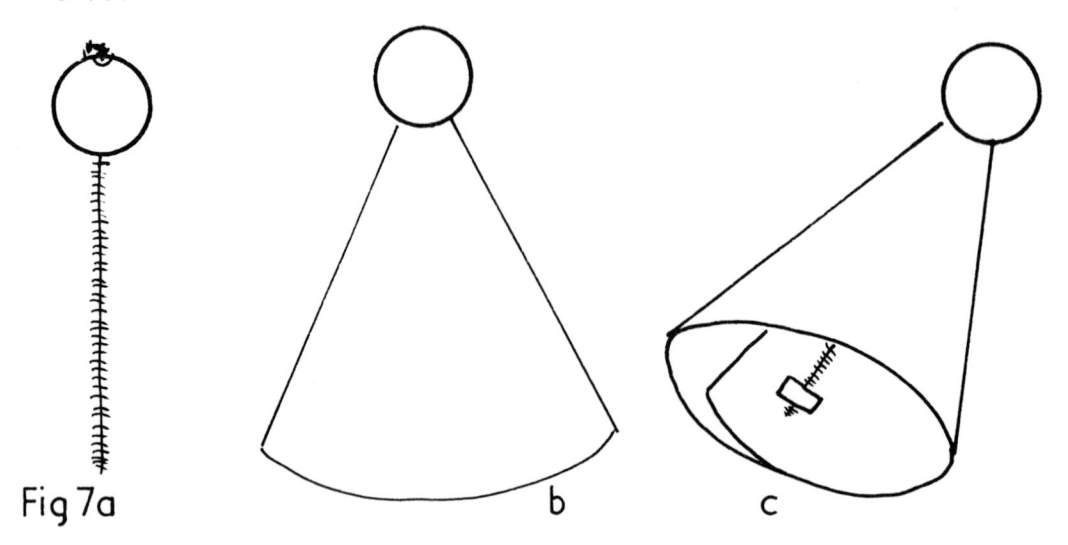

Fig 7a   b   c

To dress
1. Use the pattern in Fig. 5 and cut out in thin fabric which does not fray. Wrap around the cone and secure join with adhesive.
2. Cut out two sleeves using the pattern in Fig. 8(a). Open out each sleeve and decorate with braid. This may be stuck on, Fig. 8(b).
3. Fold the sleeves as in Fig. 8(a) and stick along the lower edge.
4. Thread the two sleeves on to a pipe-cleaner and secure to back of figure, Fig. 9(a), with adhesive. The arms can be bent into required position, Fig. 9(b).

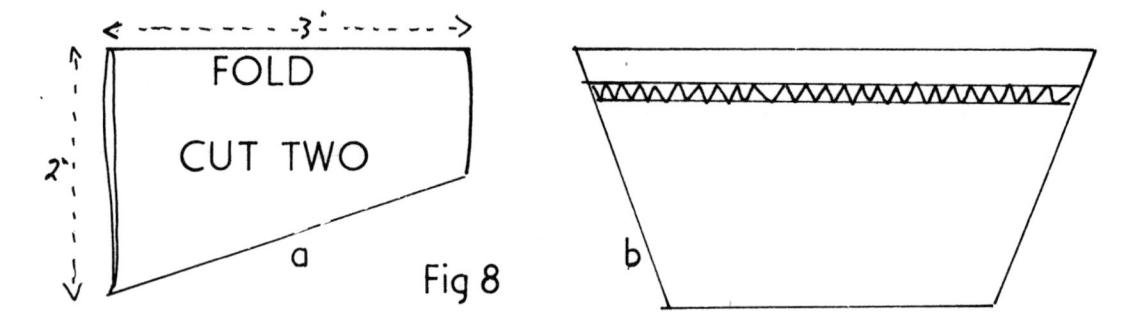

Fig 8

Unravelled wool can be used for hair, or a little piece of doll's hair (obtainable from school suppliers).

Pieces of gold or silver cake doilies are useful for making rich-looking clothes, or parts can be cut out for crowns.

a   Fig 9   b

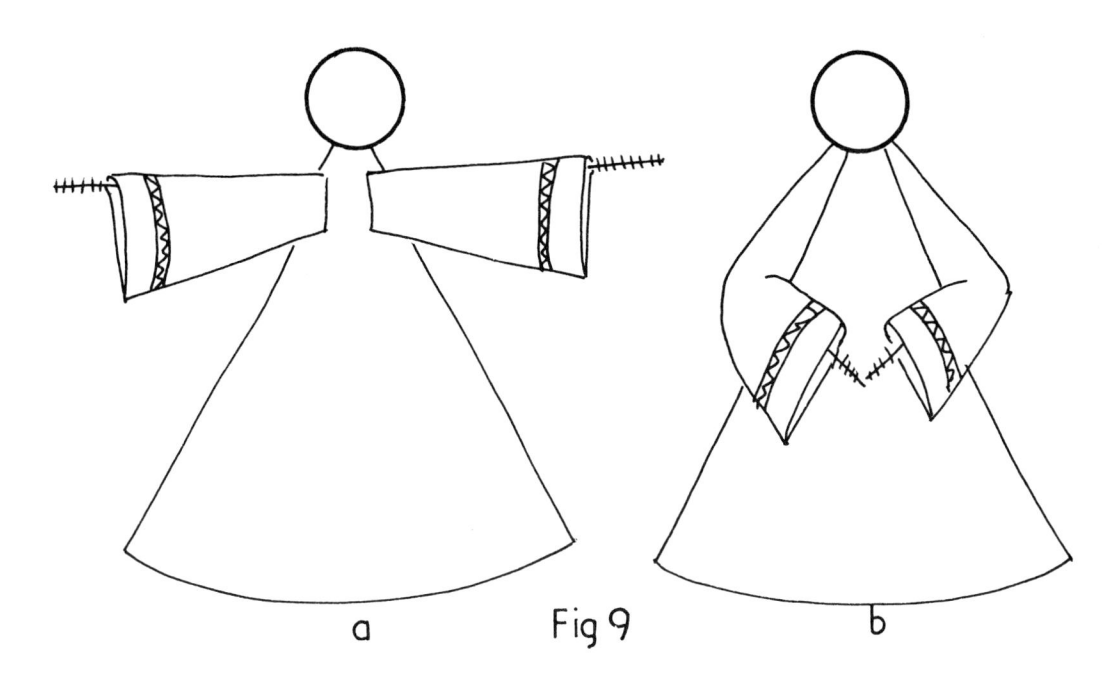

Cone figures can be used in a variety of sizes. Instead of using half a circle, Fig. 5, use a complete circle, making a slit from the outer edge to the centre. Overlap the outer edges and see what a variety of cones can be formed. Small beads are useful for the heads when the cones are small, or ping-pong balls for very large cones.

The figures may be grouped together and a setting designed and made, such as the ballroom scene from Cinderella for example. Figures of men could be made from pipe-cleaners, with beads for heads. Other ideas may be found in scenes from history or Bible stories.

For further ideas on figures see *Making and Dressing Figures* by A. V. White (Routledge & Kegan Paul).

Collage

Collage is really the building up of a design or piece of creative work from scrap materials. Very often the texture or surface of a fabric will suggest a use before one has really thought of a design. A piece of dark, rough tweed, or dark textured Crimplene may look good as the trunk of a tree. Brightly coloured, smooth fabric, as used for evening wear, would make delightful scales of a fish. The threads may even be frayed out to form the fins, as in Fig. 10.

Fig. 10 Textured fish made from transparent materials and frayed tweed. Brightly coloured shimmering material is particularly effective for the scales of a fish.

Thin, transparent fabrics, such as net or fine nylon, may be placed layer upon layer and cut to irregular shapes, thus changing the depth or tone of colour. This idea is useful for clouds, water, etc.

Collect together several thin fabrics and see how the colours change when placed on different coloured backgrounds. When a fabric is lying flat the colour may look entirely different from the colour shown when the fabric is suspended. The colour can also change according to the direction of the light which falls upon it.

The fabrics may be held in place with adhesive or stitching; this may be done either by hand or machine. More colour can be added by stitching, or by thread held on to a background with adhesive. Use an orange-stick or cocktail-stick to apply the adhesive as you will then be less likely to mark the work by using too much adhesive. Make full use of braids, buttons, beads and sequins to give further enrichment.

If the panel is to be carried out entirely with adhesive, the background may be prepared by first cutting out a piece of cardboard the size of the finished work. If you want a circular panel, then cut a lid from a box and cover with fabric, see page 110.

Ideas for collage may be found by linking the work with history. The Bayeux Tapestry is one of the finest examples of "a diary written with a needle". Perhaps a visit to a museum may make you long to carry out a panel on a theme centred on a certain item or items seen there. A visit to a hot-house containing tropical plants, or an aviary, may also give you some ideas, or perhaps brass-rubbings from a local church, or a church in another part of the country.

Do not say, "We have nothing where I live". Recently I was told by a young woman – "I cannot find any natural objects because I live in Liverpool". Well, very often in a big city there is more opportunity to look at nature than in the country. In Liverpool we have:

Tropical greenhouses like those at Kew Gardens.
Birdhouses.
Open-air aviaries.
Pets' corners where a large variety of animal life can be seen. I usually see my first lambs of spring here.
Trees of all kinds, because there are preservation orders on them so that we have miles of tree-lined roads.

We also have one of the finest museums outside London, which shows real examples of plant life from the sea-shore, and wonderful aquaria.

Well, what have you got? Obtain a local handbook of the place where you live and find out more about it.

TEXTURED FISH

Try using small pieces of fabric on a background of sugar-paper or a piece of brown paper. Draw a fish, not the kind seen in a supermarket, but the kind seen in an aquarium, or look for a book in the library and see what a lot of different fish there are in the world.

Maybe you will draw a fish like Fig. 11. Cut out pieces of fabric to represent scales and start by pasting the lower edge of each scale on to the fish, working from the tail towards the head. Use fabric for the tail.

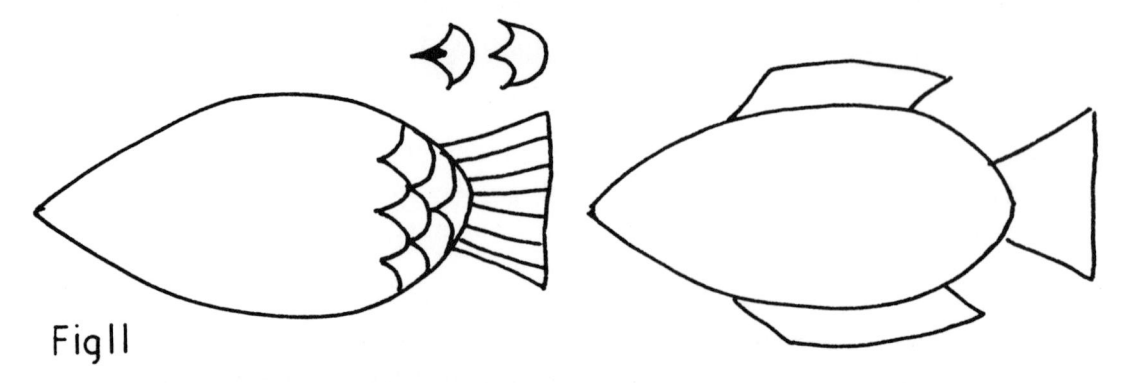

Fig 11

By working in a group a picture of an aquarium can be made. It would be necessary to have several individual pictures of fish already made of fabric. These could be cut out and arranged on a back-cloth, which can be of paper. Use threads (thick ones) to represent weeds growing from the bottom of the tank. Tweeds or coarse material could be cut into rock shapes for the bottom of the tank.

Maybe the fish are swimming round a treasure chest at the bottom of the sea!

This idea of small pieces of fabric can also be used for birds, insects, flowers, etc.

FLOWERS

For a flower with two rows of petals, Fig. 12, first draw the outer circle of the flower and cut pieces of fabric to represent petals. Paste only the lower edge of each petal. Gradually make the petals smaller and perhaps use a button for the centre of the flower.

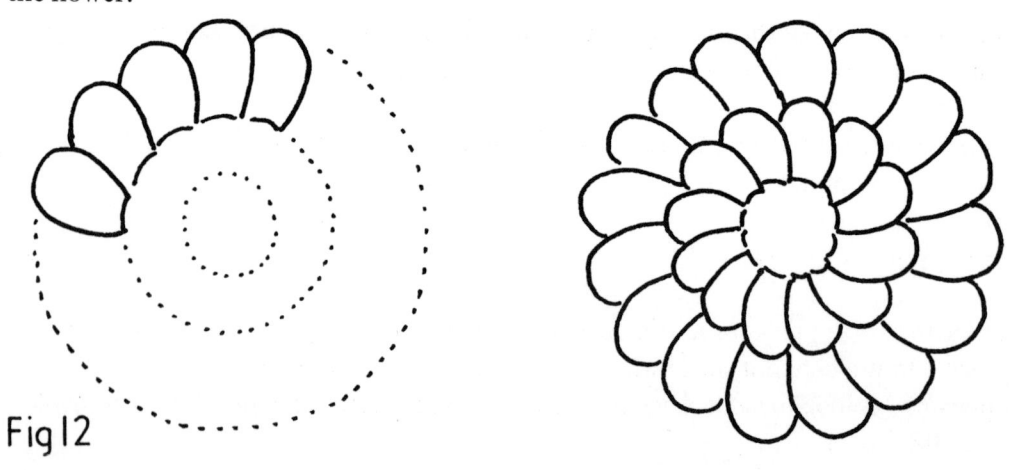

Fig 12

Other varieties of flowers can be made in a similar way, using threads from tweeds for the stems of the flowers.

The petal shape can also be used to make an attractive plaque, Fig. 13. Cut out petals in a non-fray fabric or if the fabric frays, back it with iron-on Vilene. Beads and curtain hooks may also be added. The petals may be cut out of thin transparent fabrics. If two or three rows of different-sized petals are cut out of the same coloured fabric, an interesting effect can be obtained when the petals overlap.

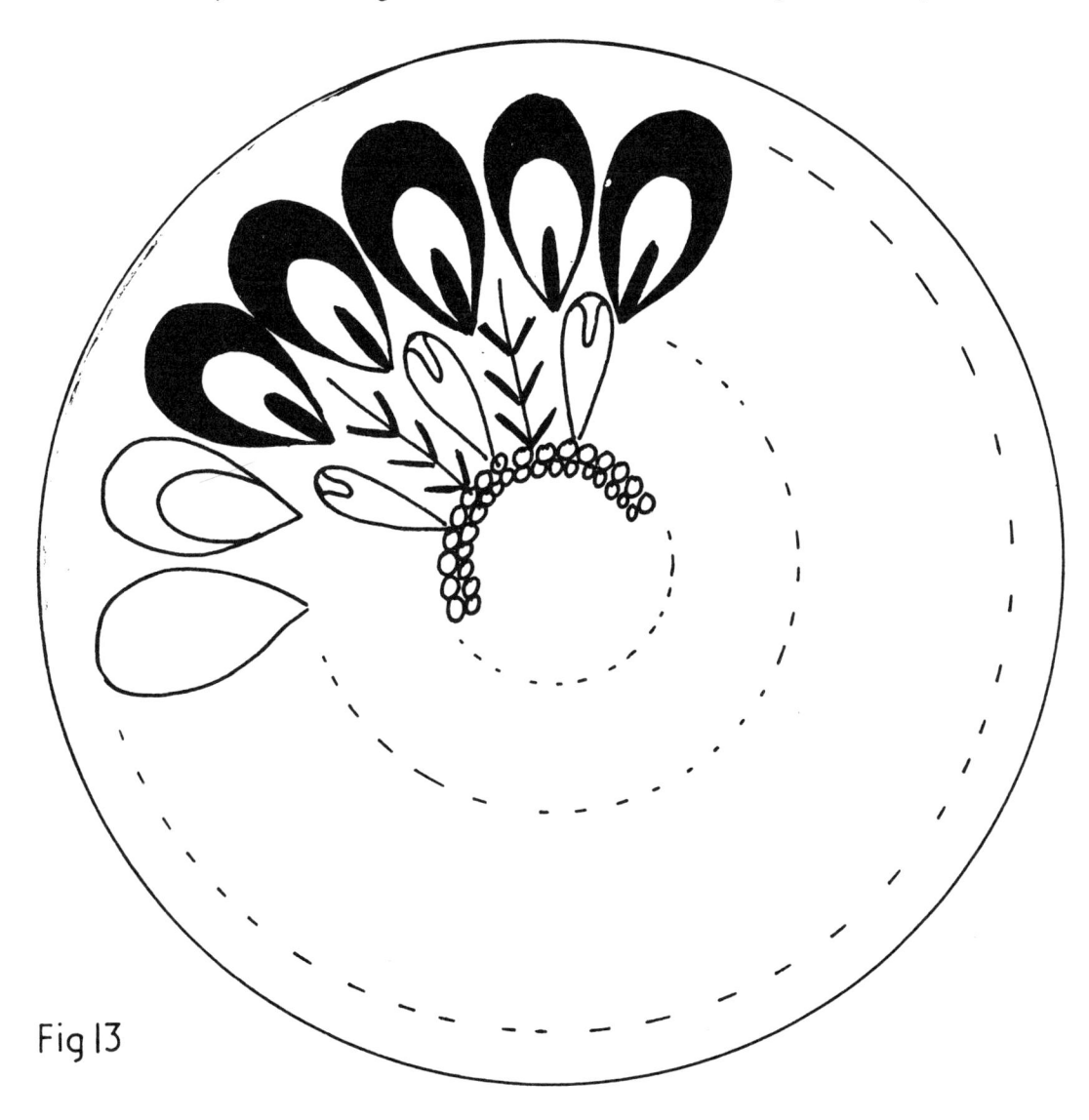

Fig 13

Designs of various size circles, Fig. 14, may be built up by using transparent fabrics, such as net or thin nylon. Let the shapes overlap a great deal so that the colour change of the fabrics can be seen. This idea can be tried out first using coloured tissue papers.

The texture of fabric can depict a very wide range of creatures, such as prehistoric monsters, creatures which we would find in a hot climate, for example crocodiles, reptiles, gaily-coloured birds, etc.

Books for reference

Alligators and Crocodiles, Herbert S. Zim (World's Work Children's Book)
Zoo Quest to Madagascar, David Attenborough (Lutterworth Press)
Digging for Dinosaurs, W. E. Swinton (Bodley Head)
Walt Disney Wonders of the Animal World (Nelson)
Fishes of the World (George G. Harrap)
Living Insects of the World, A. B. Klots and E. B. Klots (Hamish Hamilton)
Design with String, Mary Seyd (Batsford)
Dolls of the World, Gwen White (Mills & Boon)
Dress, James Laver (Murray)

TEXTURE AND COLOUR

Have a look in a bit-bag and see if you can collect a selection of fabrics of the same colour but different in texture. Some fabrics have a smooth surface which may also be shiny, others may be rough, or may be rough on one side and smooth on the other. There are fabrics with a pile surface and these have colours which look deeper, and among these fabrics you will find velvet, brushed nylon or fur fabrics. The colours of fabrics are sometimes difficult to name because a yellow, when

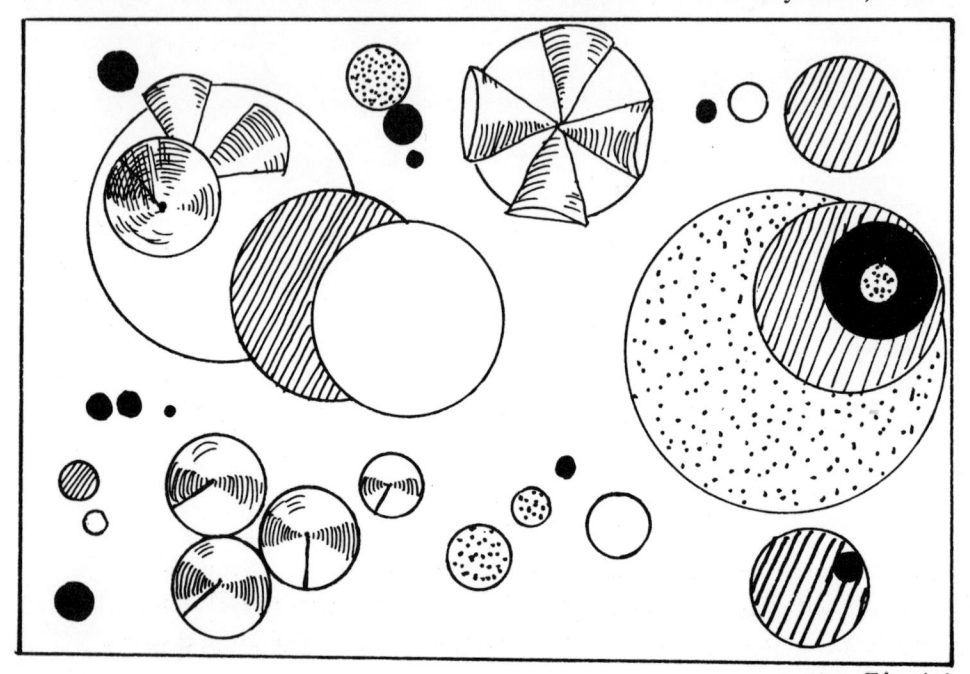

Fig 14

mixed with a little blue in the weave or dye of the fabric, looks slightly green. Therefore some greens are a very yellow-green or maybe the yellow looks more like orange.

Maybe two or three of you can group together to make a panel by cutting out circles of various sizes, using the different textures (Fig. 14). For very small

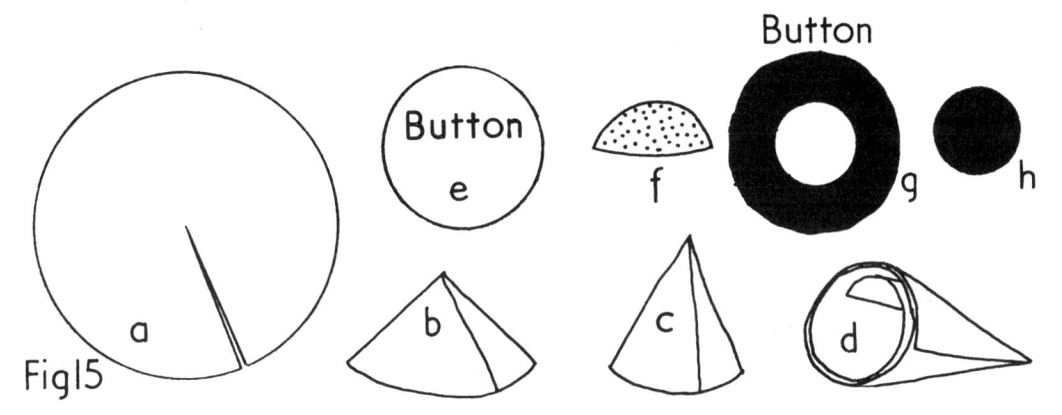

Fig 15

circles try covering buttons with one of the fabrics. Put Copydex on to the button and stick on the fabric, then cut away surplus material (Fig. 15(*g*) and (*h*)).

If you have a collection of buttons you will see how different are the shapes. Some are flat on both sides, some are flat on one side and dome-shaped on the other. The dome-shaped ones look most attractive when covered with fabric, Fig. 15(*f*). Velvet is ideal because when stuck on to a button it cannot fray as it normally does. If buttons of the same size are covered with various thicknesses of fabric then some buttons will appear smaller and others larger because of the fabric.

Choose a back-cloth of a reasonable size and arrange the cut-out shapes to form a pleasing design, then attach to the background with adhesive. To complete the panel a few beads and sequins may be added.

A panel could be built up from square and oblong shapes. Parts of these shapes could be cut and folded back. In the final arrangement the squares and oblongs can overlap.

YO-YOs

A "Yo-Yo" is a straight strip of fabric of a set size, gathered to form a circle, the outer edges of which may be slightly raised or flat.

Look at a collection of waste materials and select those which are not printed. They may have a woven design and this means that another colour, or several colours, may be introduced. The fabric may look dark on the reverse side and bright and shiny on the front. Such fabrics are often used for evening wear or curtains. These fabrics, when frayed a little to form a fringe, look more delicate in colour at the frayed edge than on the main area of the fabric, and great use can be made of this effect as can be seen in the panel, Colour Plate 8. The reverse side of the fabric may also be used. This may be a much deeper shade than the right side and could therefore be used to form the centre of a flower. Fig. 17 on page 17 shows clearly the stages of making such a flower. Pile fabrics may also be included in this type of work as the pile can be removed at the edge thus forming a fringe.

All strips of fabric used must be cut by the straight thread; a thread must run parallel with each cut edge. The making up of Yo-Yos is given opposite.

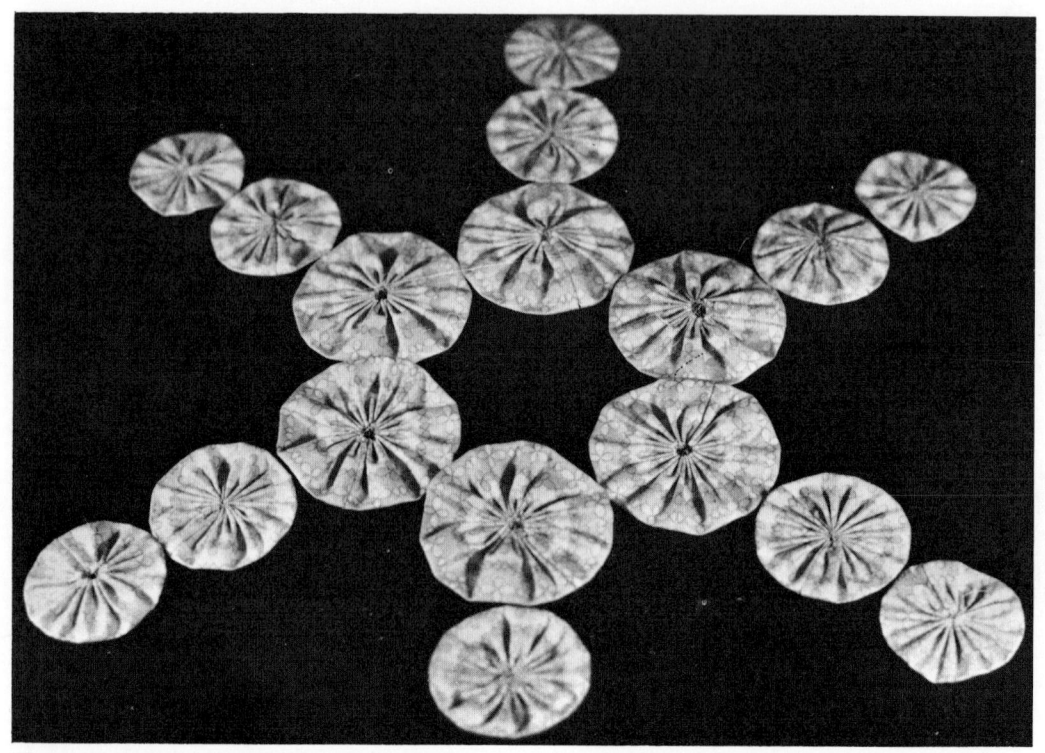

Fig. 16 Patterned fabric is here used to make Yo-Yos of graduated sizes. Note that the pattern should not be too large.

There are many variations on this theme and one can build up three-dimensional designs with graduated layers and the final design of the arrangement may be based on nature.

Pieces of crochet-work may also be added to give variety of colour and shape. It is not necessary to keep crochet-work flat, but small balls may be made by stuffing a crochet circle with threads and drawing up the circle to form a ball. A mobile may be made using Yo-Yos of a variety of sizes, but they should always be made in pairs by sticking or stitching two Yo-Yos together, back to back, before suspending.

To make flat Yo-Yos use materials which may be plain or patterned. Patterned fabrics, both printed and woven, may be used providing the fabric is no thicker than ordinary cotton. The size of the pattern on the fabric should vary according to the size of the Yo-Yos being made. When cutting out patterned fabric certain colours of the print may be emphasised by cutting along a particular line of pattern, or stripe. Fig. 16 shows how a patterned fabric can look when the Yo-Yos are graduated in size.

Yo-Yos may be joined together to form a fabric suitable for a doll's bed, or they can be arranged to form a design, especially if a variety of sizes is used and some are made of plain fabric. Perhaps some could be covered with net, having patterned ones all in the same arrangement.

STAGES OF MAKING YO-YOs

Double flower

1. The length of fabric should equal $3\frac{1}{2}$ times the diameter of flower. The width can vary according to design.
2. Fray the fabric along both straight edges.

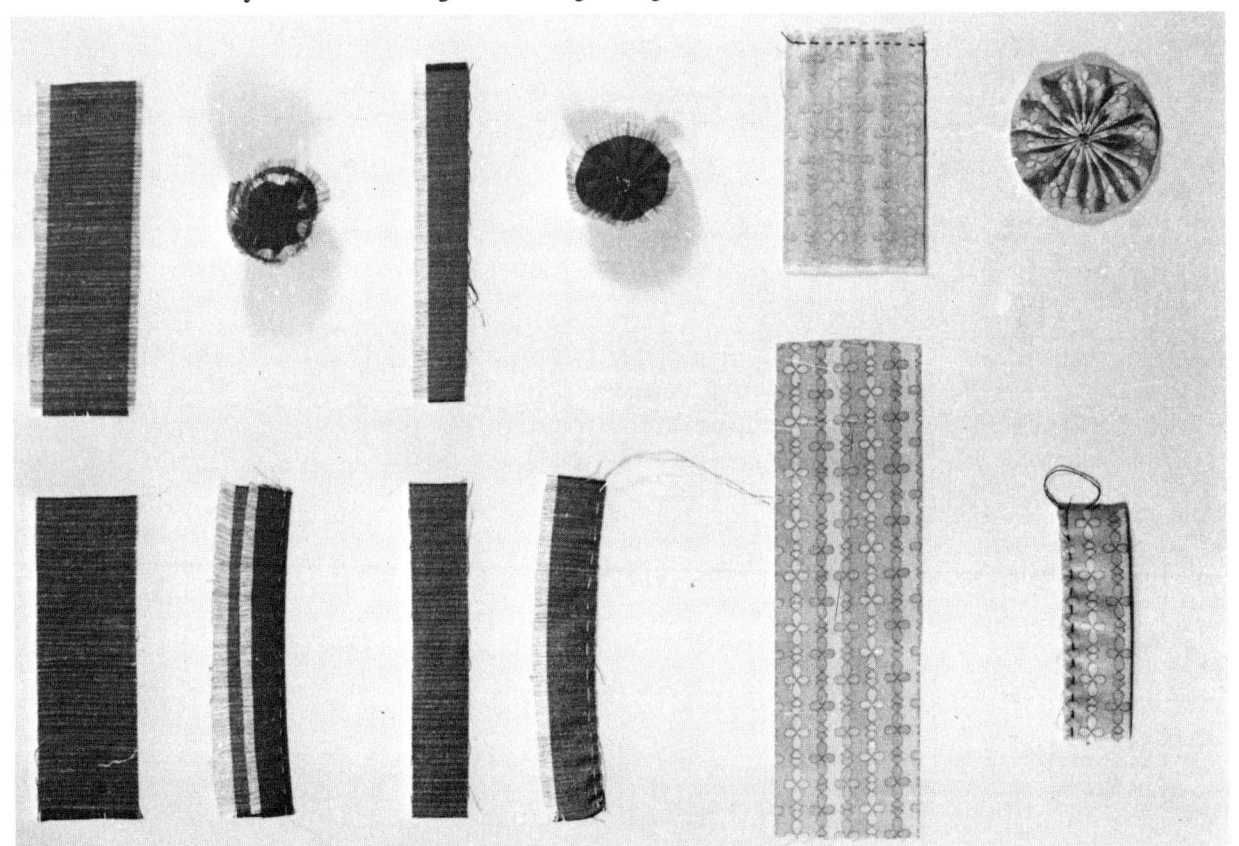

Fig. 17 Various methods of making Yo-Yos.

3. Fold over one-third of the fabric.
4. Run-stitch along the fold.
   Pull up the thread to form a flower. The ends of fabric will overlap.

Single flower
1. Cut the fabric as above but make width narrower.
2. Fray the top edge.
3. Run-stitch along the lower edge.
4. Pull up the thread to form a flower and secure the end.

Flat Yo-Yo
1. The strip of fabric is $3\frac{1}{2}$ times the diameter of flower, plus turnings. The width is equal to the diameter ($7\frac{1}{2} \times 1\frac{1}{4}$ in. or 19×3 cm).
2. Join fabric to form a cylinder. Press turnings open.
3. Fold fabric in half and run-stitch along the lower edge.
4. Pull up thread to form a flower and secure end.

ROUND PLAQUE

Materials required
Piece of cardboard, size of plaque.
Fabric large enough to cover cardboard.
Small circle of brightly-coloured felt.
Waste materials such as beads, buttons, curtain-hooks, rings, etc.
Tube of adhesive.

To make
1. Cover the cardboard with the fabric, see page 110.
2. Place the bright felt circle into the centre and stick into position.
3. Arrange curtain-hooks to form a design. (If rusty, spray with silver paint.) Make use of buttons or beads. Stick into position with adhesive.

Three-dimensional panels can be built up in many ways. Frayed fabrics as used for Yo-Yos (Colour Plate 9) or Tie-and-Dye (Colour Plate 8), or slightly raised effects obtained as on Cute Little Miss (Colour Plate 2), when the dress and sleeves are slightly padded.

Try collecting waste materials like the following: Toilet-roll tubes; cheese cartons, buttons, bottle-tops, curtain-rings, etc.

Cut the toilet-roll tube so that it is not so tall and try arranging the various shapes.

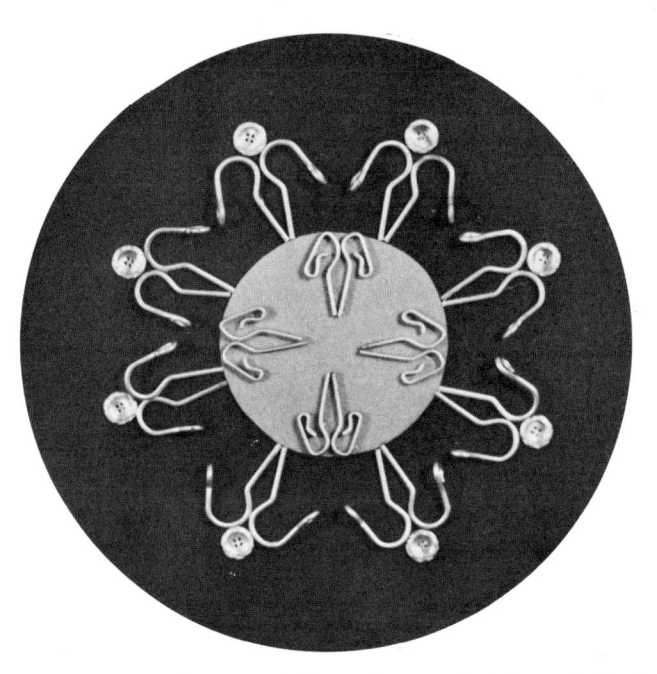

Fig. 18   Fabric-covered plaque decorated with curtain hooks and buttons.

A piece of tube on top of a cheese box; a button on top of a bottle-top. Arrange these on to a background as mentioned on page 15. Next try adding colour; cover some curtain-rings with loop-stitch; perhaps wind wool over the toilet-roll tube; cover some of the bottle-tops with fabric. Use frayed fabrics as for Yo-Yos but fray out more threads so that when the fabric is gathered up the outer edge will lie flat on the background. Place this round the outer edge of bottle-top.

Just see what fun this type of creative work is, and then you will want to do more.

CUTE LITTLE MISS (PANEL)

Materials required
Piece of 14 × 10 in. (35 × 25 cm) background fabric.
Scraps of fabric and felt (pink, black and red).

To make
Make a drawing of the girl on a piece of paper.
Trace off the shape of the face, top of body and arms; cut out in pink felt and stick on to background, Fig. 19.

Trace off the legs and cut out of black felt and stick on, Fig. 19.

Fig 19

Blouse

Cut out a straight piece of fabric for top of blouse and stick on to figure, Fig. 20. Cut out small straight strips for the sleeves. Place a row of running-stitch at top and bottom of sleeve and draw up the thread slightly, Fig. 21. Fasten off. Stick sleeves on to arms. Push under raw edge at sides of sleeve.

Trace the pattern of the bodice off the figure and cut out of fabric to match skirt. Paste into position.

Skirt

Cut out a straight piece of fabric for the skirt to match blouse. (This should be equal in depth from the waist of the figure to top of stocking.) Put a running-stitch round top of skirt and pull thread up so that it is equal in width to the waist of figure, and fasten off. Stick into position, Fig. 20. A little wadding may be put under skirt.

Fig 20

Fig 21

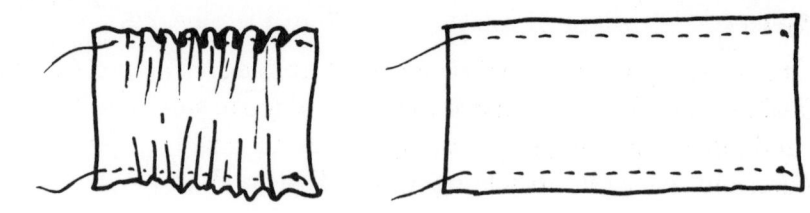

Cut out a strip of felt to overlap the raw edges of bodice and skirt. Decorate with threads.

Decorate edge of sleeve and top of stockings with threads or lace. An apron may be added if you like.

Face

To make the face cut out two red circles of felt for cheeks and a red mouth, and stick on to face, Fig. 22(*a*). Cut out black felt eye-lashes, Fig. 22(*b*) and stick on to face. Make plaits of thread for hair, Fig. 22(*c*), and arrange round face. Attach with adhesive.

Many ideas for dress on panels can be obtained from books on historic costume or peasant costume. The fabrics may be printed to your own design, giving an individual touch to a costume. The clothing on the figures may be slightly padded to give a three-dimensional effect. There is no need to cut all the pieces of fabric flat; in fact a figure of Henry VIII looks splendid when slightly padded. Rich

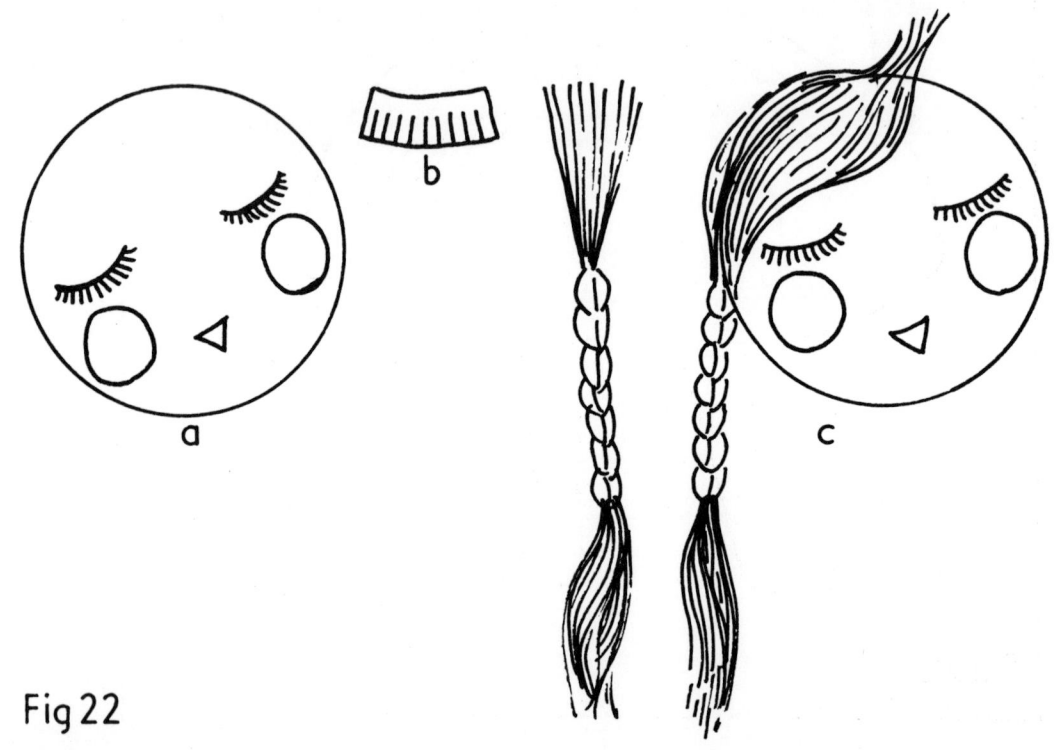

Fig 22

fabrics, such as velvet, look extremely well if you slightly gather them instead of merely painting lines on, or working rows of embroidery stitches to represent fullness.

A group of figures could be arranged in archways of the same architectural period as the costumes. The archways could be made up of applied fabrics.

For ideas, look at the following books:

Peasant Costumes of the World by Kathleen Mann.
Dolls of the World by Gwen White.
Any "History of Costume" books by James Laver.

Visit old churches and look for the brasses on the tombs. Try to obtain permission to take brass-rubbings as these are excellent for design.

Toying with fabrics and threads

Have you ever tried to pull the threads out of a piece of loosely woven tweed and then looked carefully at them? Some are quite thick and often quite different in colour from the actual fabric. These threads can be used like paints to give colour to illustrations. Sheep's wool can also be used because this is thread before it is spun and woven into cloth. In this section are a few ideas showing how these threads can be used.

When you have carried out your idea for a panel mount it on to stiff cardboard, but cut the card $\frac{1}{2}$ in. smaller than the panel (see page 110).

LION

An attractive panel can be quickly made of a lion's head. The actual face of the lion is quite small but the mane is the important feature. This can be built up from scraps of knitting yarns and also threads which have been unravelled from tweeds, see Colour Plate 3.

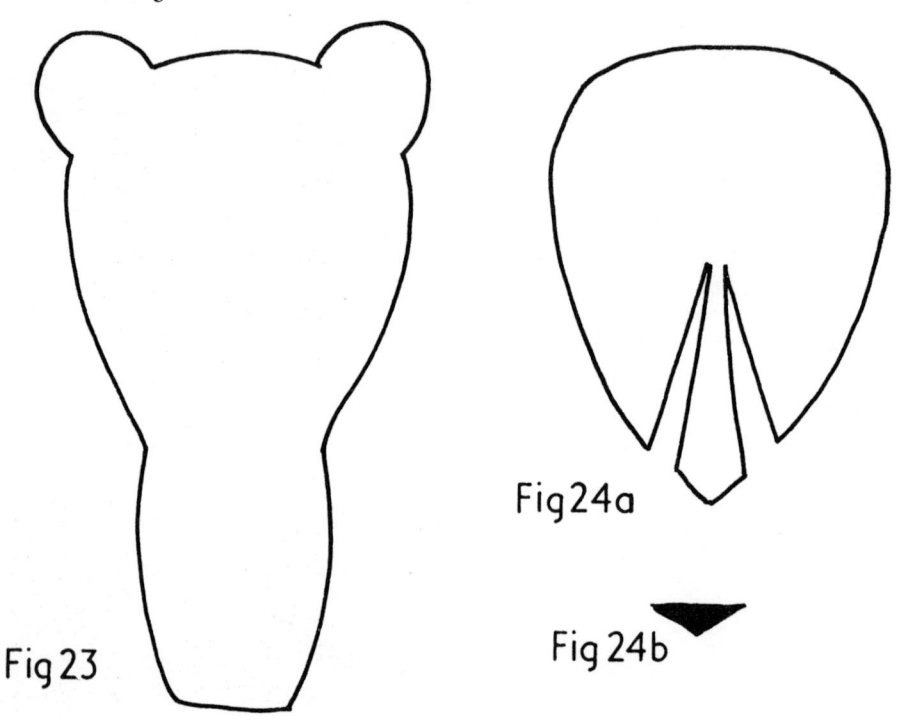

Fig 23

Fig 24a

Fig 24b

1. *Left:* Parrot collage. The pieces of fabric were purposely left frayed and jagged to achieve the effect of feathers.

2. *Above:* Cute Little Miss collage. The effect can be made three-dimensional by padding the dress and sleeves slightly.

3. *Below:* Lion and hedgehog collage.

4. Tie-dyed snail and cat.

5. Tie-dyed reptile.

Materials required

12 × 9½ in. (31 × 24 cm) fabric for background (dark colour).
3½ × 2½ in. (9 × 6 cm) white felt or firm fabric.
2½ × 2 in. (6 × 5 cm) dull gold felt or firm fabric.
Scraps of knitting yarns or unravelled threads.
Tube of adhesive.

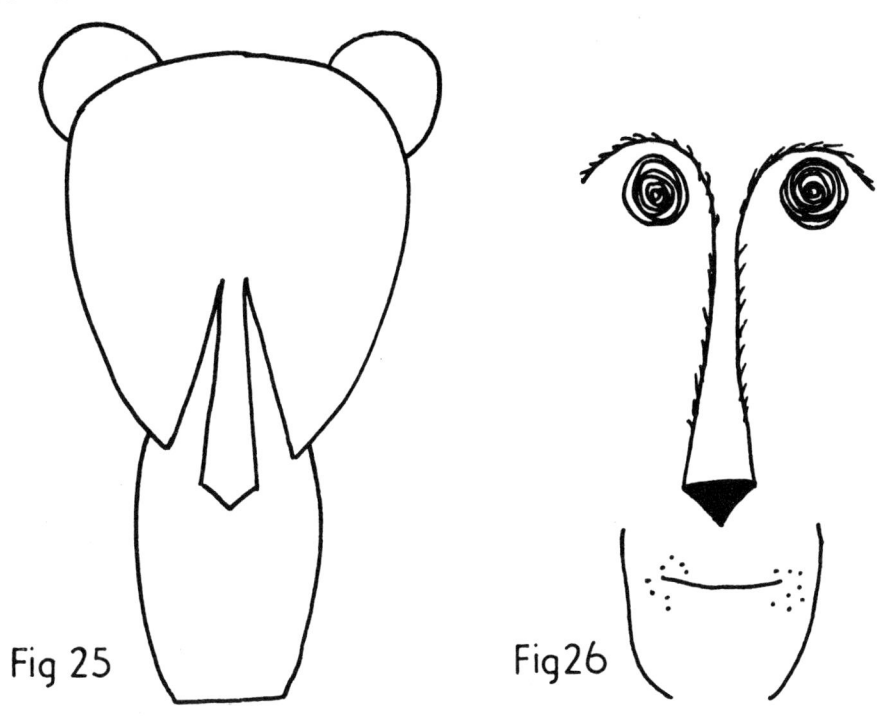

Fig 25

Fig 26

Cutting out

1. Using the pattern for the face (Fig. 23) cut out in white felt.
2. Using the pattern for the face (Fig. 24(a)) cut out in the dull gold fabric.
3. Cut out a nose in black felt (Fig. 24(b)).

To make

1. Place the white face into position on the background fabric, leaving a little more space at the bottom than the top and stick into position.
2. Place the dull gold face on top of the white (Fig. 25) and stick down.
3. Make the features by sticking on the black felt nose (Fig. 26).
4. Use the knitting wool to form the features. Start with the eyebrow and continue down to the nose; stick into position.
5. Make the eyes (Fig. 26) by winding dark wool round and round to form a circle and stick down. Stick a small yellow circle of felt on top of the dark eye and put a dot in the centre of the yellow circle with a pencil.
6. Stick on a line of thread for mouth and put dots at the end of the mouth, using a pencil.

Mane

Arrange lengths of wool and unravelled threads to form a mane. Use short pieces for under the chin and long pieces to flow from the top of the head. Mohair wool is good for this.

HEDGEHOG

A hedgehog is a delightful creature. His body is quite small but his spikes make him look large. A great variety of threads can be used to represent his spikes, and small pieces of straw can also be used, see Colour Plate 3.

Materials required

8 × 10 in. (20 × 26 cm) fabric for background (dark colour).
5 × 3 in. (13 × 8 cm) beige felt.
Scrap of black-and-white felt.
Scraps of knitting yarns and unravelled threads, also small pieces of straw.
Tube of adhesive.

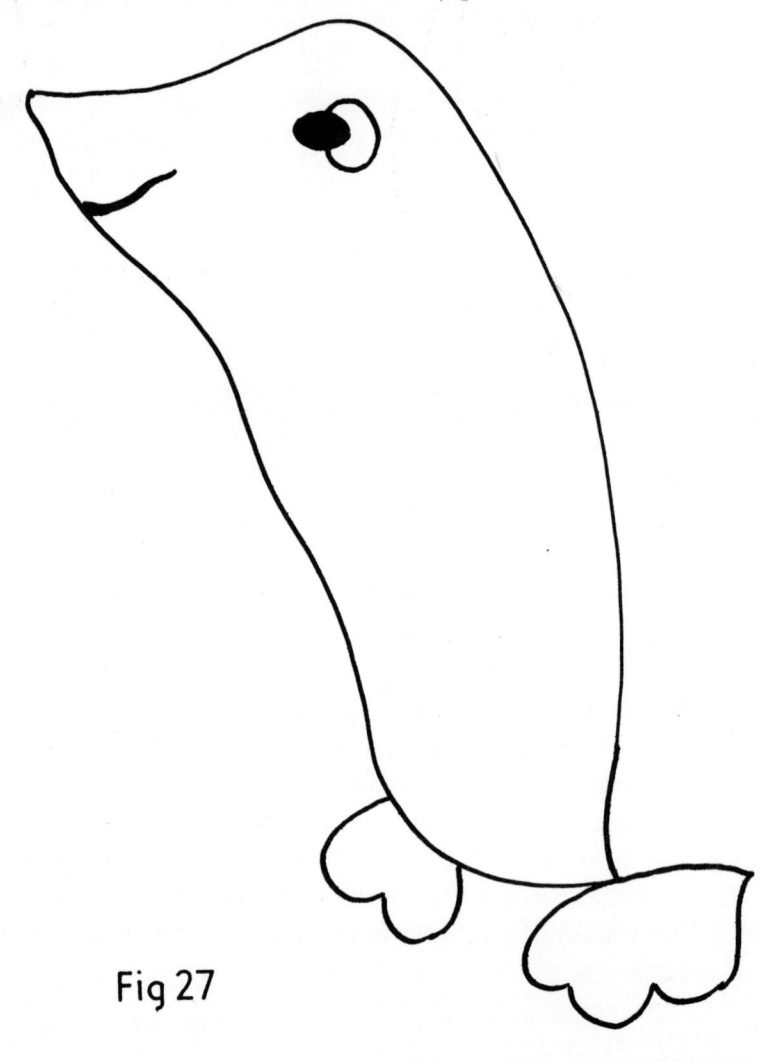

Fig 27

Pattern and cutting out

Trace off the pattern of the body and feet, and cut out in the beige felt, Fig. 27.

To make

1. Place the body piece on to the background. The nose should be 1½ in. (4 cm) in from the side, and 2¼ in. (6 cm) up from the lower edge. There should be a slight slope of the body on the background, see Colour Plate 3. Secure with adhesive.
2. Place feet into position and stick. Shade in the toes and the underside of the body, using a felt-tip pen.
3. To make the features, cut out a narrow strip of black felt for mouth, Fig. 28(a). Cut out one white eye and one black, Fig. 28(b) and (c), arrange as in Fig. 28(d) and stick into position.
4. The spikes are short near the head and longer over the rest of the body. Use a piece of chalk to draw an outline of the hedgehog.
5. Cut the threads in various lengths and arrange for spikes. Secure all threads with adhesive, but the straw need only be secured at base and then it will stand away from the body like spikes.

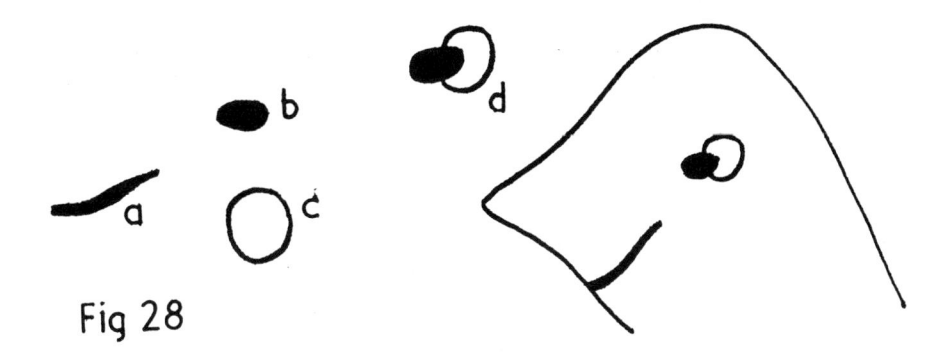

Fig 28

INSECT

Materials required

A piece of cardboard covered with fabric for base of panel (see page 110).
Scrap of orange tweed.
Scrap of black tweed.
Six pipe-cleaners, dyed black.
Two black buttons.

This attractive creature is made from tweed which frays easily. The shape of body and head is built up from layers of fabric as seen in Fig. 29.
The original shapes are those in Fig. 30, Nos. 1–17. Four of these pieces were cut out of black tweed.

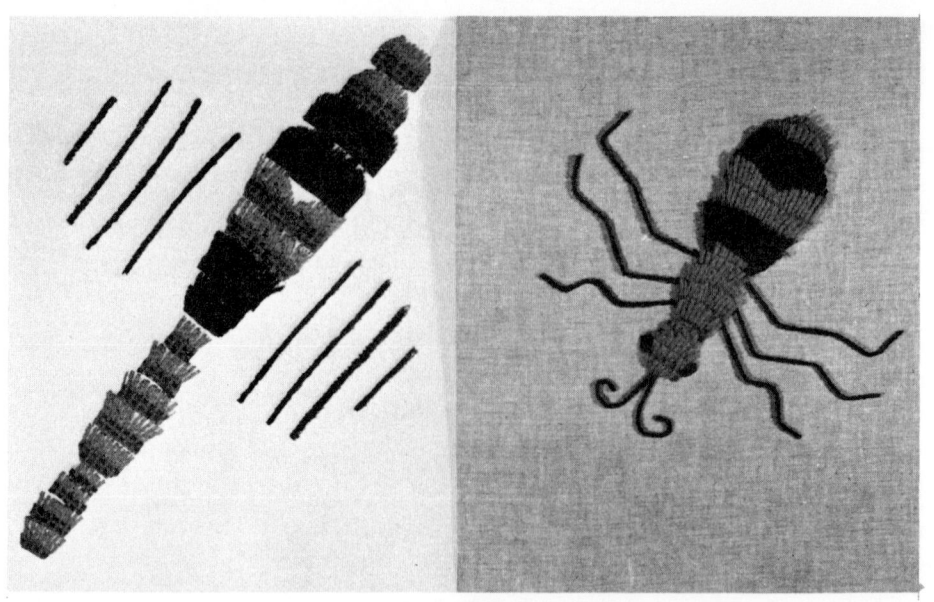

Fig. 29 An insect collage made from bits of frayed tweed and pipe-cleaners.

Cutting out

It may look like a lot of pattern pieces, but you only require a long straight strip of fabric and cut it to the length of each of the shapes. All fabric must be cut to the straight of the threads, and a portion frayed away.

To make

Arrange the pieces, starting at the tail, and gradually build upwards, each piece overlapping the previous one. The fabrics are stuck down at the base with adhesive. Two buttons form the eyes and pipe-cleaners dyed black form legs and feelers. You can improve the shape of the body if you trim it after it has been mounted. Try out this method for other insects and creatures.

Once we have seen the possibilities of using threads which can be removed from fabrics, and also how fabrics which fray can be used to obtain a fur effect on the body of an insect, these ideas can be combined or developed separately to enable panels to be made inspired by insects, including winged creatures. Here great use can be made of thin transparent fabrics, such as net. The fine jersey fabrics are inclined to roll at the edge when cut into small pieces.

Butterflies and moths are very attractive in design. Look at *Living Insects of the World* by A. B. Klots and E. B. Klots, published by Hamish Hamilton. This book not only shows moths fully grown but also moths in the early stages before the wings are formed. These are very simple in shape but colourful, and they lend themselves to the making of panels.

Fig 30

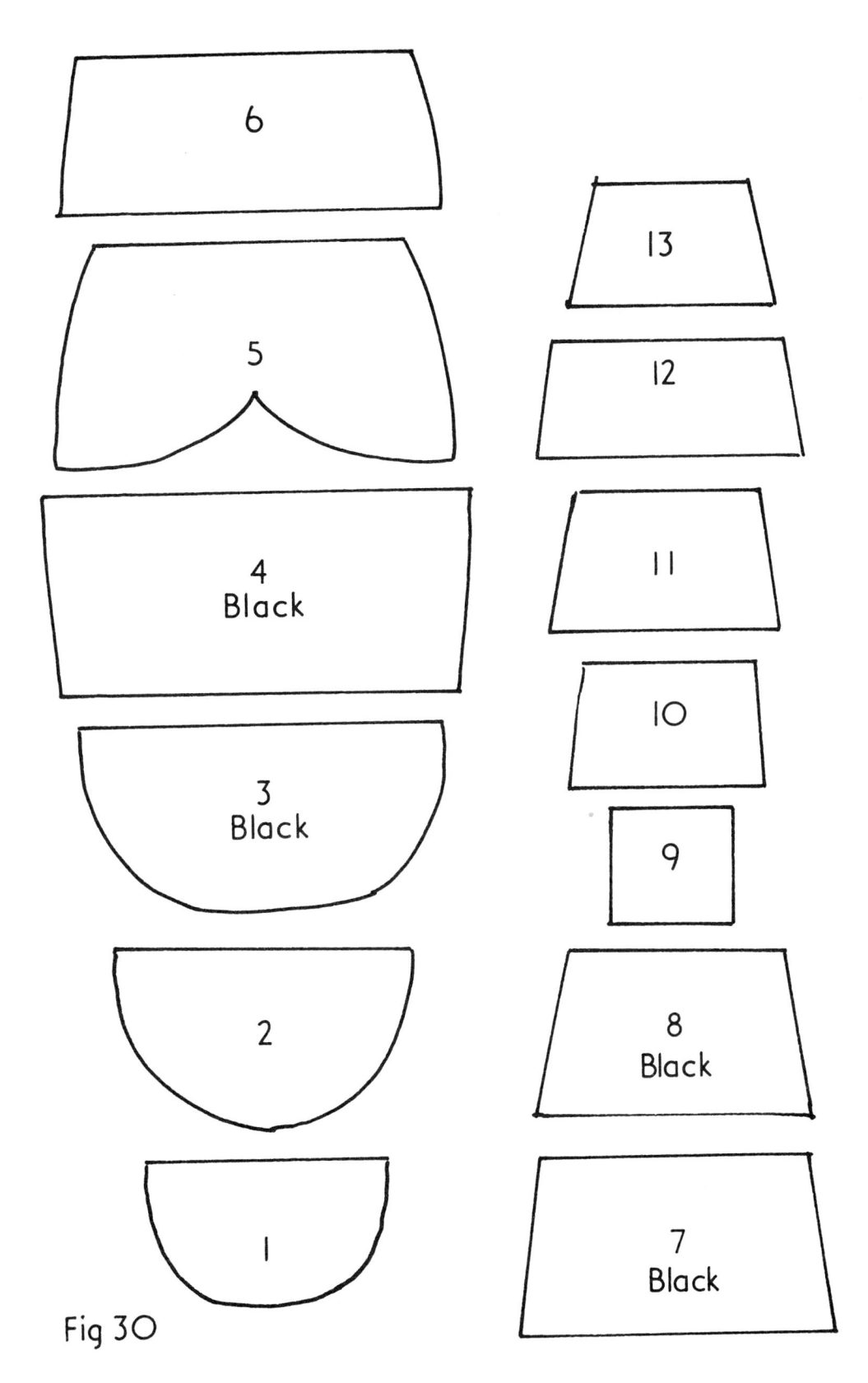

29

Fig 30

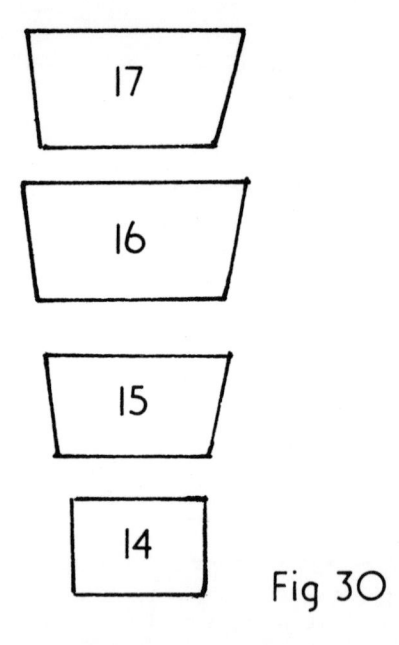

Although in this section I have not made use of beads and sequins, and lurex threads, these should be used whenever a rich effect is desired.

There is no need to make individual panels of animals and insects. They could be grouped together with work from other sections of the book, so that a large screen or wall-hanging could be made. The back-cloth could be partially painted if desired.

Creating texture with cut threads

Fabrics which are loosely woven, such as tweeds, and those fabrics which can easily be unravelled, are really great fun to use. It is amazing what a range of colours may be found in a piece of fabric when one starts to destroy it by unravelling the threads, some of which may be quite thick.

These threads may be grouped together in colours and cut up into small pieces the size of a pea. They then may be applied to a design, which may be natural or abstract. The desired surface area can be applied with paste and then the cut threads stuck on to it. The threads may also be cut very finely and mixed with a little paste and applied to a design with a brush.

The threads could be cut in lengths of 15–20 cm and then applied to a background to form a textured fabric suitable for an animal's head.

3-D patchwork

Patchwork is the joining together of small pieces of fabric, often in a variety of colours, to make a larger piece. You may have seen a patchwork quilt, perhaps in a museum. Often the patches were joined together to form a flower or geometric design. In Victorian times cushion covers and pincushions were often made of rich fabrics, such as silk and taffeta. The geometric shapes used in patchwork are Hexagons, Pentagons, Octagons, Diamonds, Triangles and Long Diamonds.

Materials required

Template, Fig. 31(*a*).
A piece of thin card.
Piece of fabric 3 × 10 in. (8 × 23 cm) for each completed flower section. There are ten flower sections to make the complete 3-D patchwork (Colour Plate 6). It is more interesting if each flower section is a different colour, or several flowers may be made of one colour.

Ten circles of card (1·5 cm diameter).

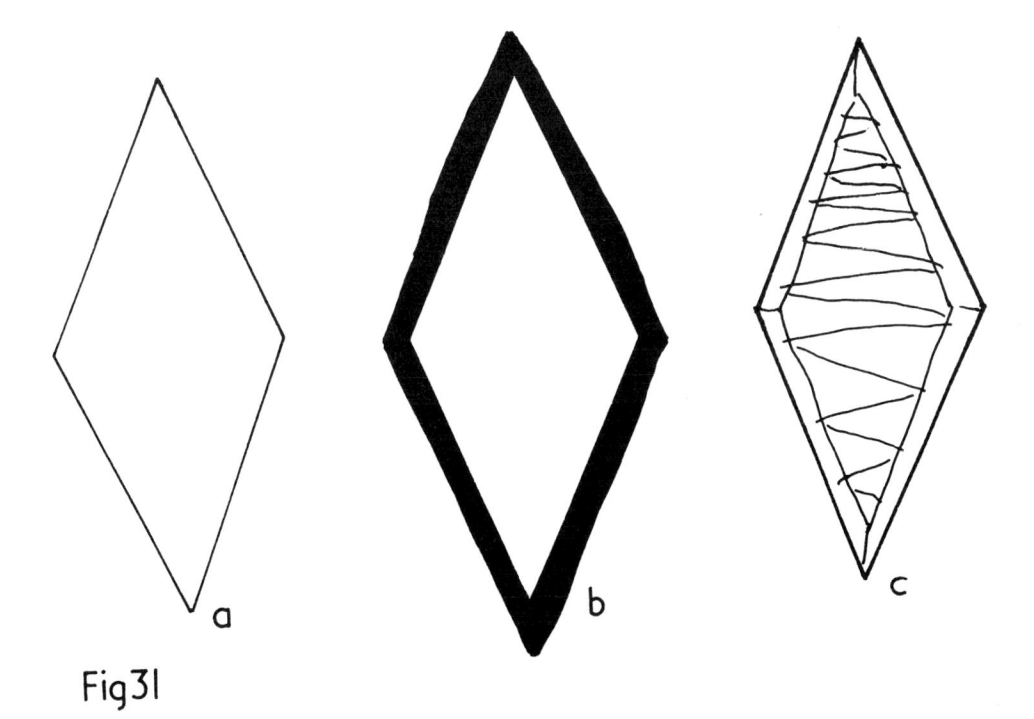

Fig 31

Preparation

1. Cut out five pieces of card the size of Fig. 31(*a*). (This is the number required to make one flower section.)
2. Cut out five fabric diamonds as in Fig. 31(*b*), allowing 5-mm turnings.
3. Bring the turnings over the card and stitch with a type of lacing as in Fig. 31(*c*).
4. To make a flower, place the two right sides of two diamond-shaped pieces together, and join one side by oversewing, Fig. 32(*a*).
5. Join on another section, Fig. 32(*b*).

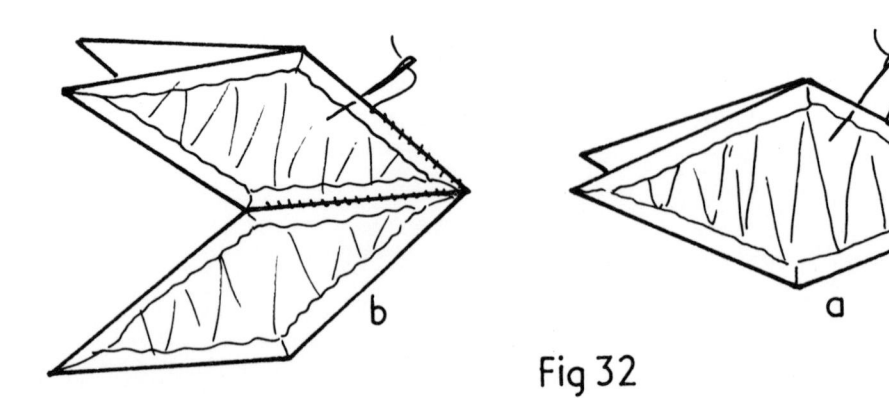

Fig 32

6. Take another colour and join the sections together to form a flower, Fig. 33.
7. To make the 3-D patchwork another nine flowers are required. After these are made they are joined together. Join two flowers together starting at point (*a*) and working downwards and up to the next point (*b*), Fig. 34. Then join on another flower and repeat until all pieces are assembled.
8. Stick a covered circle into the centre of each flower, as in Colour Plate 60, for the large 3-D flower. The smaller one has tiny cones of fabric stuck into each centre.

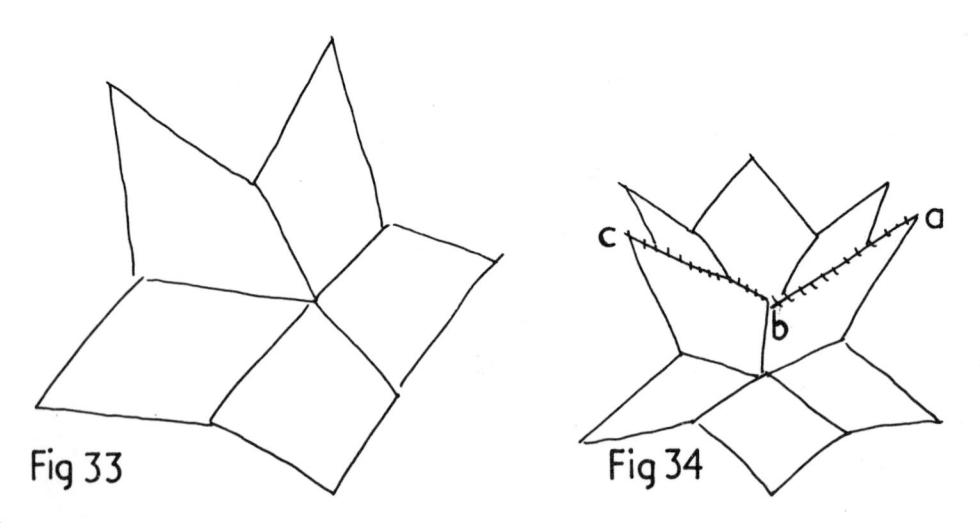

Fig 33

Fig 34

For other ideas the backs of each flower section could also be covered in fabric and the flowers arranged in a different formation, or suspended on a metal frame.

Other shapes may also be used and the fabric stuck on to the card, but instead of stitching sections together, stick them. For this, allow extra card so that it can be folded under and stuck to the next section.

Things you can do with a circle

A MOBILE FISH

Materials required
A 4-in. (10-cm) circle in Vilene, or stiff fabric which does not fray. Collect anything which is round – drawing-pins, coins, bottle-tops.

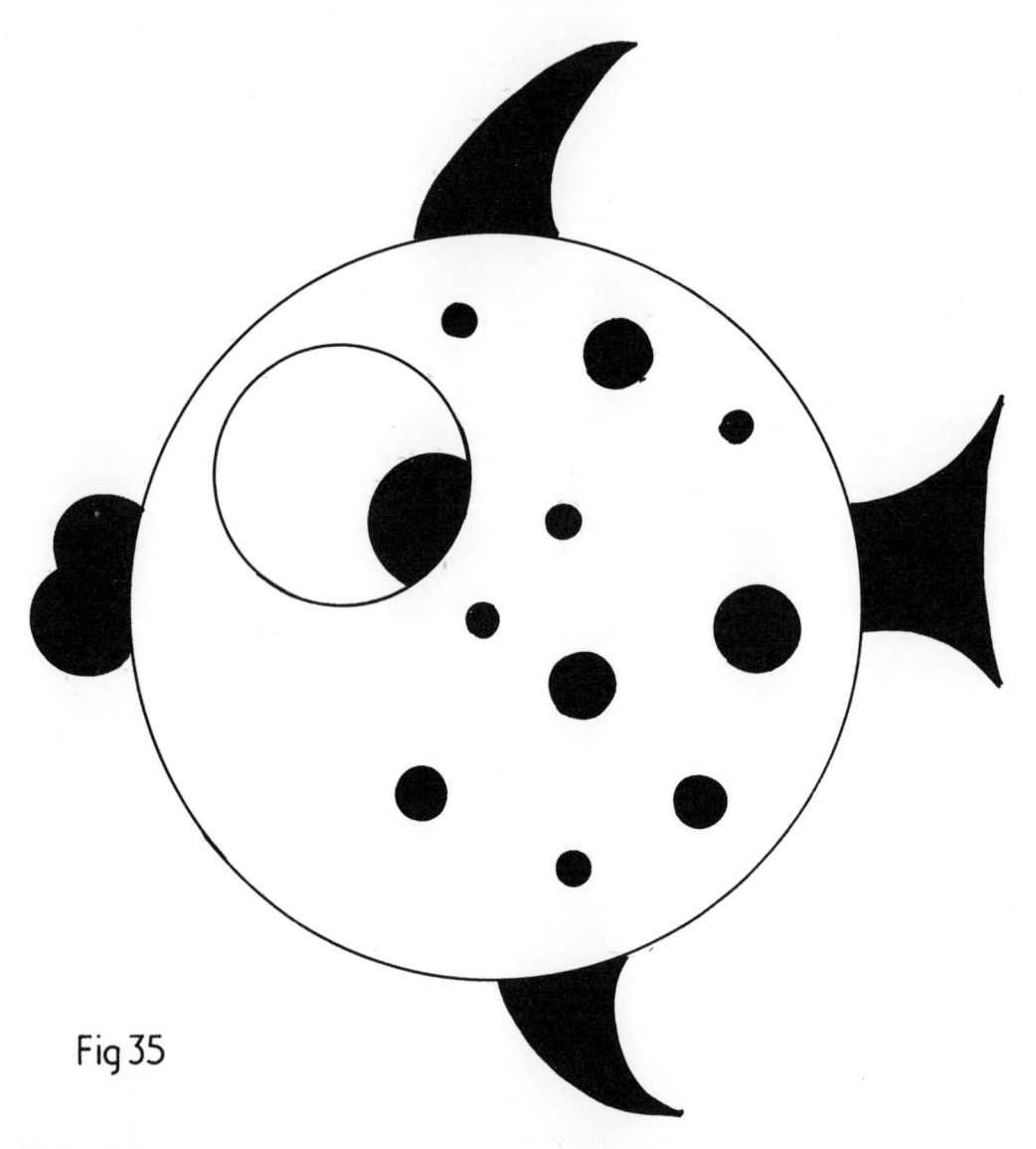

Fig 35

To make
1. Draw around the largest object for eye, on to the fish.
2. Use smaller coin for the other part of the eye.
3. Draw spots on the fish using various other smaller objects.
4. Trace off shape of mouth, tail and fins.
5. Cut out in black felt and stick or stitch on to fish.

Fig 36

To make fish mobile
1. Make one large fish, the size of the one shown in Fig. 35.

2. Make a variety of sizes of fish, using smaller circles for the body, and making the eyes and spots also smaller.
3. Thread a cotton through the top fin of the fish and suspend from a coat-hanger. Arrange to have the fish suspended from various heights, Fig. 36.

TOY FISH

Materials required

Two 4-in. (10-cm) circles of felt or bonded fabric.
Scraps of felt for eye, fins and tail.
Kapok for stuffing.

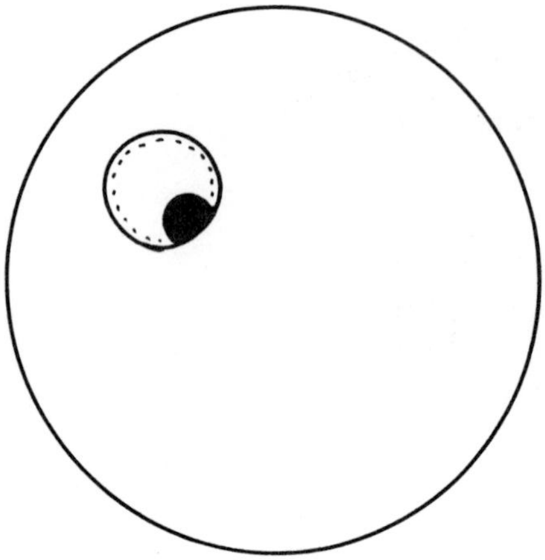

Fig 37 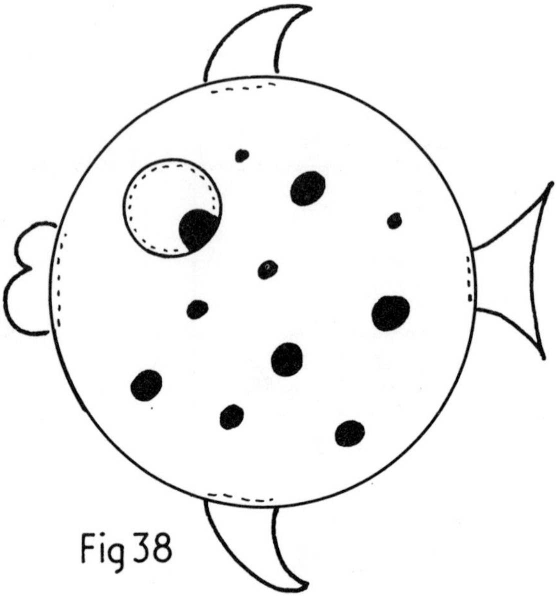   Fig 38

To make

1. Cut felt out for eye, using shape as in Fig. 37. Stitch on to one large circle using running-stitch.
2. Decorate the fish with spots cut out in felt, and stick them on, or embroider, Fig. 38.
3. Cut mouth, fins and tail out in felt and stitch to one circle.
4. Place the two circles together and join with running-stitch, leaving a gap. Stuff and then stitch up the gap.

TUDOR ROSE PINCUSHION

Materials required

3-in. (7·5-cm) circle of black felt, Fig. 39.
3-in. (7·5-cm) circle of red felt cut to shape as in Fig. 40.
Kapok for stuffing.

Fig 39

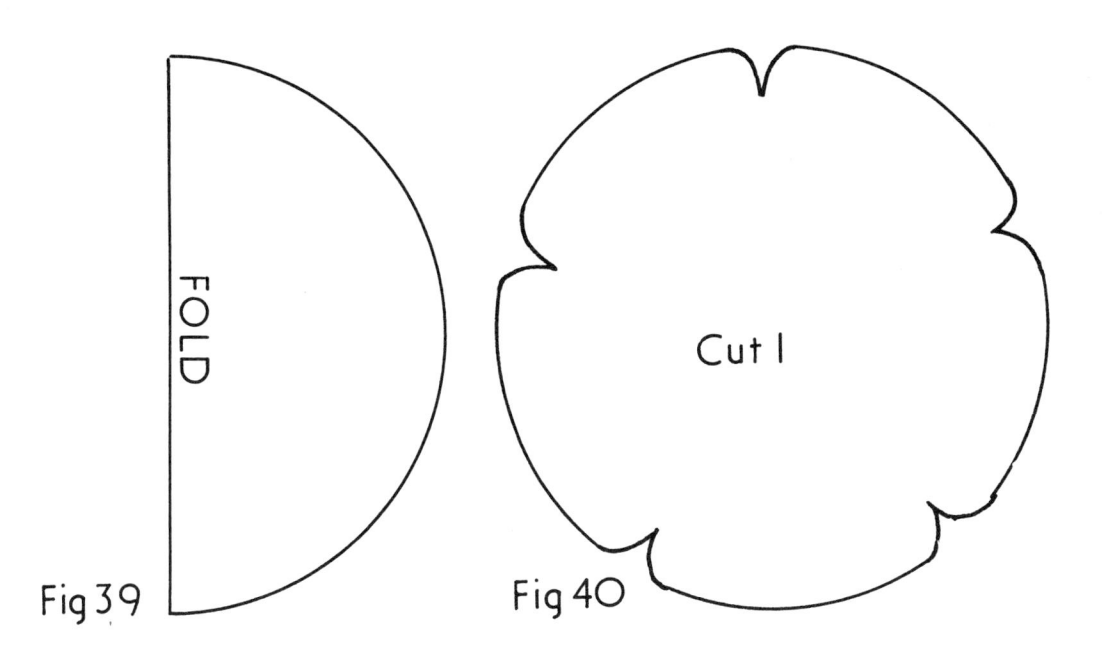

Fig 40 Cut 1

To make

1. Put a row of running-stitches near to the edge of the black circle. Do not fasten off the end of the thread but draw up to make the edges of the circle curve over slightly, Fig. 41. Fasten off.
2. Pin to red felt as in Fig. 42 and stitch round the edge. Stuff before completing the stitching.
3. The pincushion can be decorated with straight stitches as shown in Fig. 42.

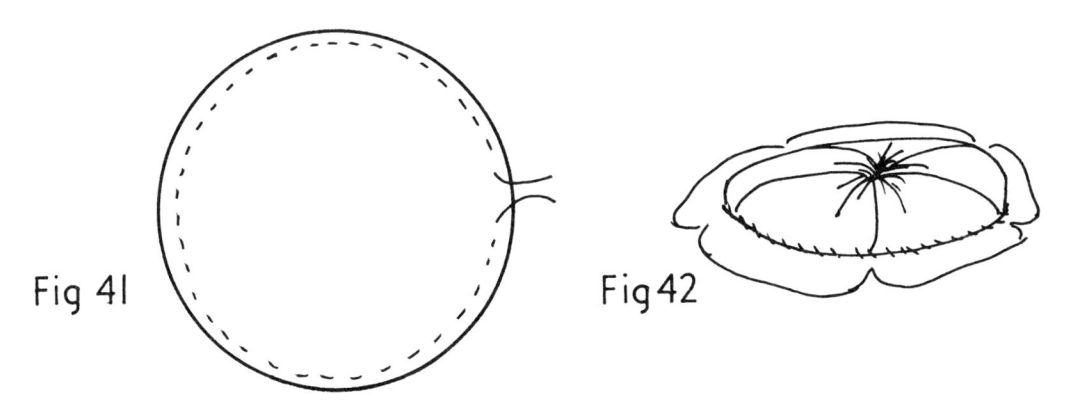

Fig 41

Fig 42

DESIGN YOUR OWN PINCUSHION

Cut out a 4-in. (10-cm) circle of paper. Fold in half, Fig. 43. Fold again, Fig. 44. Fold again, Fig. 45, and draw a petal shape. Cut out and open out the paper, Fig. 46. This is just an example – you can vary it to suit yourself, and choose your own colours.

Fig 43

Fig 44

Fig 45 Fig 46

Fig 47

Materials required

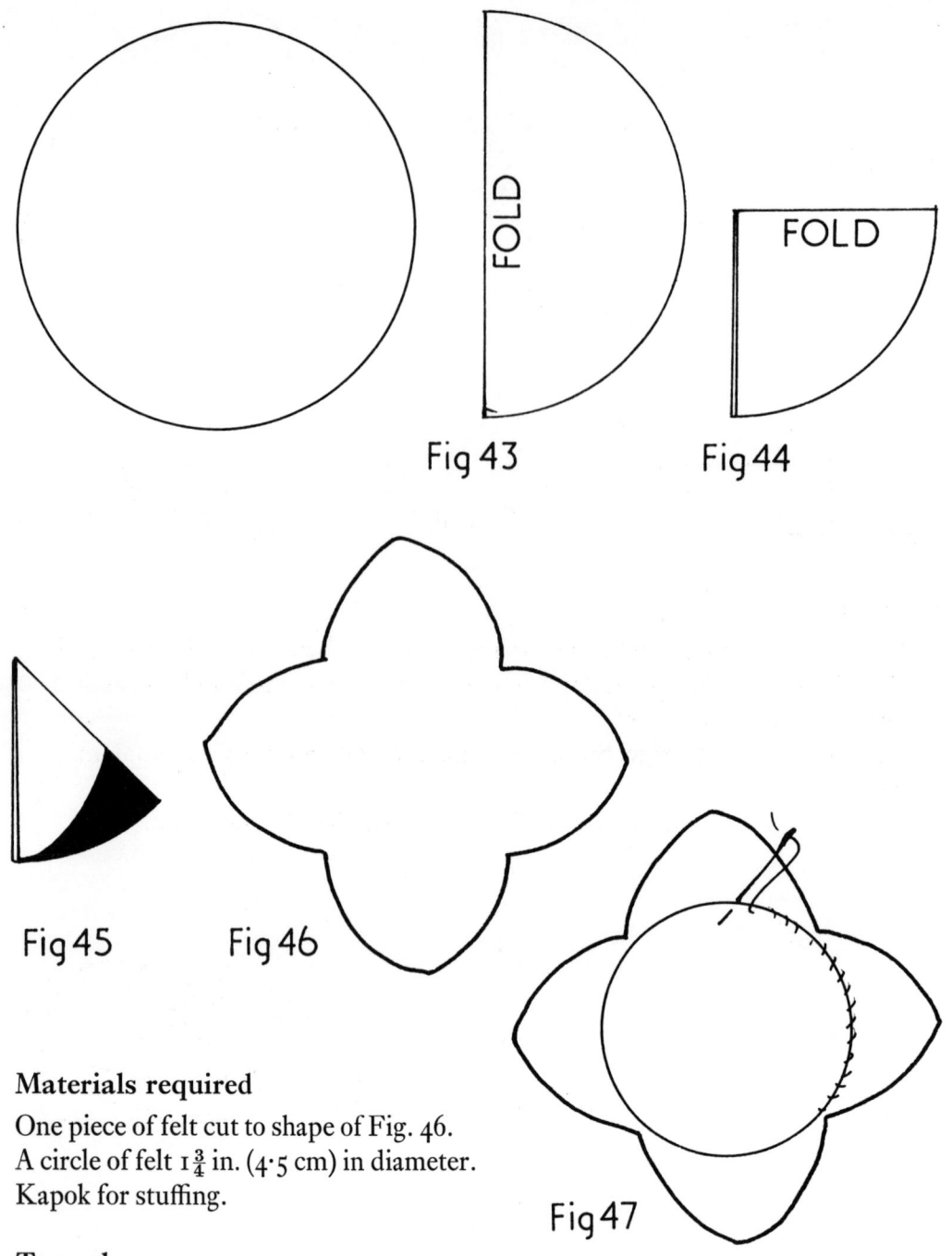

One piece of felt cut to shape of Fig. 46.
A circle of felt 1¾ in. (4·5 cm) in diameter.
Kapok for stuffing.

To make

Place the circle into position, Fig. 47, and secure by stitching the two together. Before completing the stitching stuff with kapok.

Note : The pincushion could be embroidered but the small circle should be embroidered before joining to the petal piece. This type of pincushion can be worn on the wrist if stitched to a band of elastic.

CURIOUS CURVY CREATURE

Materials required

Piece of felt 11 × 4 in. (28 × 10 cm). I used orange, but of course you can have any colour you prefer.
Scrap of white and black felt.
Kapok for stuffing.
Pipe-cleaner.
Trace off the pattern, Fig. 48.

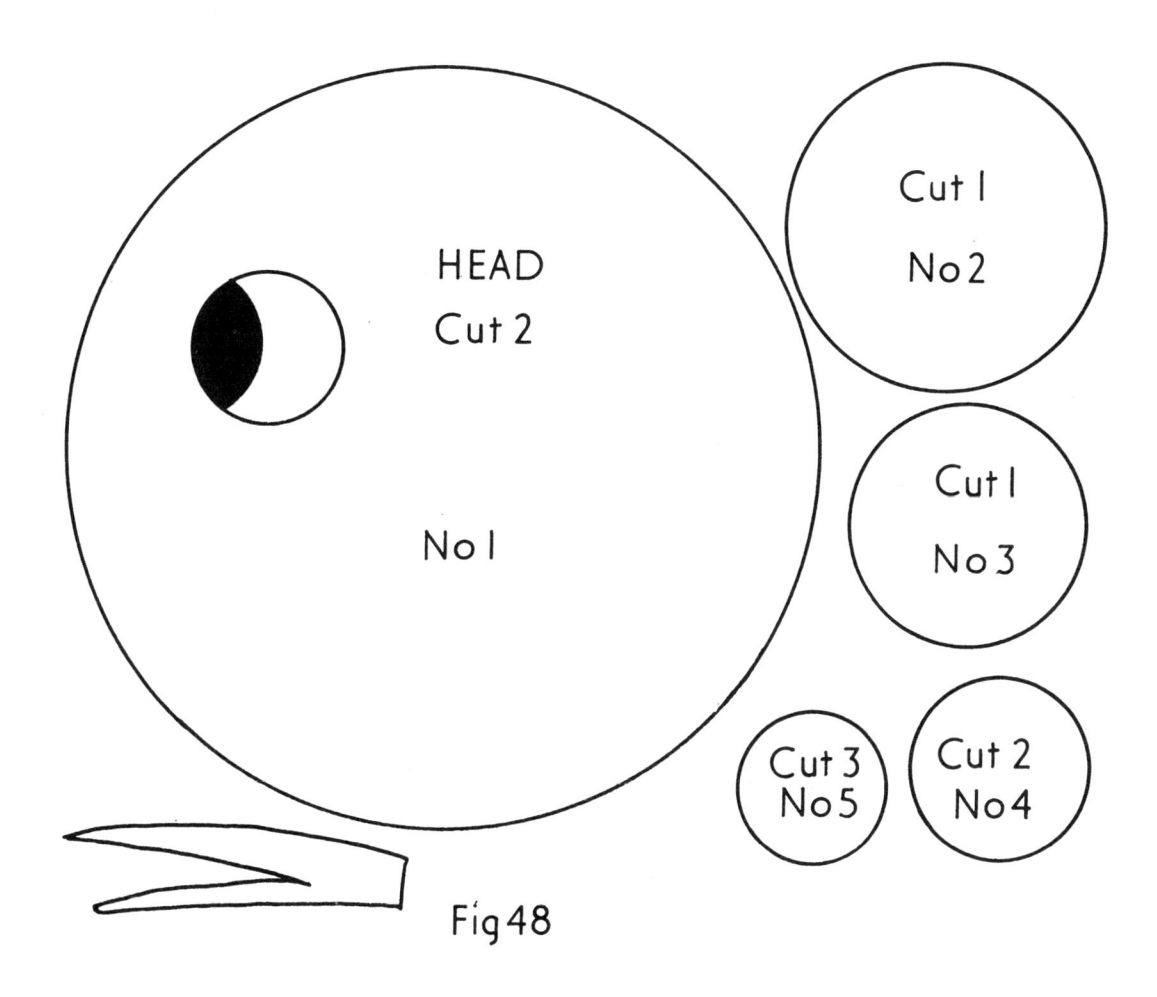

Fig 48

To cut out

1. Cut out two circles for head. Then cut: One circle of No. 2.
   One circle of No. 3. Two circles of No. 4. Three circles of No. 5. Follow layout in Fig. 49.
2. Using the black felt cut out a beak and eye section, Fig. 50.
3. Cut out two white eyes in felt, Fig. 51.

Layout Diagram   ORANGE FELT

HEAD   HEAD   No 2   4   4   3   5   5   5

Fig 49

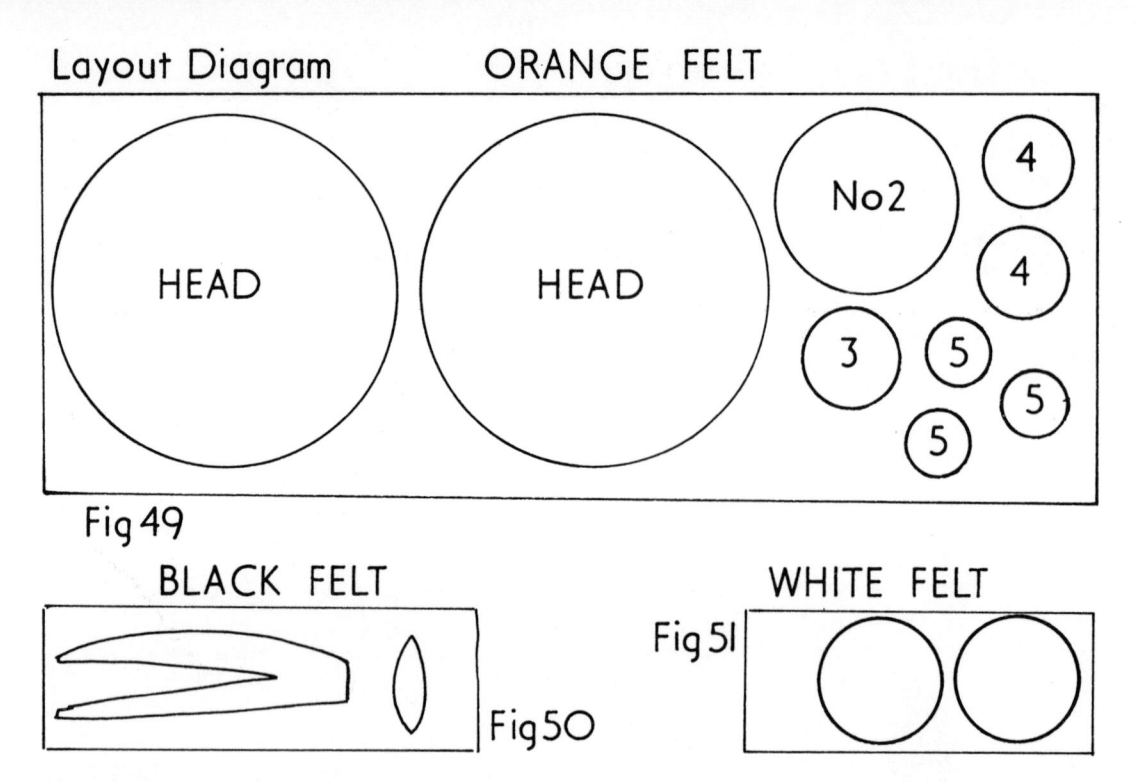

BLACK FELT

Fig 50

WHITE FELT

Fig 51

To make
1. Stitch on a black beak to the head, Fig. 52.
2. Join the two head circles together as in Fig. 53, starting at Point A. Stuff firmly before completing the stitching, and insert pipe-cleaner at A. Then stitch up the end securely.

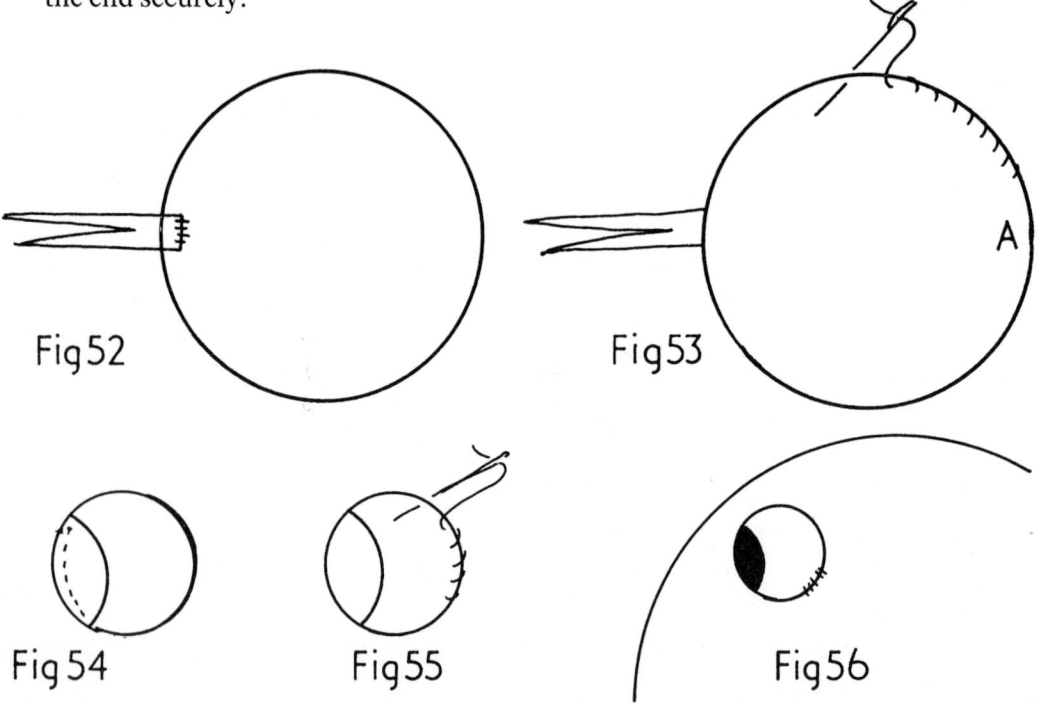

Fig 52

Fig 53   A

Fig 54   Fig 55   Fig 56

6. Three-dimensional patchwork.

7. Peacock collage. Note the variety of materials used.

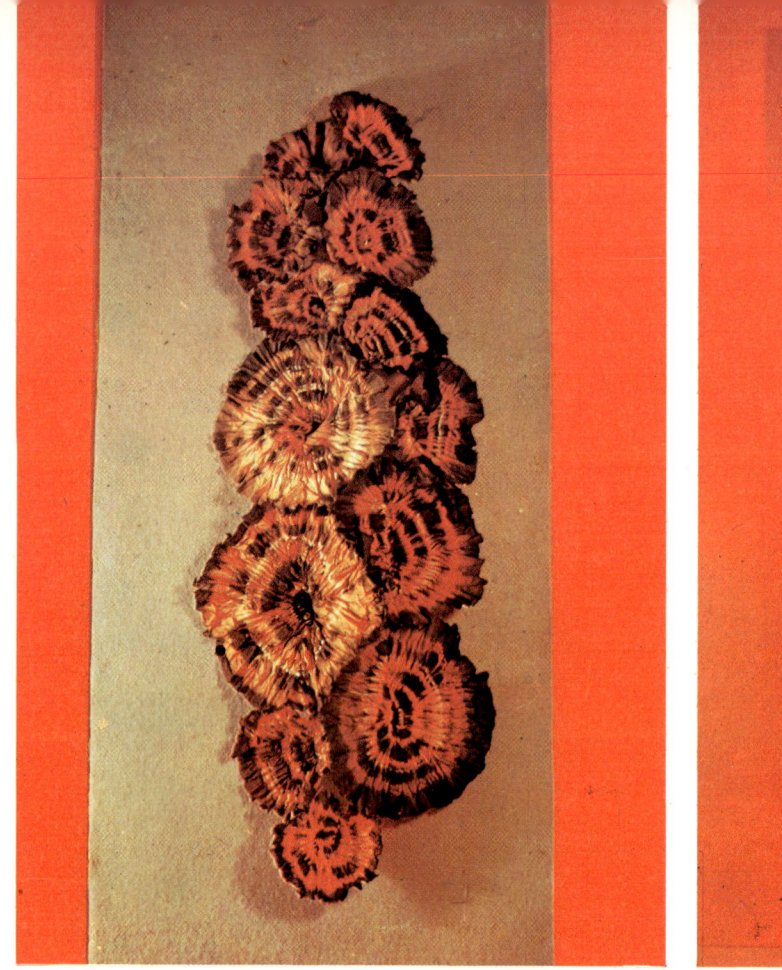

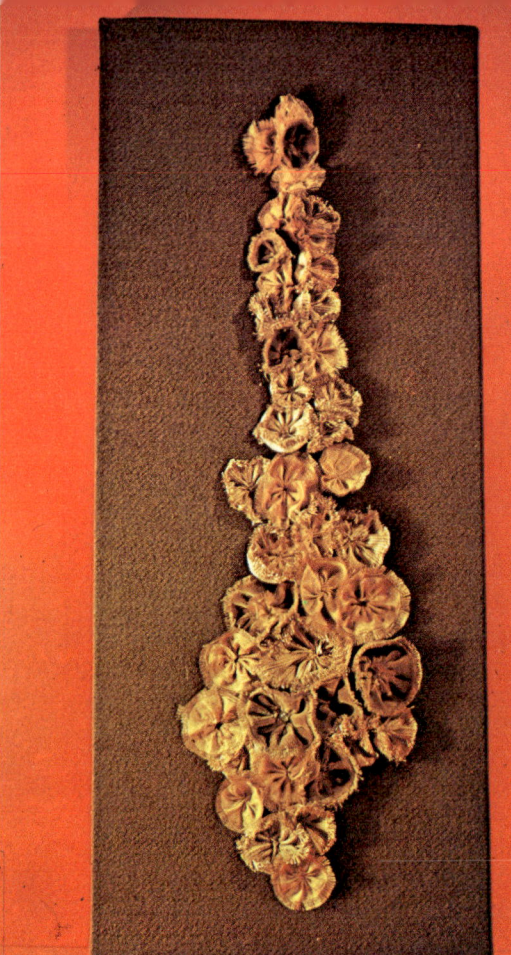

8. *Left above:* Tie-dyed Yo-Yo collage. Note the way the colour becomes more delicate at the frayed edges of the fabric. 9. *Right above:* Yo-Yo collage. 10. *Below:* Geometrical designs worked out on fabric-covered plaques with lines of thread. Sequins and pieces of fabric can also be added.

Fig 57

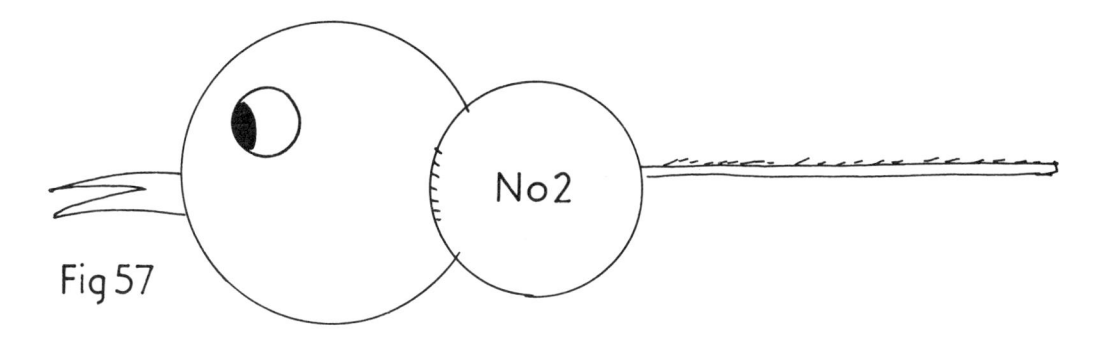

3. Place black eye section on to white circle and stitch, Figs. 54 and 55.
4. Stitch the eye to the head with a few stitches, Fig. 56.
5. Stitch No. 2 circles on to part of the body and stitch to pipe-cleaner, Fig. 57.
6. Join the remainder of the circles to the pipe-cleaner to form a tail. Overlap each one, grading the size downwards, Fig. 58.

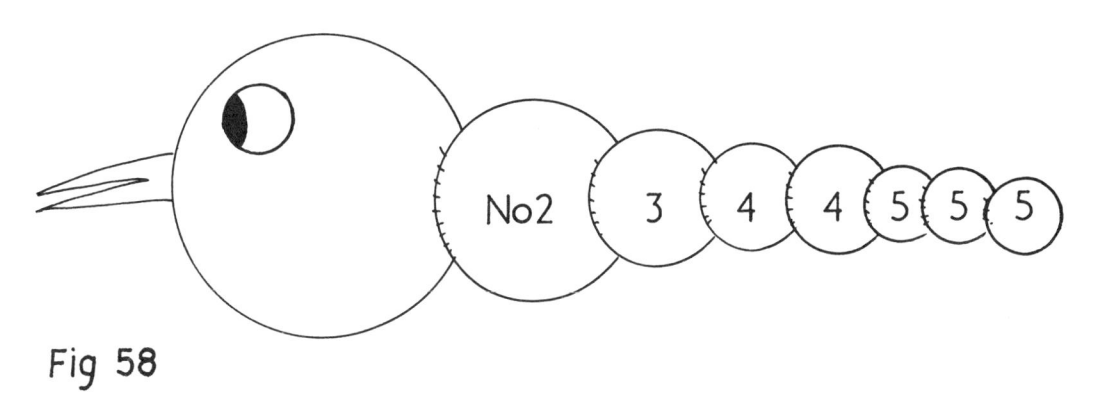

Fig 58

Books for reference

Primary Embroidery Stitches and Designs, A. V. White (Routledge & Kegan Paul)
Toys for your Delight, Winsome Douglass (Mills & Boon)
Performing Toys, A. V. White (Mills & Boon)

Things you can do with a triangle

TRIANGULAR FISH

A large triangle with a smaller one attached to it can look like a fish.

Fig. 59 From left to right – Pencil man (take his hat off and put pencils in), Curious Curvy Creature and a mobile fish.

Materials required

A piece of felt 5 × 5 in. (12 × 12 cm) and another piece 2 × 4 in. (5 × 10 cm).

To make

1. Trace off the outline of the fish and cut out in felt, Fig. 60.
2. Trace off the inner shape of the fish and cut out in felt, Fig. 60.
3. Using a leather punch and a scrap of felt (of a colour different from that used for the body), cut out some spots.
4. Place body of fish on to larger fish, Fig. 61. Pin and run-stitch round. Leave an opening near tail. Stuff, then complete the stitching.
5. Stick on the spots, also pieces of felt for eyes and mouth, Fig. 62.

Fig 62

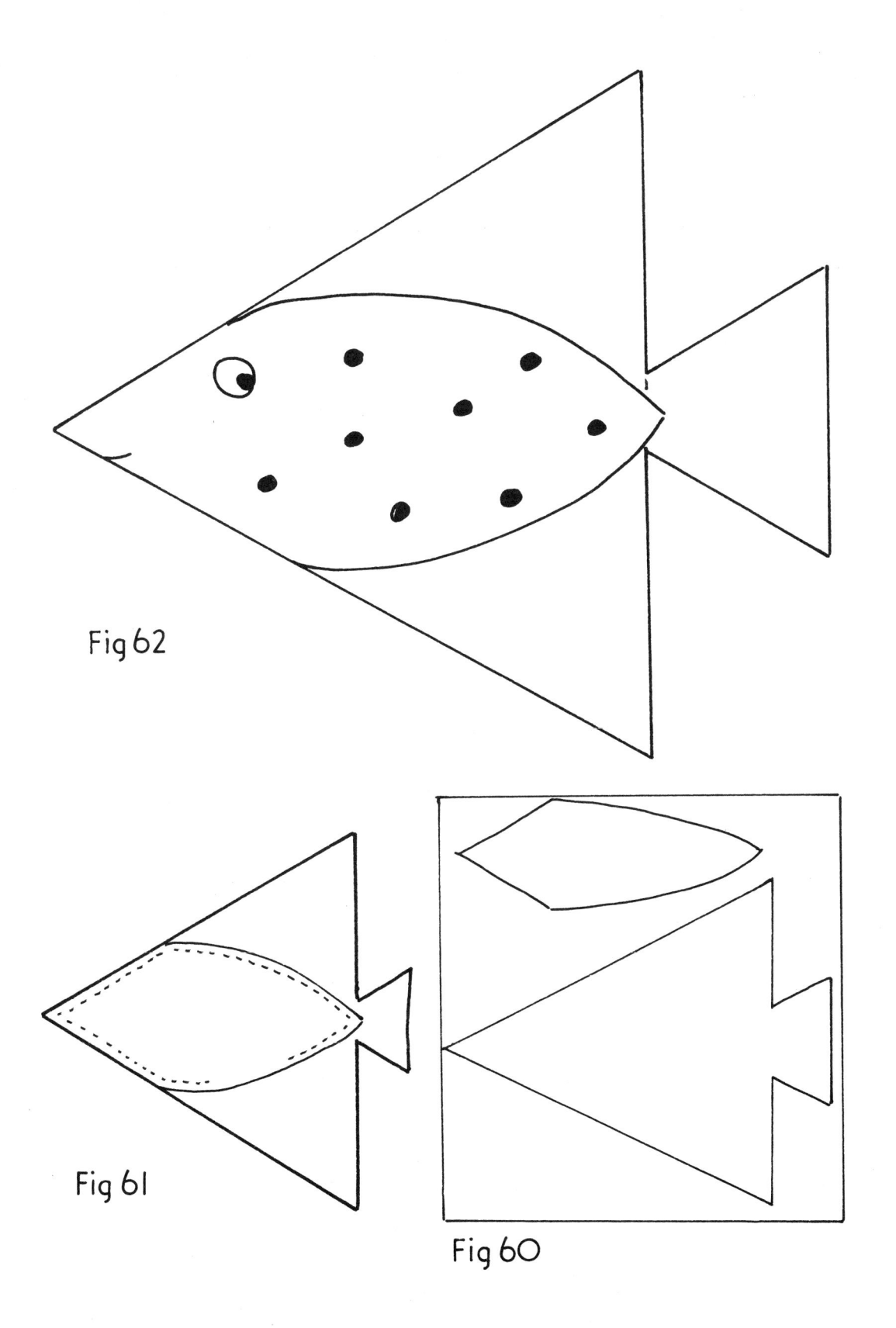

Fig 61

Fig 60

EMBROIDERED FISH

Embroider a spot design on body before joining together. Embroider the fins.

Look for ideas in *Primary Embroidery Stitches and Designs* by A. V. White (Routledge & Kegan Paul).

Here are three sizes of triangles, Fig. 63.
They can be arranged to form a design other than a fish. Here are three trees, Fig. 64. You could embroider these shapes on to a mat, or cut out the shapes in felt and apply them to a larger piece and make a flower-pot cover.

A Flying Fish was made from triangles of two different sizes, see *Performing Toys* (Mills & Boon).

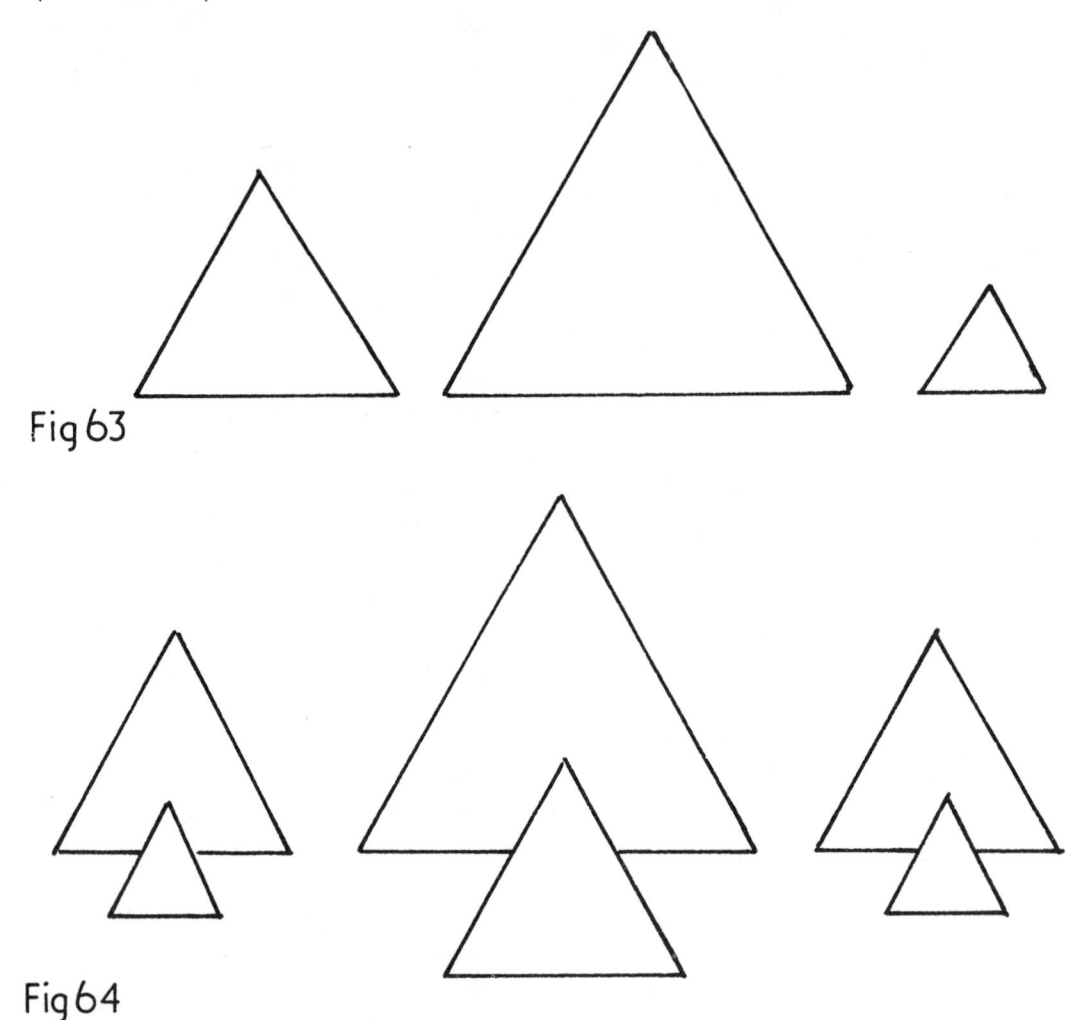

Fig 63

Fig 64

Binca canvas

This type of fabric is easy to embroider because it is woven with holes in the weave. The fabric is generally known as Binca, but other names may be used, according to the suppliers. Sometimes it is thought to be expensive and not really a fabric suitable for creative work. In the past too many mats, dressing-table sets, traycloths, etc. were made with very simple, unimaginative stitchery because other ideas were considered too difficult, and this was so when the whole class had to do the same thing.

I hope that the ideas given in the following pages will set you off to do some planning for yourself with the aid of pencil and squared paper, and later with a small piece of Binca. If it is undyed, e.g. cream, it is much cheaper and is 40 in. wide. Use a blunt-ended needle, i.e. a tapestry needle, as this will go through the holes more quickly than a needle with a sharp point. Use a coarse embroidery cotton such as Clark's Anchor Soft Embroidery.

Fig. 65 Three hangings – clown, dog and bear – made from Binca canvas using a variety of stitches.

There is no need to know a great deal about stitches to be able to make wonderful patterns. Just try out a little cross-stitch, or better still zigzag stitch. There are over a hundred different patterns which have a row of zigzag as part of the foundation of the design and although this may sound strange, once you get carried away with ideas you will soon see what fun it can be. Mathematical straight-stitch patterns may also be worked on this canvas.

Fastening on

Always leave about the depth of three squares to form a border, because the material frays, i.e. it can form a fringe. A knot may be tied, but better still pass the needle between the two layers of weave and make two small stitches, one on top of the previous one.

Fastening off

Always work two stitches on top of each other on the back of the Binca fabric, making sure that the stitches do not show on the right side.

Cross-stitch

Make a vertical stitch as in Fig. 66(a), and a diagonal stitch, Fig. 66(b). This forms a cross-stitch. Continue working as in Figs. 66(a), (b) and (c). It is important that the upper stitches should all slant in the same direction.

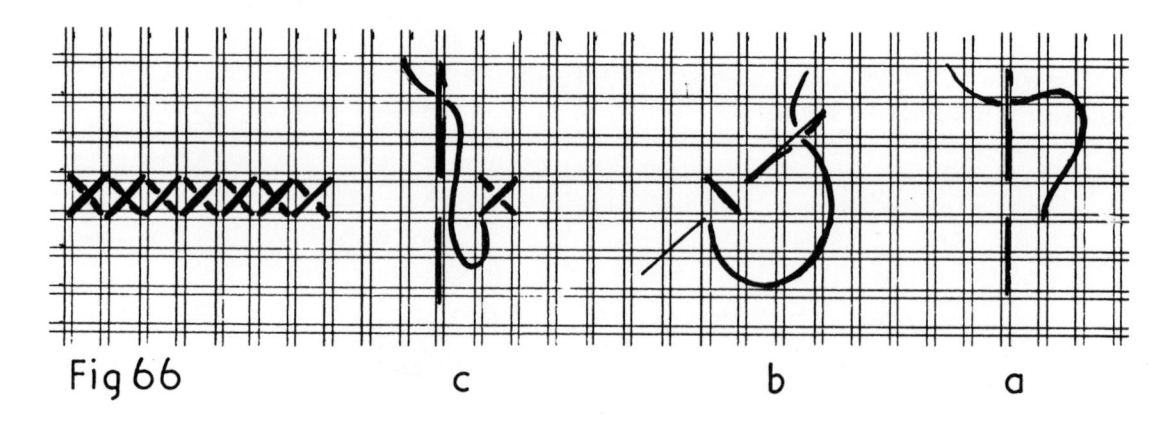

Fig 66   c   b   a

Borders of cross-stitch can be planned on graph paper. Fig. 67(b) and (c) shows how designs can be built up from a basic border, Fig. 67(a). Other ideas are illustrated in Fig. 67(d), (e) and (f).

Make your own design for panels, etc. Fig. 68(a) shows how a boy and two girls might look if they were doing a folk dance. Perhaps you could make a picture with animals, Fig. 68(b). Maybe you prefer to draw trains, as in Fig. 68(c).

Fig 67

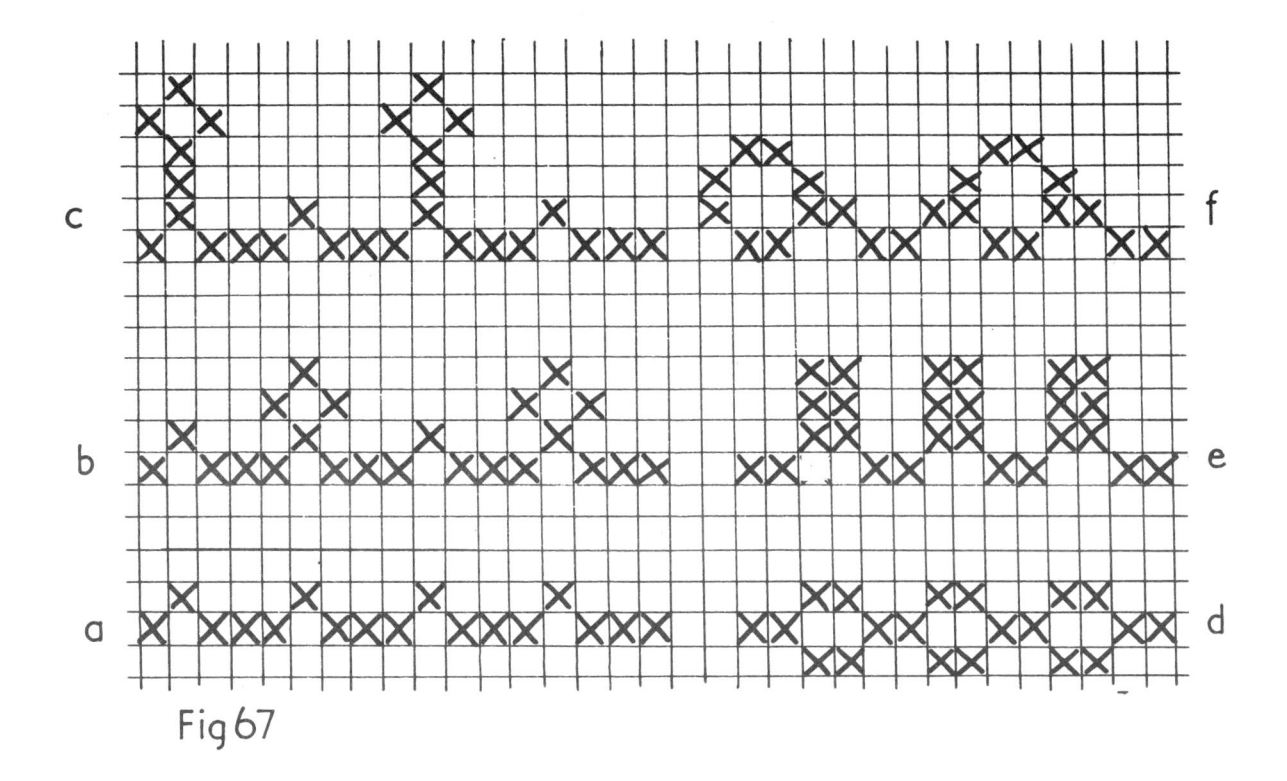

Zigzag stitch

Pick up two squares on the top row but note the position of the needle and thread, Fig. 69(a). Put the needle into the base of the previous stitch and pick up two squares, Fig. 69(b). The stitch should give a continuous line, as in Fig. 69(c).

Borders can be built up from zigzag stitch. Straight stitches can be added as in Fig. 70(a), then another row of zigzag, Fig. 70(b).

Vertical fly-stitch

Bring the needle out on to the right side of the fabric and insert the needle two squares to the right and bring out as in Fig. 71(a), with thread under point of needle.

Insert the needle into the canvas one square lower down and bring out as in Fig. 71(b). Repeat to form a vertical line, Fig. 71(c).

Motifs can be built up as in Fig. 72(a), (b) and (c), using four fly-stitches for the centre. A larger motif can be made from Fig. 73(a) to Fig. 73(b) and further enlarged to Fig. 73(c).

a

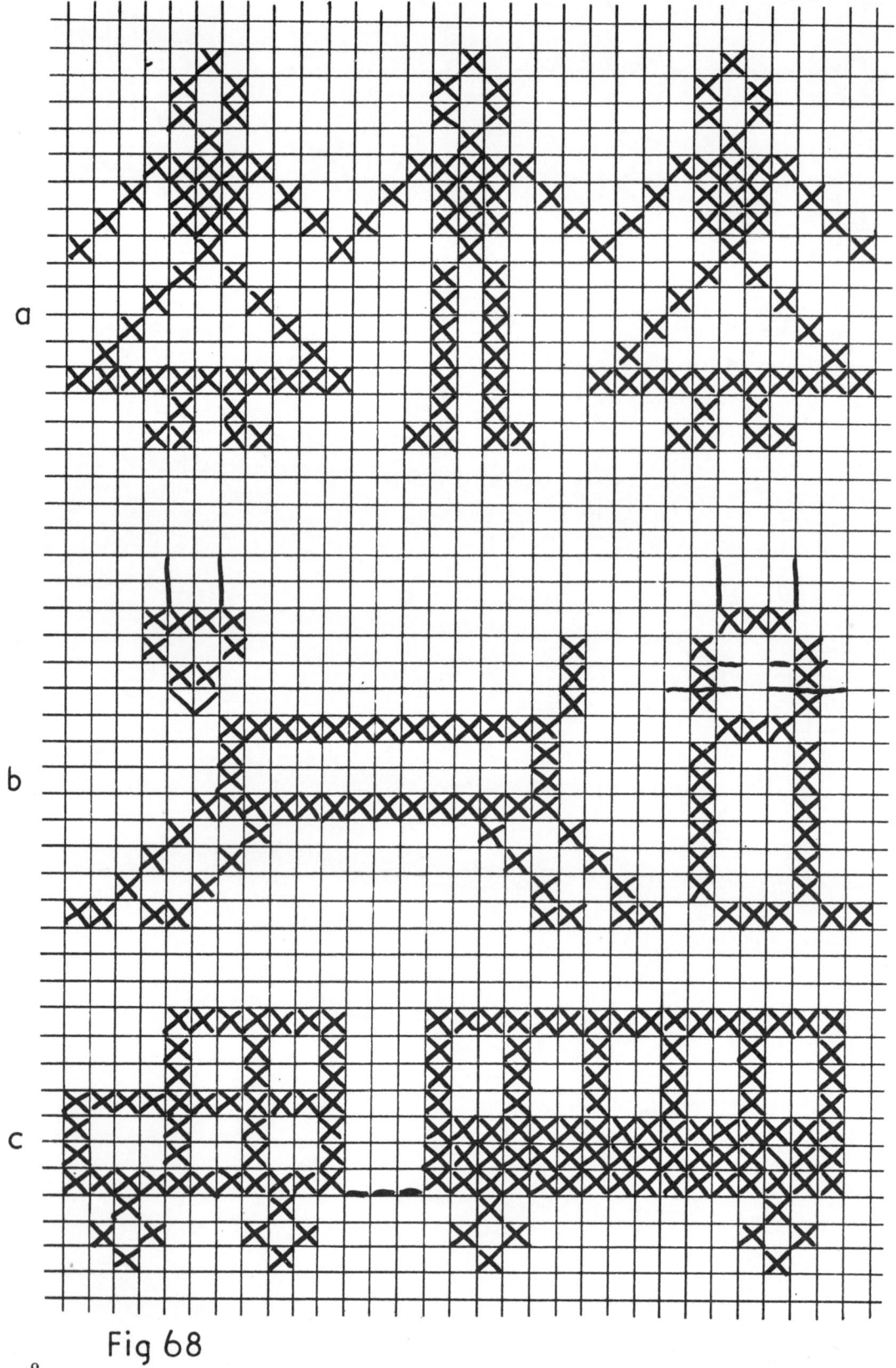

b

c

Fig 68

Fig 69 c   b   a

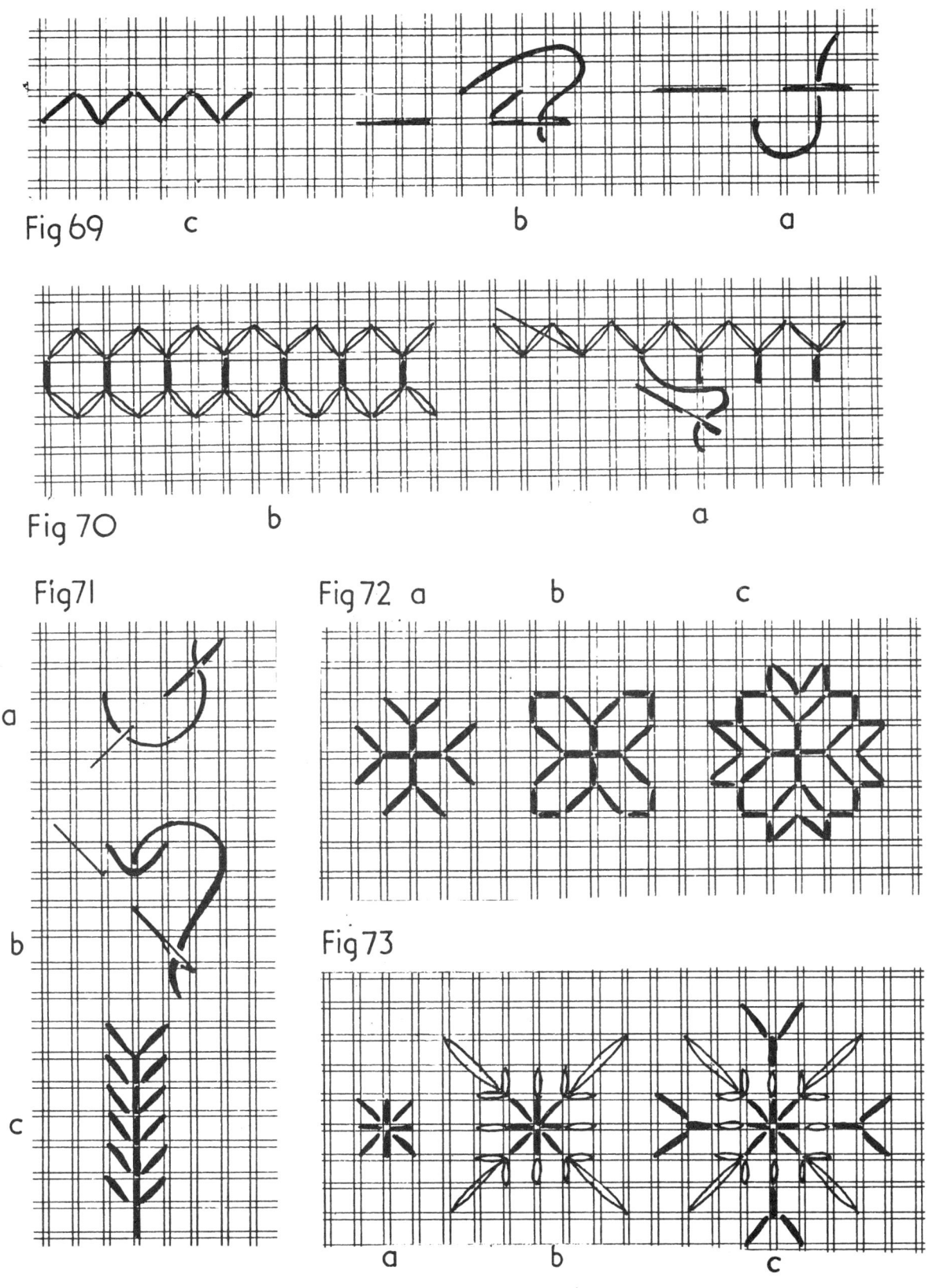

Fig 70 b   a

Fig 71

a

b

c

Fig 72 a   b   c

Fig 73

a   b   c

49

Fly-stitch

Insert needle as in Fig. 74(*a*), keeping the thread under the point, and pull through. Push the needle diagonally into the fabric as in Fig. 74(*b*). Continue working to form a solid band, Fig. 74(*c*).

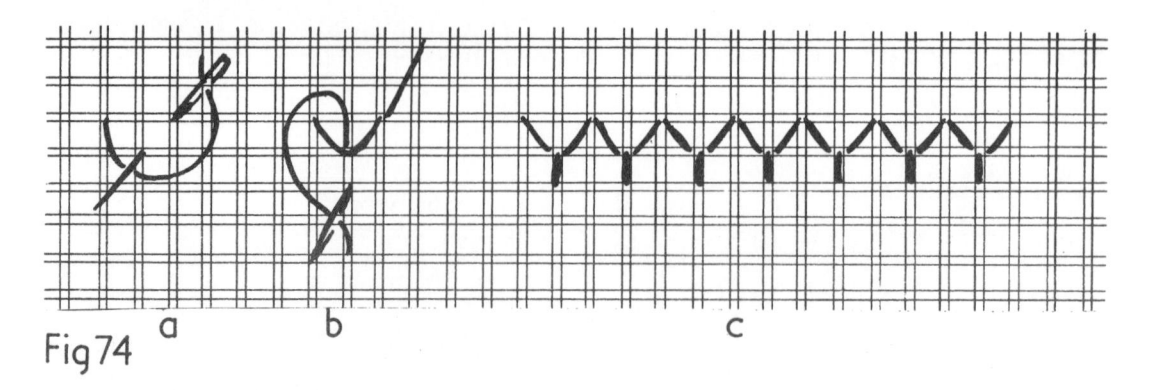

Fig 74   a   b   c

There are two different ways of turning a corner with zigzag stitch, Fig. 75 and Fig. 76. The inside border designs also show how corners can be turned.

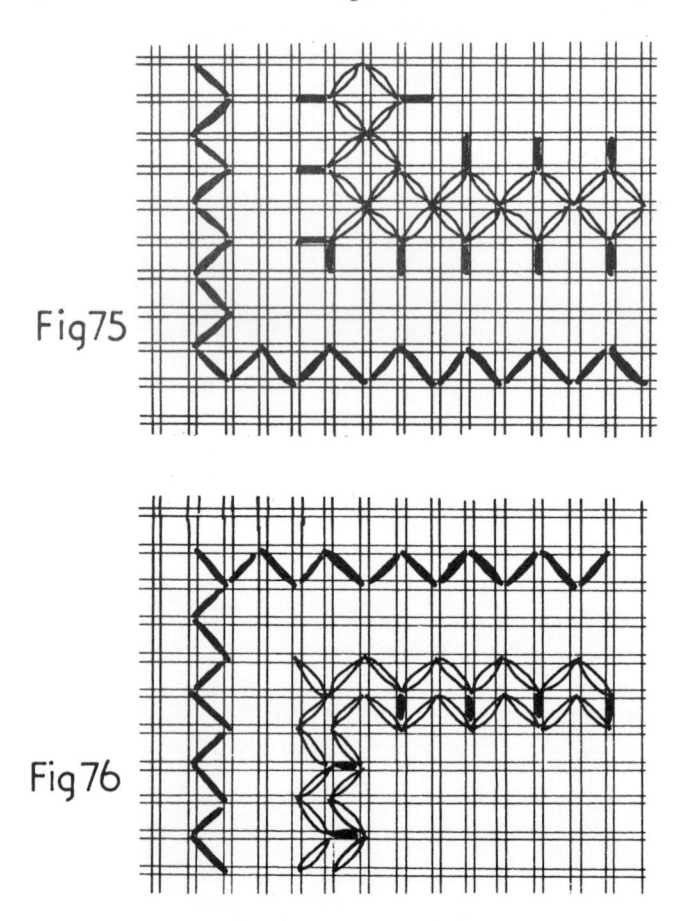

Fig 75

Fig 76

Hangings or pictures can be designed quickly by using straight stitches or cross-stitch. The design of the dog, Fig. 77, is based on straight stitches of varying lengths; also the clown in Fig. 65. Thick thread was used for the outline and finer thread for the filling. The leg pattern is that of Fig. 68 and the feet have a pattern of thick french knots.

Perhaps you would prefer to make a picture of buildings you have seen, as in Fig. 78.

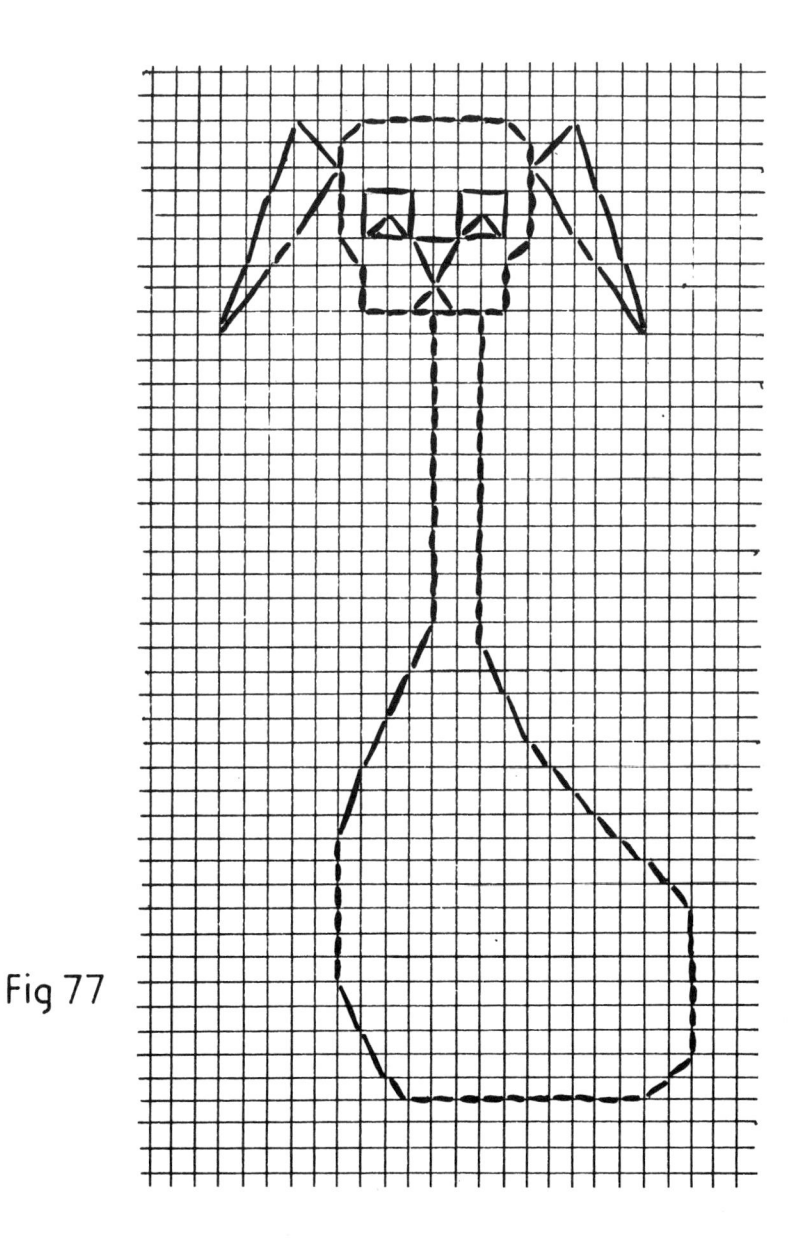

Fig 77

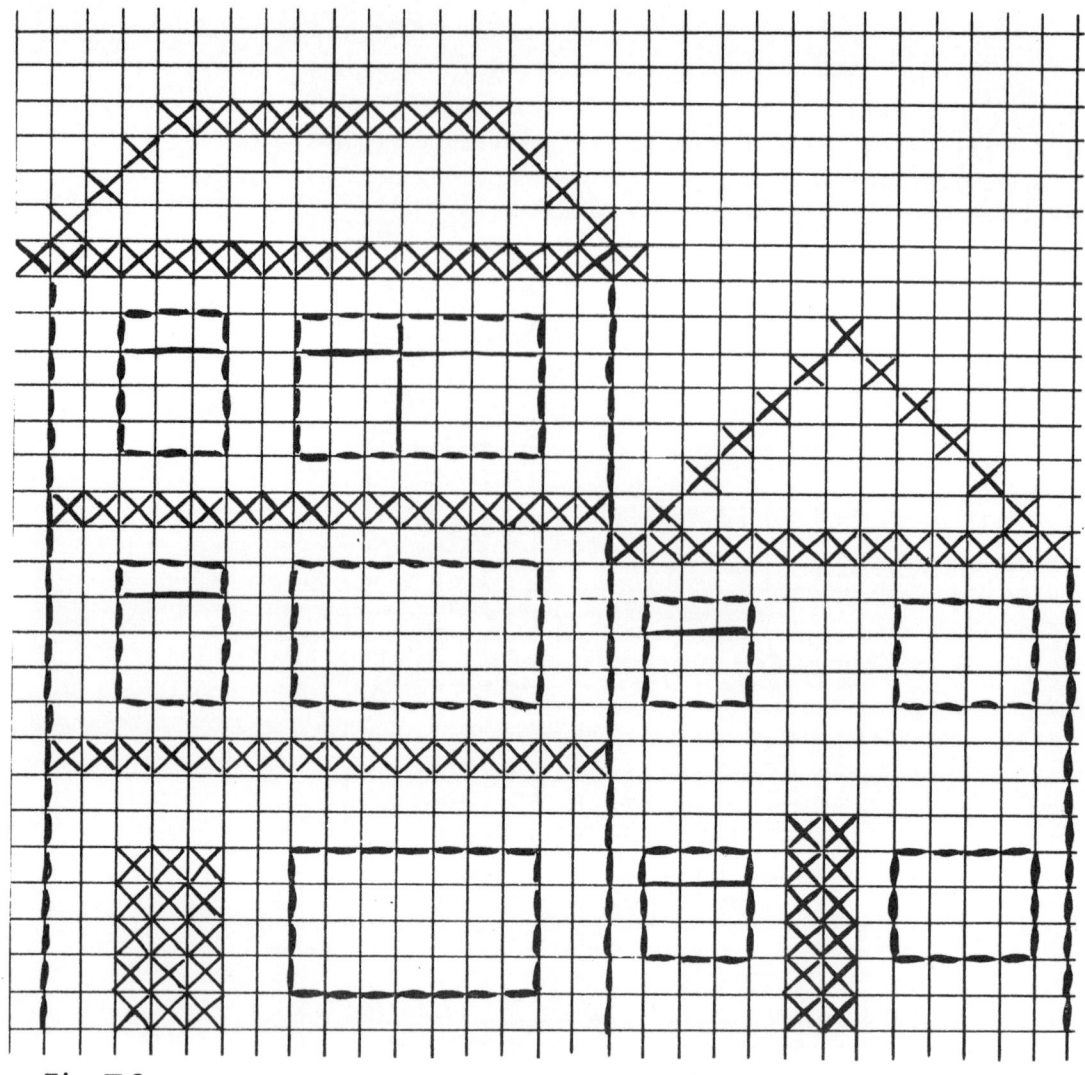

Fig 78

BINCA MAT

Materials required

11¾ × 15¾ in. (30 × 40 cm) Binca canvas.
Clark's Anchor Soft Embroidery Cotton in two different colours.
Tapestry needle.

To make

Work a row of zigzag stitch, Fig. 69, page 49, three rows of squares in from the edge.
Work a second row to form diamond shapes.

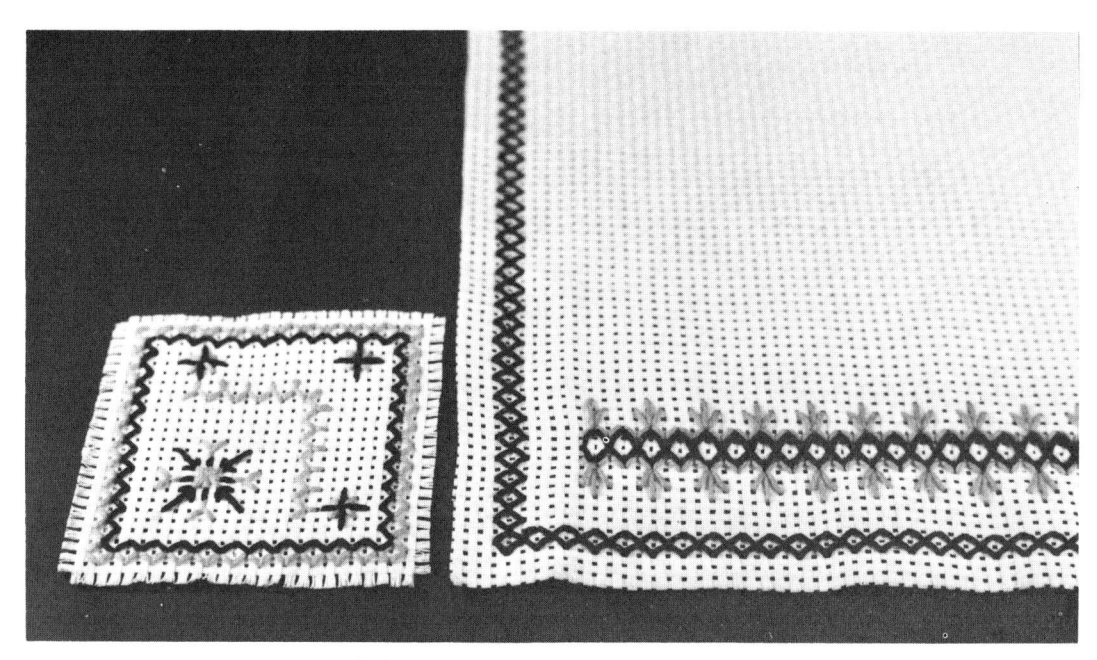

Fig. 79 Two mats made of Binca canvas.

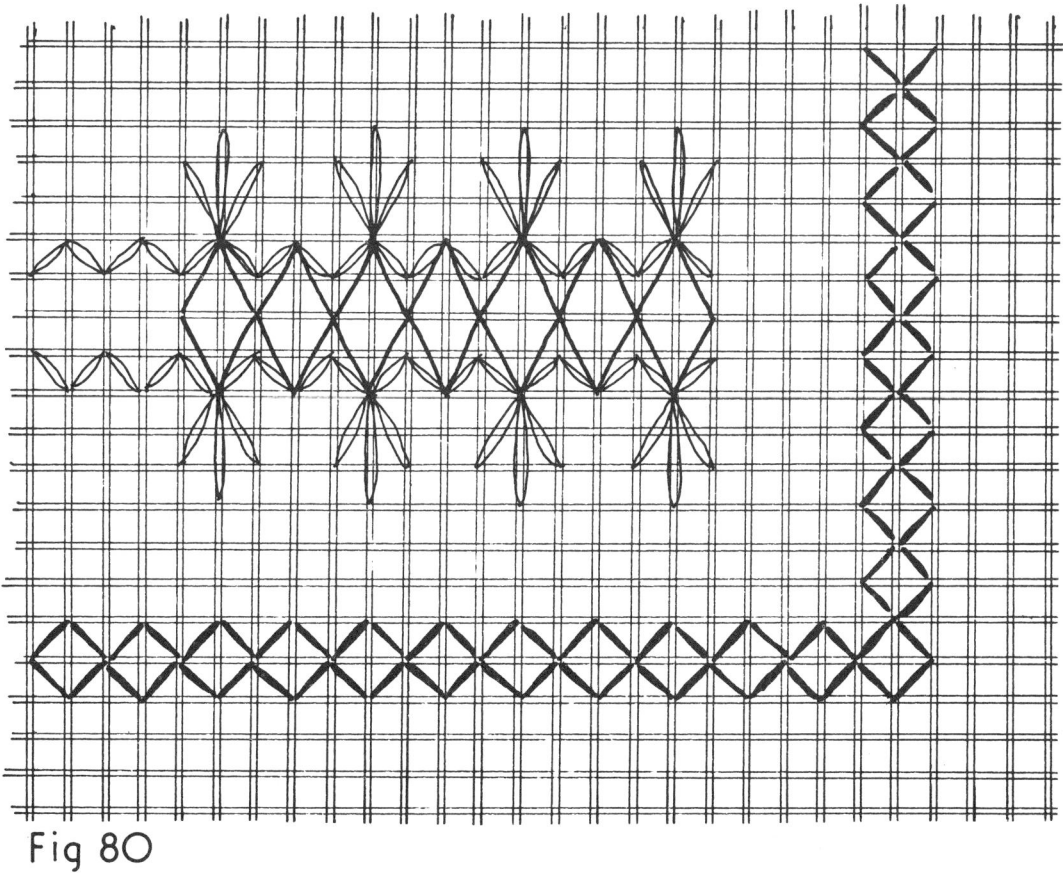

Fig 80

The border design consists of two rows of zigzag stitch worked in a contrasting colour, Fig. 80. The two rows are worked with a space of two squares between each row.

Two rows of zigzag stitch are worked over two squares, Fig. 80, using the previous row of stitches to form part of the centre design. The outer edge of the border is made up with three straight stitches radiating from a centre hole.

Books for reference

Primary Embroidery Stitches and Designs, A. V. White (Routledge & Kegan Paul)
Blackwork Embroidery of Today, A. V. White (Mills & Boon)
Blackwork Embroidery, Geddes & McNeill (Mills & Boon).

Tie-and-dye

If we take a piece of plain, thin fabric and bind with thread, or rubber-bands, or hold it tight with clothes-pegs, then place the fabric into a dye bath for fifteen minutes or so, we find that when the fabric is removed and the bands or pegs taken out, where the pegs or ties were the dye did not penetrate. When the fabric is fully opened out a type of pattern is formed The pattern is governed by the way a resist is formed against the dye. This can be varied by the number of clothes-pegs used, and their position, and also by the way the fabric is held by the ties or bands.

Try using a piece of old cotton sheeting (i.e. a fabric which has been washed many times), also a piece of plain new cotton fabric. Tie both pieces of fabric in the same shapes and see what effect the old fabric has over the new, or vice versa.

Always rinse the fabrics well before untying. See what a variety of patterns you can achieve by pleating the fabric in different ways, or knotting. Maybe you could try both on one piece of fabric.

Having used plastic pegs in one arrangement, try out other patterns. Do not limit yourself to straight pieces of fabric; cut out circles and see what can be done with this shape.

See what effect a second colour will have on the previous dye, but first rearrange the pattern of the clothes-pegs or rubber-bands. If some areas are to be left to show the original colour, then leave in some of the pegs and bands.

Although cotton fabric is the one mentioned for these experiments, it most certainly is not the only fabric. If you look around for other pieces of plain material you may find some are knitted and others woven. Try out ideas of your own, and see what interesting results you can obtain by using plain fabrics, also textured fabrics, Crimplene, for instance.

In the following pages instructions are given on how to plan the tying and dyeing of fabrics and making them up into panels, toys, etc. These are only ideas and other patterns could be carried out for the same articles.

A plan of the tie-and-dye ideas may be made so that on one piece of fabric you may have some patterns formed by stitchery and others by pleating, and by clothes-pegs.

Three-dimensional tie-and-dye need not be mounted as in Colour Plate 8 but arranged so that the designs can be mounted within a skeleton frame and pulled taut.

An immense variety of ideas and techniques can be found in *Tie-and-Dye As a Present-Day Craft* by Anne Maile – virtually the "Bible" of tie-dyeing – and in *Tie-and-Dye Made Easy* by the same author (both published by Mills & Boon).

In this section I have tried to show how a plain fabric can be decorated by tying and dyeing it, and how the fabric can be used.

The method of producing patterns by tying and dyeing is exciting both for its own sake and for the use of the fabric for embroidery. For making up the dyes follow the instructions on the packet.

Materials required

Saucepan (or bowl if using cold-water dye).
Household dyes. Cold-water or hot-water dyes can be used.
Thread for tying (any odd lengths of thick cotton thread or very thin soft string).
Suitable cloth – thin cotton which has been washed, or old sheeting.
First see what attractive results can be obtained by doing the following:

Methods of tying

A striped pattern:

1. Use a piece of fabric about 9×6 in. (23×15 cm). Fold the fabric into accordion pleats, Fig. 81. Fold into two, Fig. 82, and hold in place with rubber-bands, Fig. 83 and Fig. 84. Or, use plastic clothes-pegs of the snap-fastener variety. Place several of the pegs in to hold the pleats firm, Fig. 85. This method is only suitable for cold-water dyes.

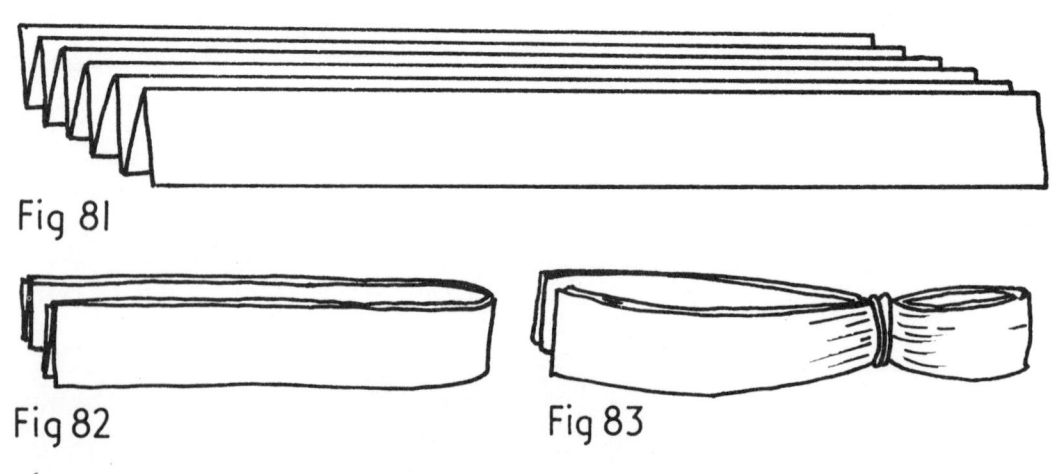

Fig 81

Fig 82   Fig 83

Fig 84

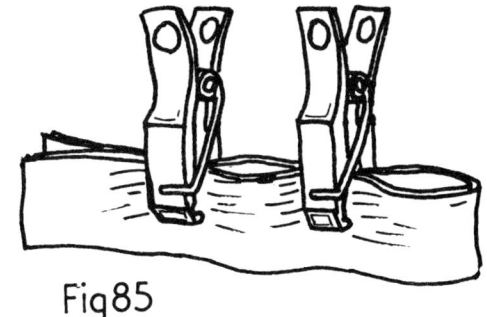

Fig 85

2. Use a piece of fabric 9 × 6 in. (23 × 15 cm) and fold it into accordion pleats, but not more than ½–¾ in. (1–1·5 cm) in depth, Fig. 86. Tie firmly in two or three places. To "tie" one really binds the thread around the fabric several times before tying very securely, Fig. 87. The pattern effect will be like Fig. 88.
3. Using a 6 in. (15 cm) square, make a spot pattern by picking up the centre of the fabric. Smooth the fabric down from the point and bind round firmly with thread, Fig. 89(a). When dyed this will give a single spot design, Fig. 89(b).

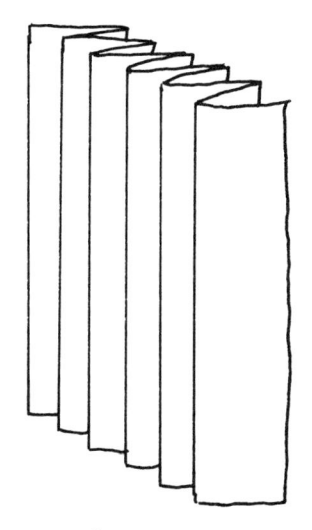

Fig 86

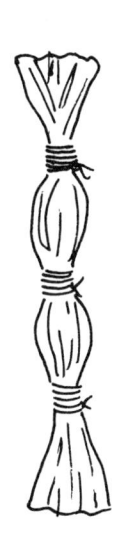

Fig 87

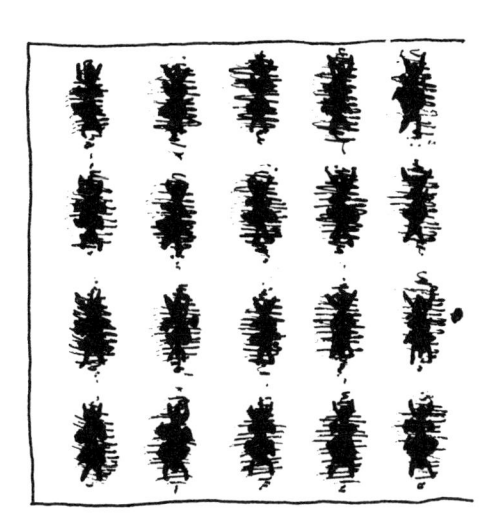

Fig 88

4. Repeat the spot pattern, but this time tie in two or three places. This gives a much larger design, Fig. 90(a) and (b).
5. A diamond design can be formed by folding the fabric diagonally. Then, using a safety-pin, pick up the double layers of fabric, working down to a point (dotted line, Fig. 91(a)) and back up again. Bind just below the pin, then remove the pin to enable the fabric to be bound really tightly, Fig. 91(b) and (c). When dyed the fabric will look like Fig. 92. Four repeats could be arranged as in Fig. 93. This could then be lightly embroidered and used as a place mat.

Fig 89 a b

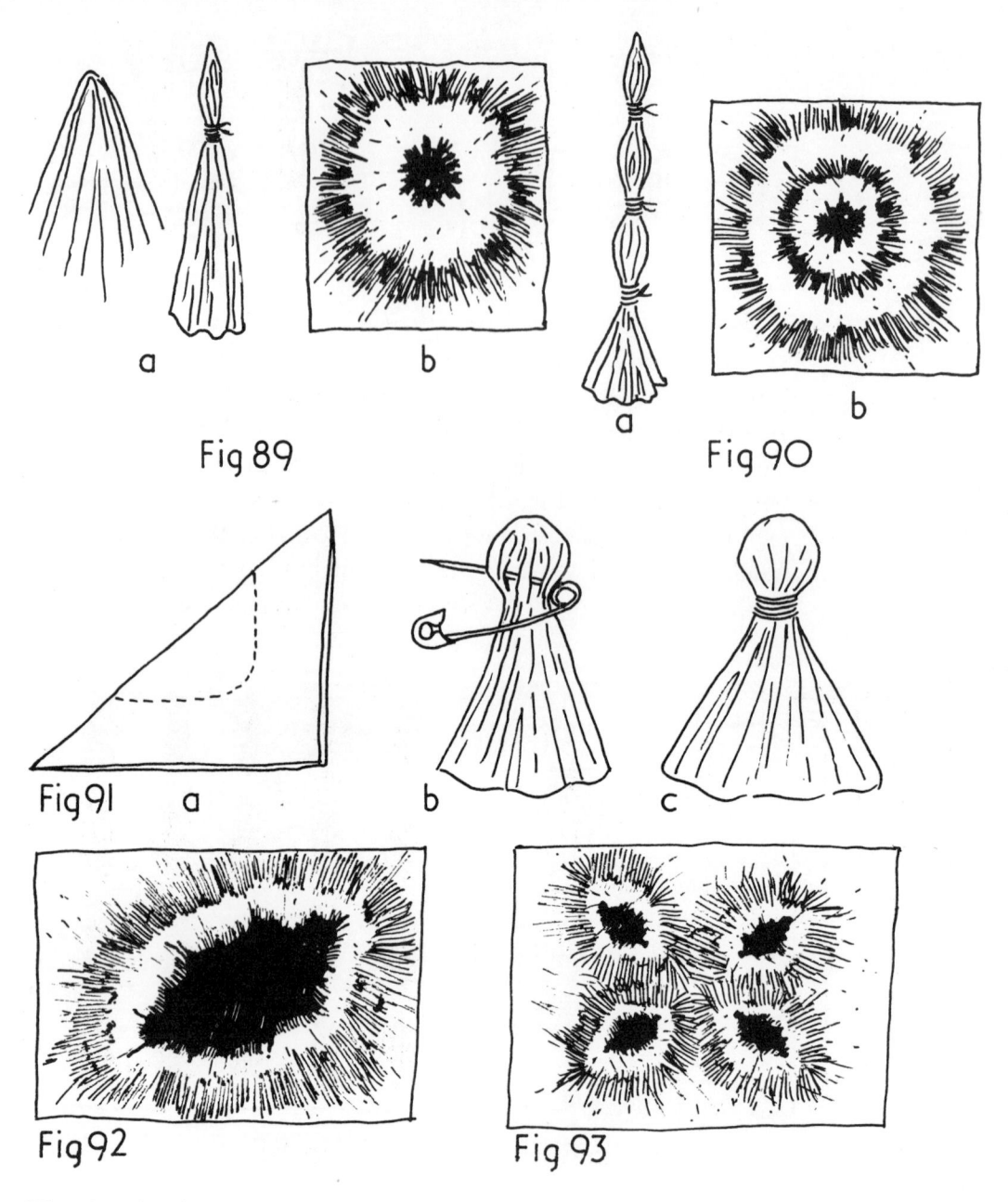

Fig 90 a b

Fig 91 a b c

Fig 92

Fig 93

The dye should be made up according to the instructions. Hot-water dyes, i.e. for fabrics which are boiled with the dye, usually have stronger colours. Cold-water dyes are very good and these again should be used after carefully reading the manufacturer's instructions. It must be remembered to add salt to the dye-bath because this makes the colour fast.

After the article has been dyed rinse well in cold water, then place on to several sheets of newspaper and untie. The fabrics may be left to dry or ironed between layers of newspaper.

Dyeing using two colours

Very interesting effects can be obtained by using more than one colour of dye. Tie the fabric in two or three places as in Fig. 94(a). Dye the fabric and afterwards bind the centre area, Fig. 94(b), for a much larger area. Next tie the fabric near the top and remove the previous tie (Fig. 94(c)) which will now reveal a white part or undyed area. This will enable this area to take the new colour. Bind the area at the lower end (Fig. 94(c)) to prevent the new colour penetrating.

If the first dye was yellow and the second red, when the fabric is finally untied then a pattern of white, yellow, orange and red should appear.

Interesting bright and dark patterns can be obtained by using orange and blue dyes.

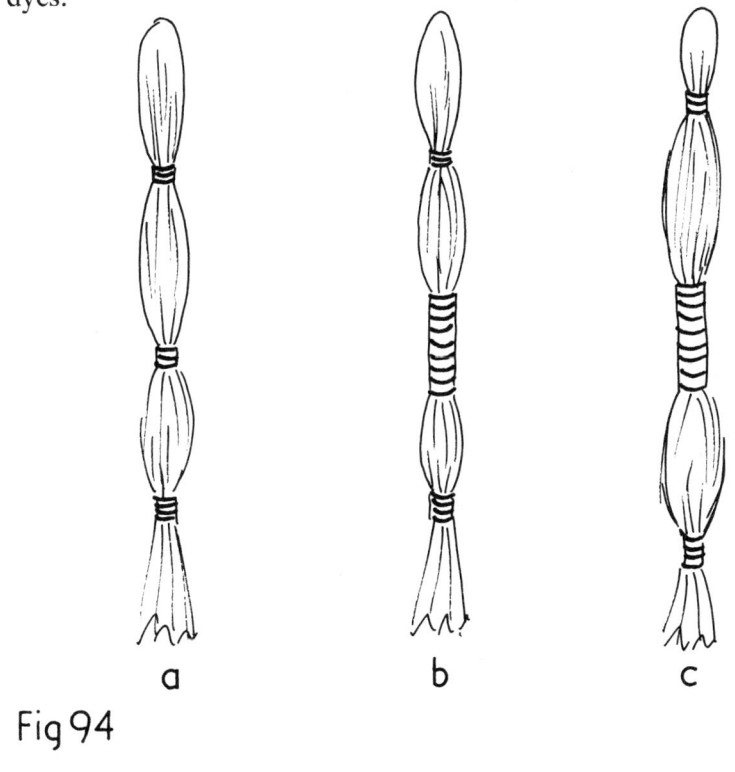

Fig 94

FISH FOR A FRIEZE

You can make a delightful spotted fish for a frieze. Draw the fish shape on to a piece of fabric and mark in the position of the spots, Fig. 95(a).

Make the spots small (maybe tie in a dried pea or pearl barley to form the dot). After the fabric has been dyed and dried, draw in the tail and fins of the fish, using a felt-tipped pen, Fig. 95(b), then cut out and mount on to a back-cloth.

Fig 95a   Fig 95b

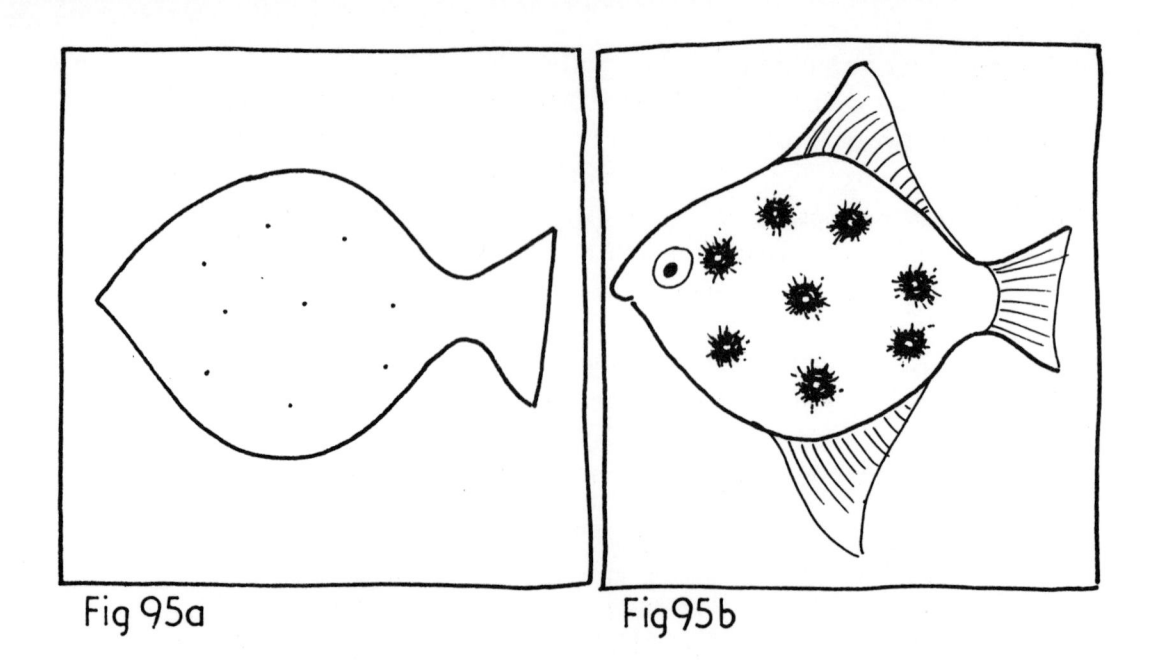

A PUPPET DRESS

Can be made by first drawing the shape of the bodice on to a piece of fabric and marking the position of the spots, Fig. 96. These are then tied (patent fasteners make good spot patterns). After the fabric has been dyed, the bodice is then cut out. The skirt of the dress is made by pleating the fabric. For pattern and making see page 81.

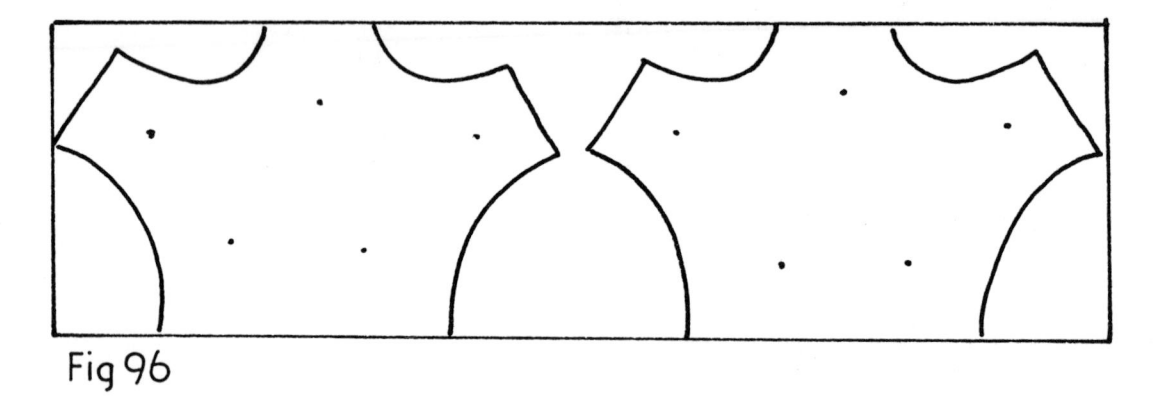

Fig 96

A PINCUSHION

A pincushion can be made from a strip of fabric which has been pleated and dyed for the sides, and a spot pattern for the top.

A NEEDLE-CASE

This may be made from a piece of fabric with a spotted pattern (see Fig. 97).

Materials required

Two pieces of fabric 4 × 7 in. (10 × 18 cm).
One piece of Vilene (for stiffening) 3 × 6 in. (7·5 × 15 cm).
Piece of felt $2\frac{1}{2}$ × $5\frac{1}{2}$ in. (6·5 × 13 cm).

Fig. 97 Tie-dyed and embroidered needle-case.

To make

On the one strip of fabric tie a spot at each end, Fig. 98. Make the spot bold by tying it twice as in Method 4, page 57. Keep the other piece untied, but put it into the same dye. This plain piece is for lining the needle-case.

Embroider around the spot pattern, using simple bold stitching such as chain-stitch (detached) or fly-stitch, or long straight stitches in a bold colour, Fig. 99.

Place the Vilene on to the wrong side of the spotted piece and pin, Fig. 100(a). Turn over the raw edge at the top on to the Vilene and tack, Fig. 100(b).

Turn under $\frac{1}{2}$-in. (1-cm) turnings of the lining and place on top of the wrong side of needle-case, pin carefully, then oversew all round, Fig. 100(c). Fold the piece of felt in half, Fig. 100(d). Fold needle-case in half. Place crease of felt to crease of inside of case, hold the two together, with two or three straight stitches.

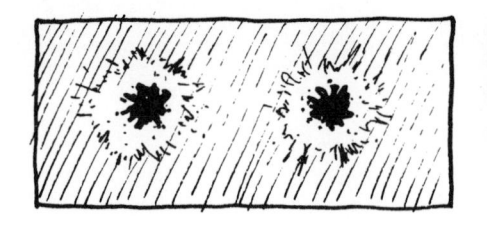

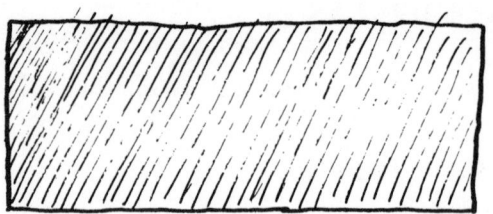

Fig 98

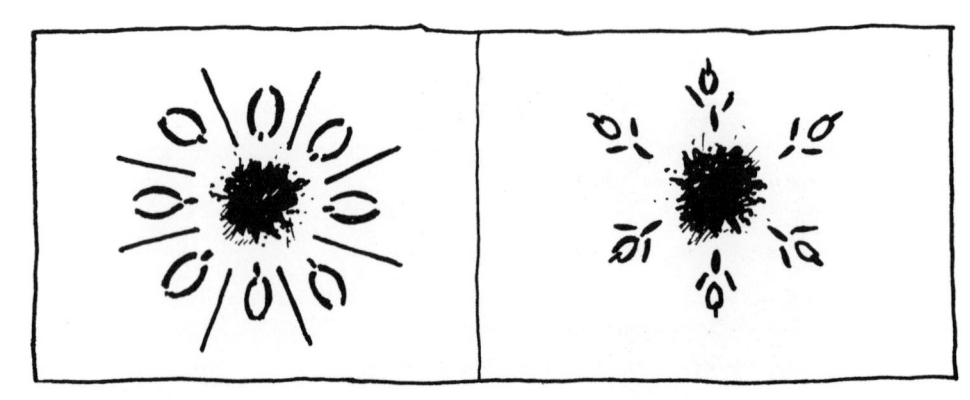

Fig 99

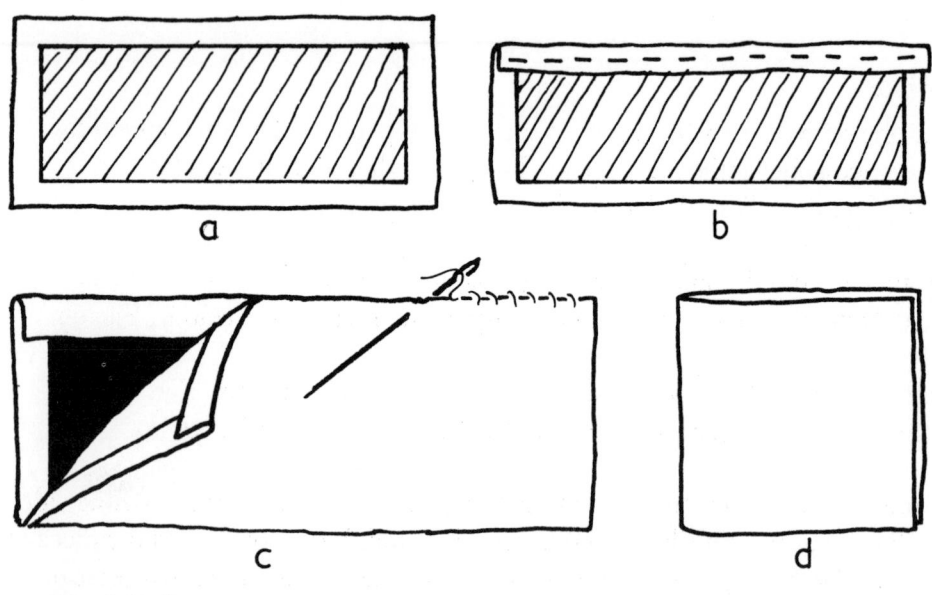

a

b

c

d

Fig 100

GYM-SHOE BAG

Materials required

12 × 21 in. (30 × 54 cm) cotton fabric.
Six plastic rings.
30-in. (75-cm) white cord.

Fig. 101 Tie-dyed and embroidered gym-shoe bag.

To make

Pleat the fabric and dye it. Press carefully, then embroider upon some of the stripes, Fig. 102, using detached chain-stitches or fly-stitch. Bands of embroidery can be carried out by using threaded running-stitch in its various forms. The embroidery thread can be quite thick so that a quick, bold result can be obtained.

Fig 102

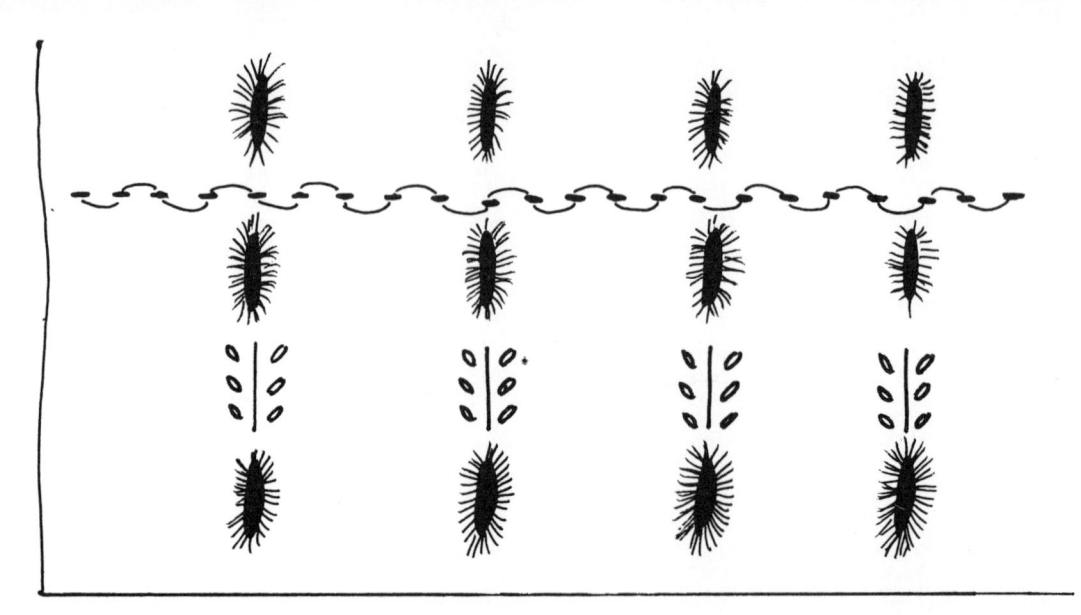

Make up the bag by using a french seam.
Turn a ¼-in. (5-mm) hem on the top edge of the bag over on to the inside, and hem.
Measure out the position of the plastic rings and stitch securely to the bag.
Thread the cord through the rings and secure with a knot or a tassel.

Tie-and-dye fabric can be so designed that it is very suitable for soft toys. A long snake-like creature could be quickly designed and made. A ladybird is a delightful

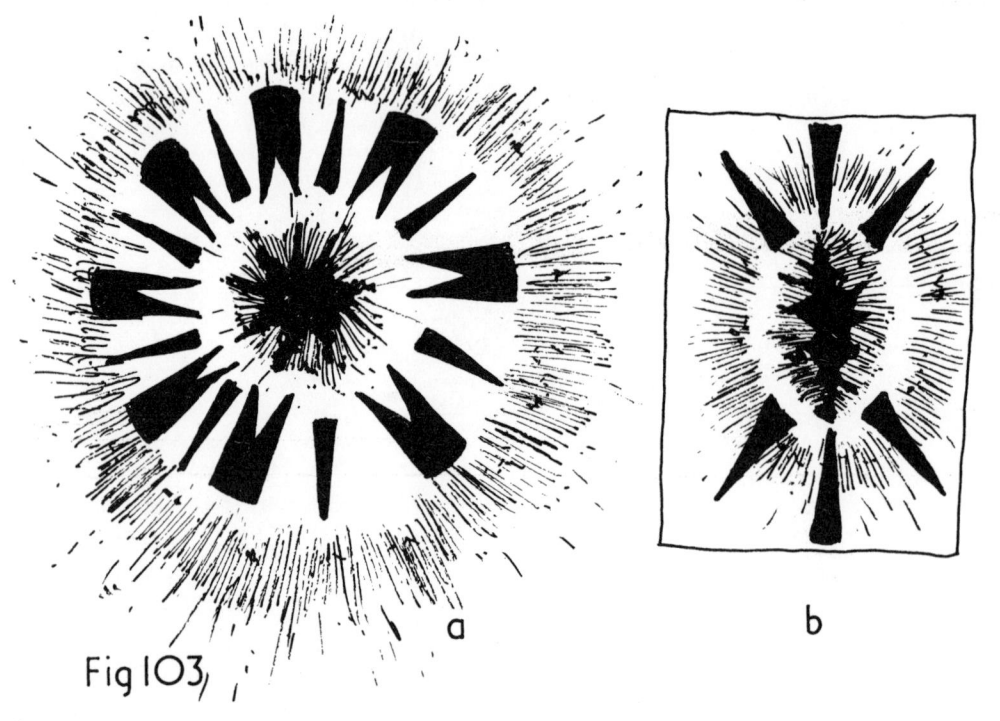

Fig 103   a   b

64

shape, with a patterned body. A snail could have a design built up of spots for the main house section, while the body could be striped and the head spotted. Some examples are given later in this chapter.

A potato print may be added to a tie-and-dye design. This should emphasise the design as in Fig. 103(a) or for an elongated design this can be developed as in Fig. 103(b).

THREE-DIMENSIONAL FLOWER PANEL

Materials required
Piece of felt or background fabric, 10½ × 26 in. (26 × 65 cm) mounted on to cardboard
4 squares of thin white cotton fabric, each 9 × 9 in. (23 × 23 cm)
2   ,,   ,, ,,   ,,   ,,   each 7 × 7 in. (18 × 18 cm)
4   ,,   ,, ,,   ,,   ,,   each 6 × 6 in. (15 × 15 cm)
3   ,,   ,, ,,   ,,   ,,   each 4 × 4 in. (10 × 10 cm)
2 dyes (one brightly-coloured, i.e. orange) and blue.

Preparation
1. Rule three squares, Fig. 104(a) on to the large pieces of fabric.
2. Run-stitch round. Do not fasten off, Fig. 104(b).
3. Draw up threads and bind round the fabric two or three times, and secure, Fig. 105(a).

   Do this to all the squares. The small ones may have only two squares drawn on them.

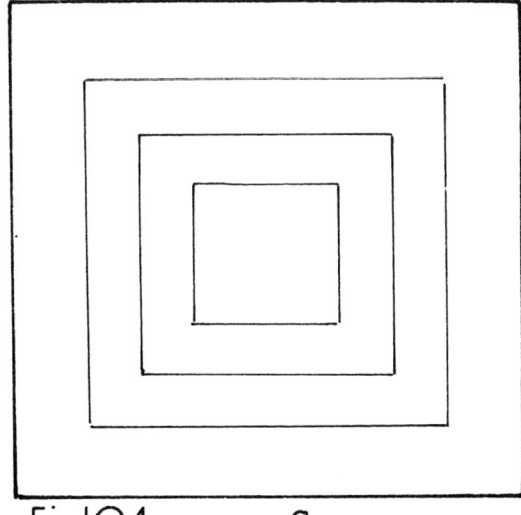

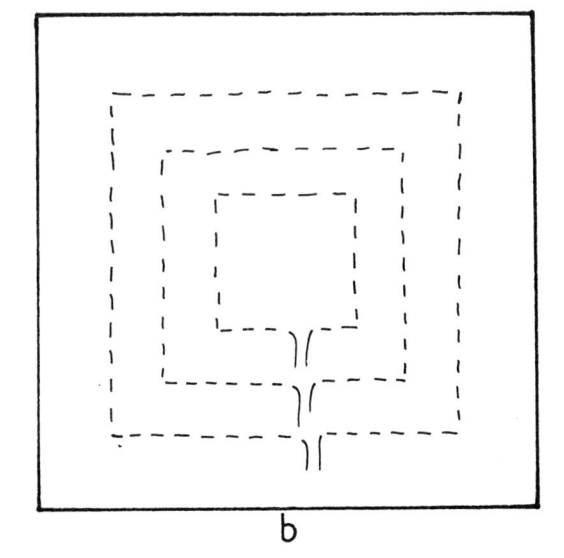

Fig 104   a   b

a   b   Fig 105

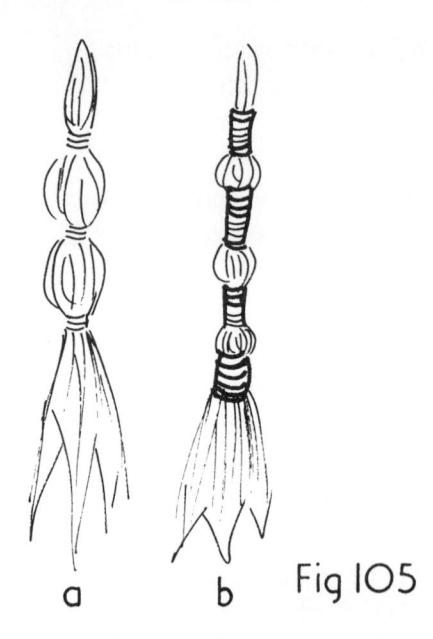

4. Dye a bright colour (orange).
5. Add further binding threads, Fig. 105(*b*).
6. Dye in blue, then leave the fabrics in the tied condition for several days.
7. Untie and remove stitching threads. Trim round the outer edge of each piece to obtain a flower shape. Turn each flower inside out so that one is looking into the brighter colour.

Arrange to form a design, keeping some of the flowers slightly closed and others opened wider. Pin to the back-cloth and when satisfied with the arrangement, stick down with adhesive, and stitch some of the flowers which are raised.

SNAIL

Materials required

Piece of cotton fabric 12 × 6 in. (30 × 15 cm) for body.
Two pieces of cotton fabric 10 in. (25 cm) square.
Kapok.
Two dyes.

Preparation

1. Mark two eyes in the body piece, Fig. 106. Make small circles of stitching and draw up and tie.
2. Pleat the fabric and tie in several places, Fig. 107.
3. Draw three circles on to each square, Fig. 108(*a*). Put a row of running-stitches

round each circle, Fig. 108(b). Draw up the stitching and bind round several times, and tie firmly, Fig. 109(a).
4. Dye the fabric a bright colour.
5. Add further bindings to each square, Fig. 109(b).
6. The body piece should also have further bindings added. Re-dye in a dark colour.
7. Untie and press flat.

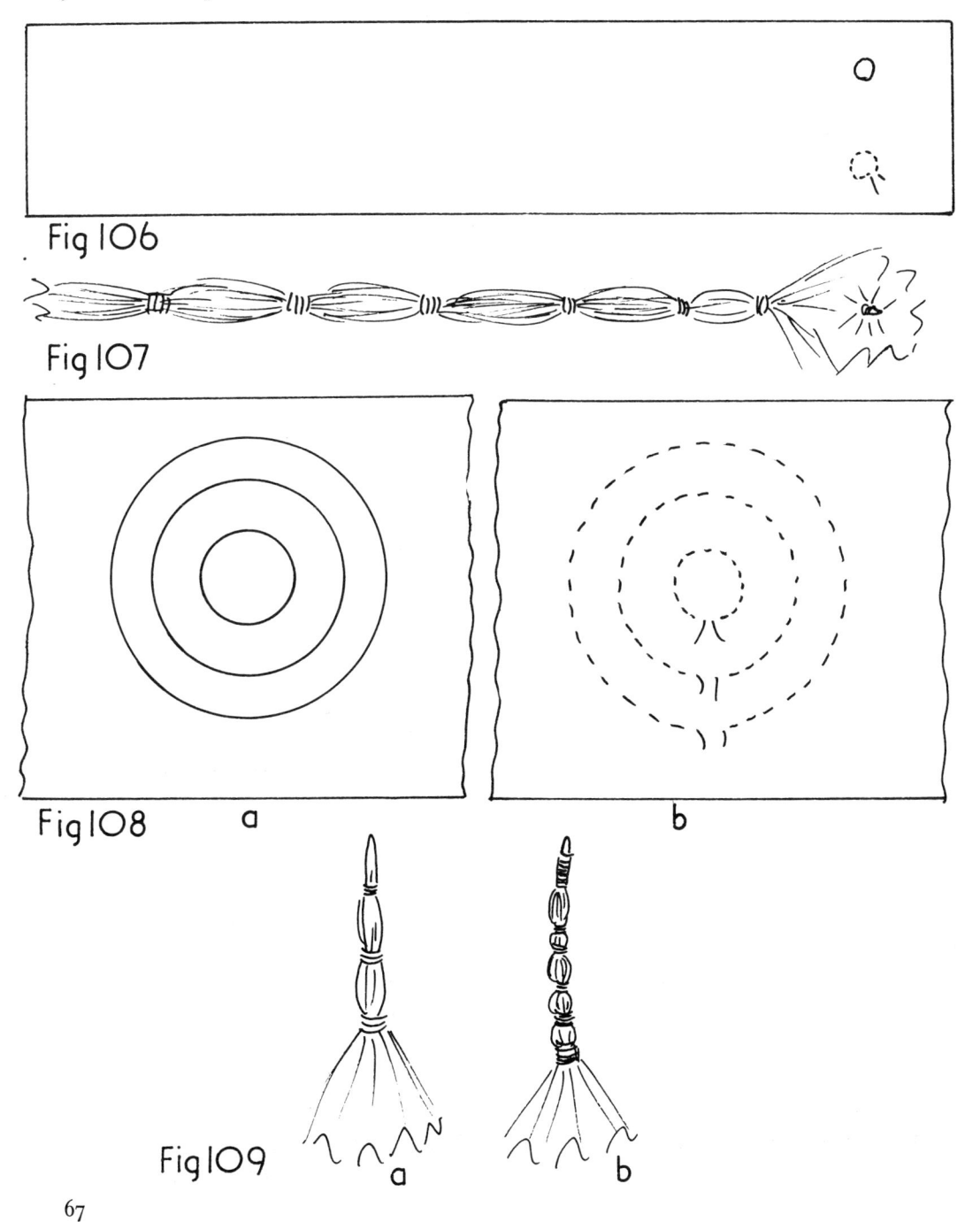

Fig 106

Fig 107

Fig 108   a   b

Fig 109   a   b

To cut out
1. Use Fig. 110 as pattern lay-out guide.
2. Trace off the pattern of the body and gusset, Fig. 111.
3. Fold the fabric in half and place on the patterns, Fig. 110, and cut out.
4. Cut a 10-in. (25-cm) circle from each square.

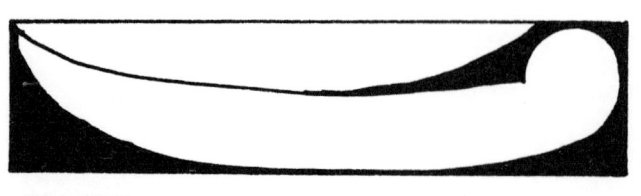

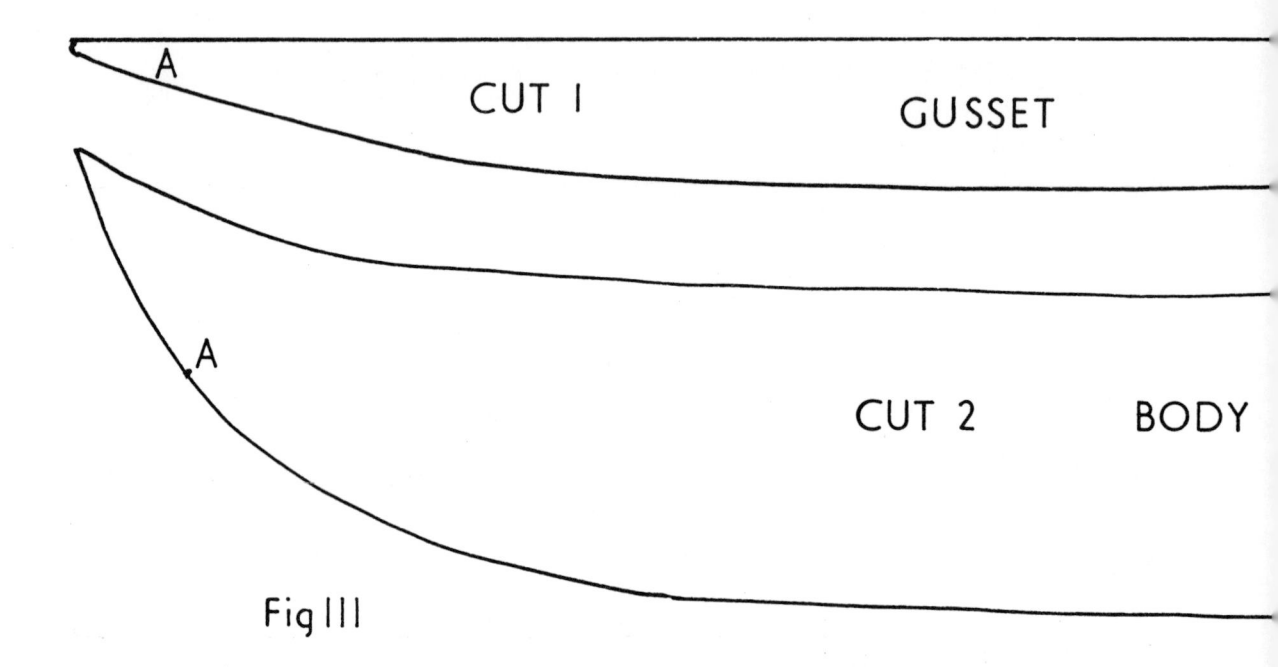

Fig 110

Fig 111

To make
1. Place A of gusset to A of one body piece, Fig. 112, and stitch along to B.
2. Join the other side of the body to gusset.
3. Join the two body pieces, Fig. 113, leaving an opening along the top. Snip turnings.
4. Turn inside out and stuff firmly, then stitch up opening.
5. Place the two right sides of the circles together and stitch, leaving an opening of about 3 in. (8 cm).
   Turn right side out and stuff firmly before stitching up opening.
6. Place the snail's house on top of body and stitch firmly. (See Colour Plate 4.)

Fig 112

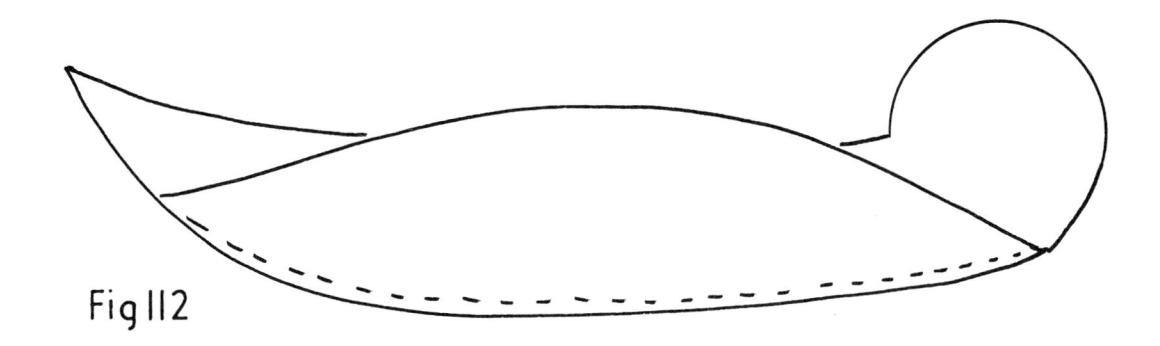

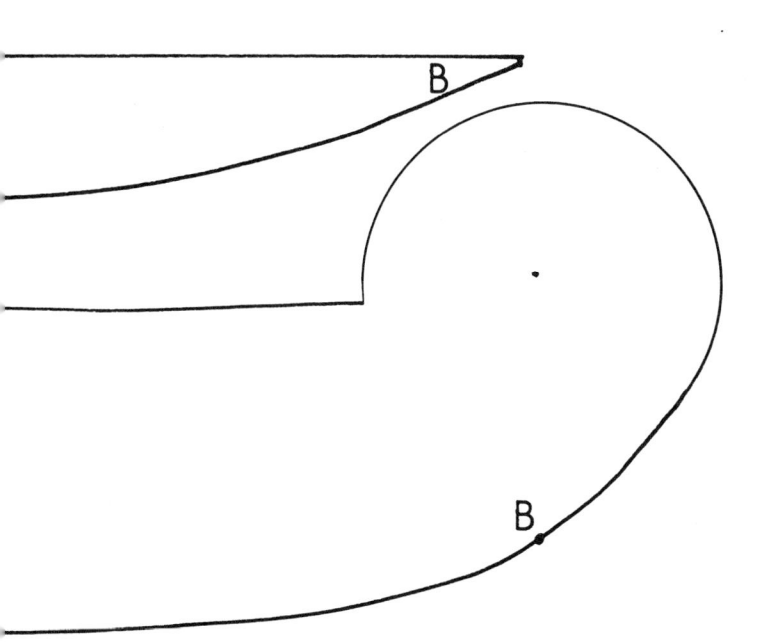

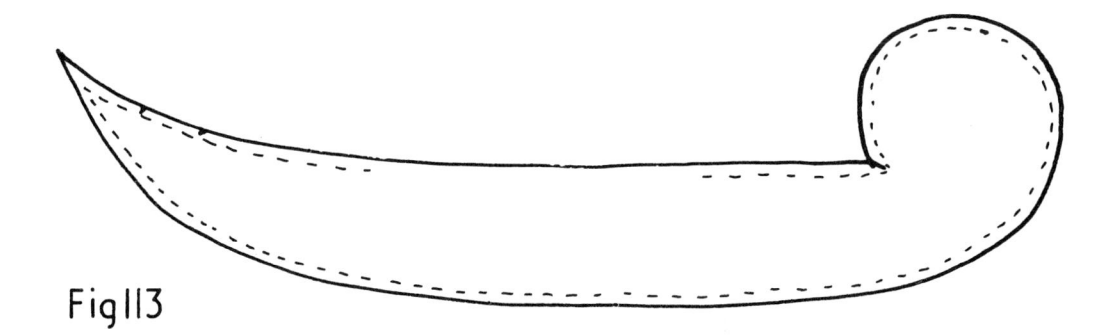

B

B

Fig 113

TOY CAT

Materials required
White cotton, 12 × 24 in. (30 × 60 cm).
Kapok for stuffing.
Red dye and brown dye.
Plain paper, 12 × 12 in. (30 × 30 cm).

Pattern
Draw out the pattern from the chart, Fig. 114, on to the paper and cut out. Mark the dots for the centre of each design.
Draw round the pattern on to the fabric twice, Fig. 115, and mark the dots for the design.

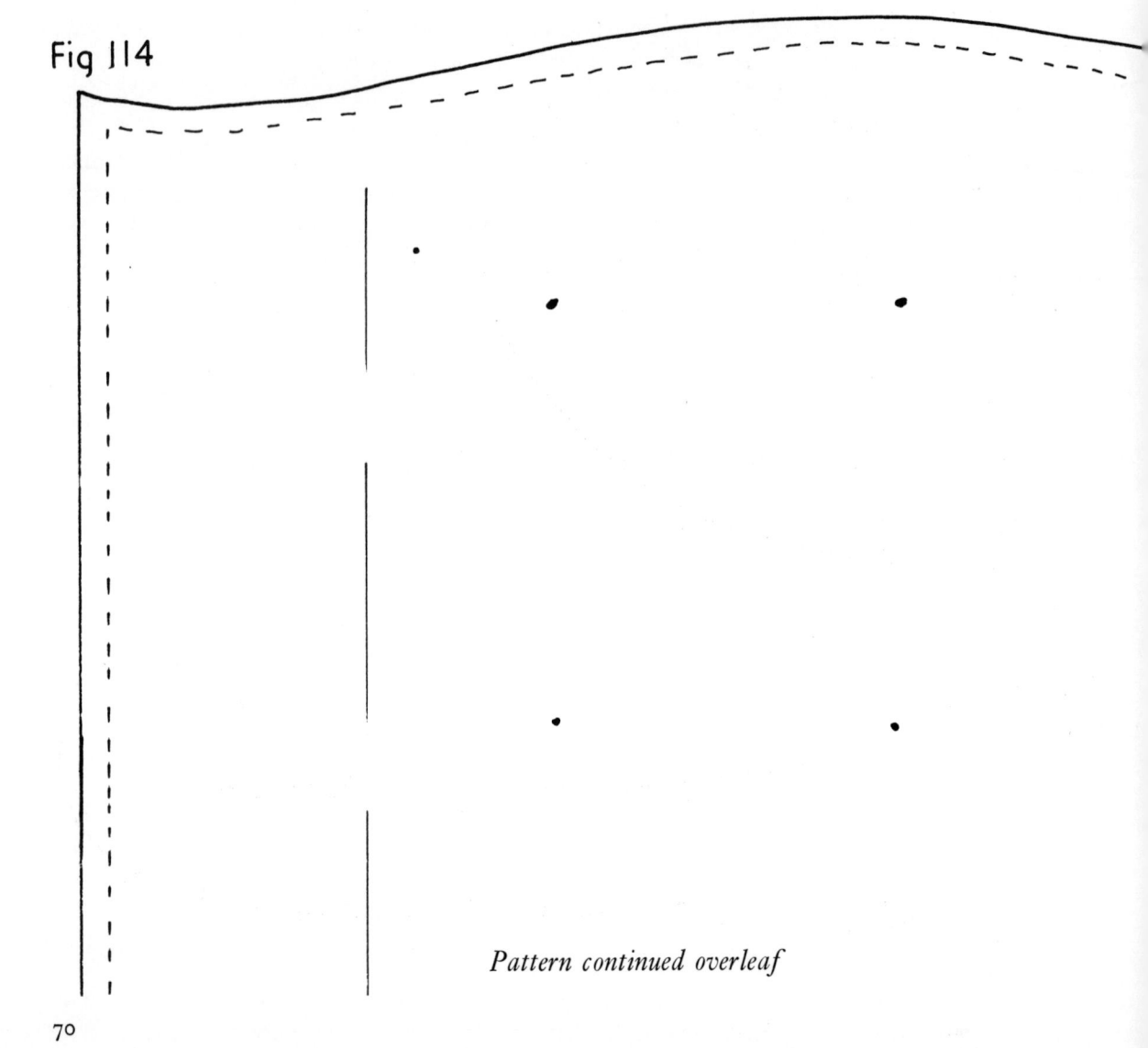

Fig 114

Pattern continued overleaf

fig 115

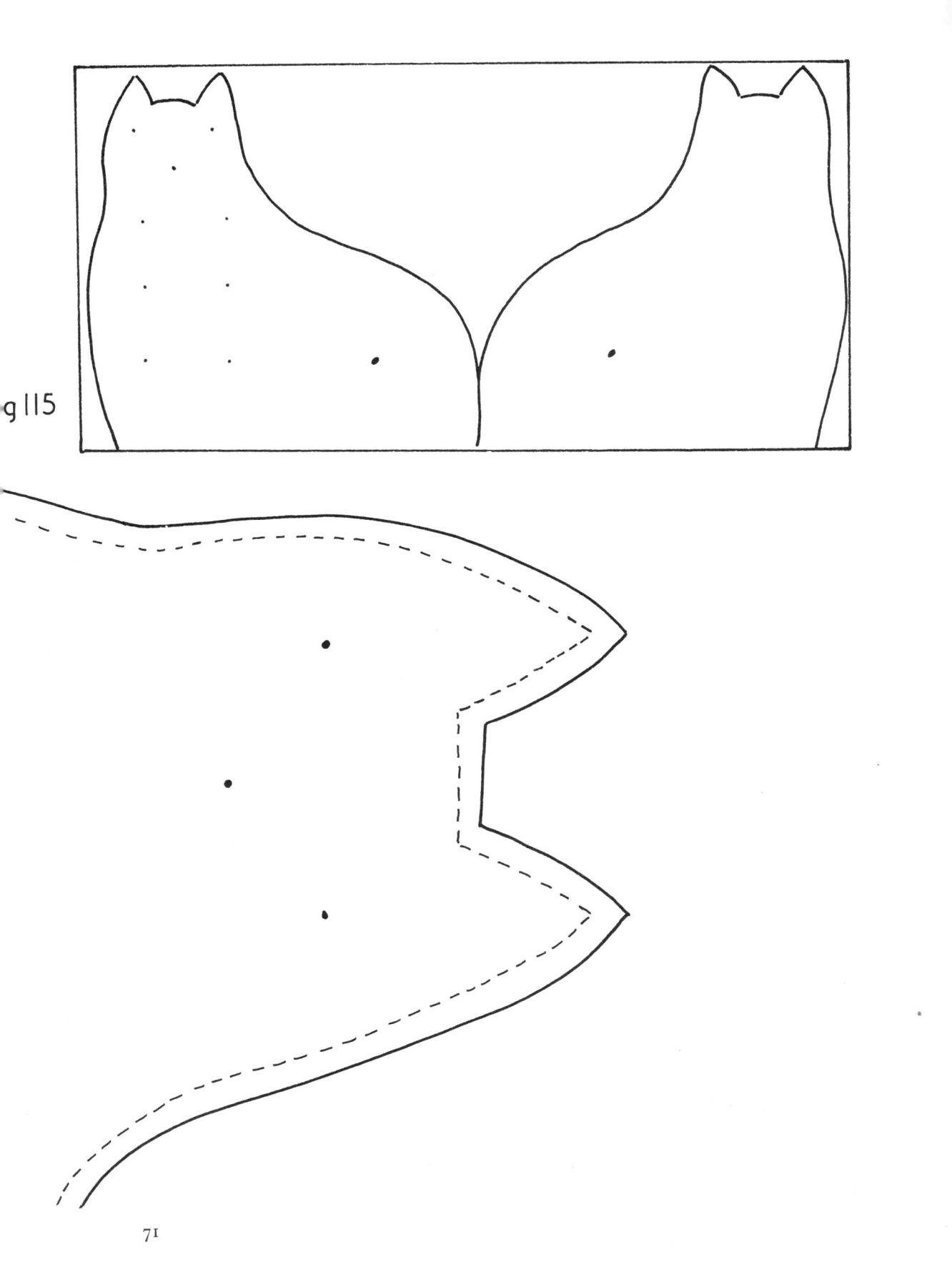

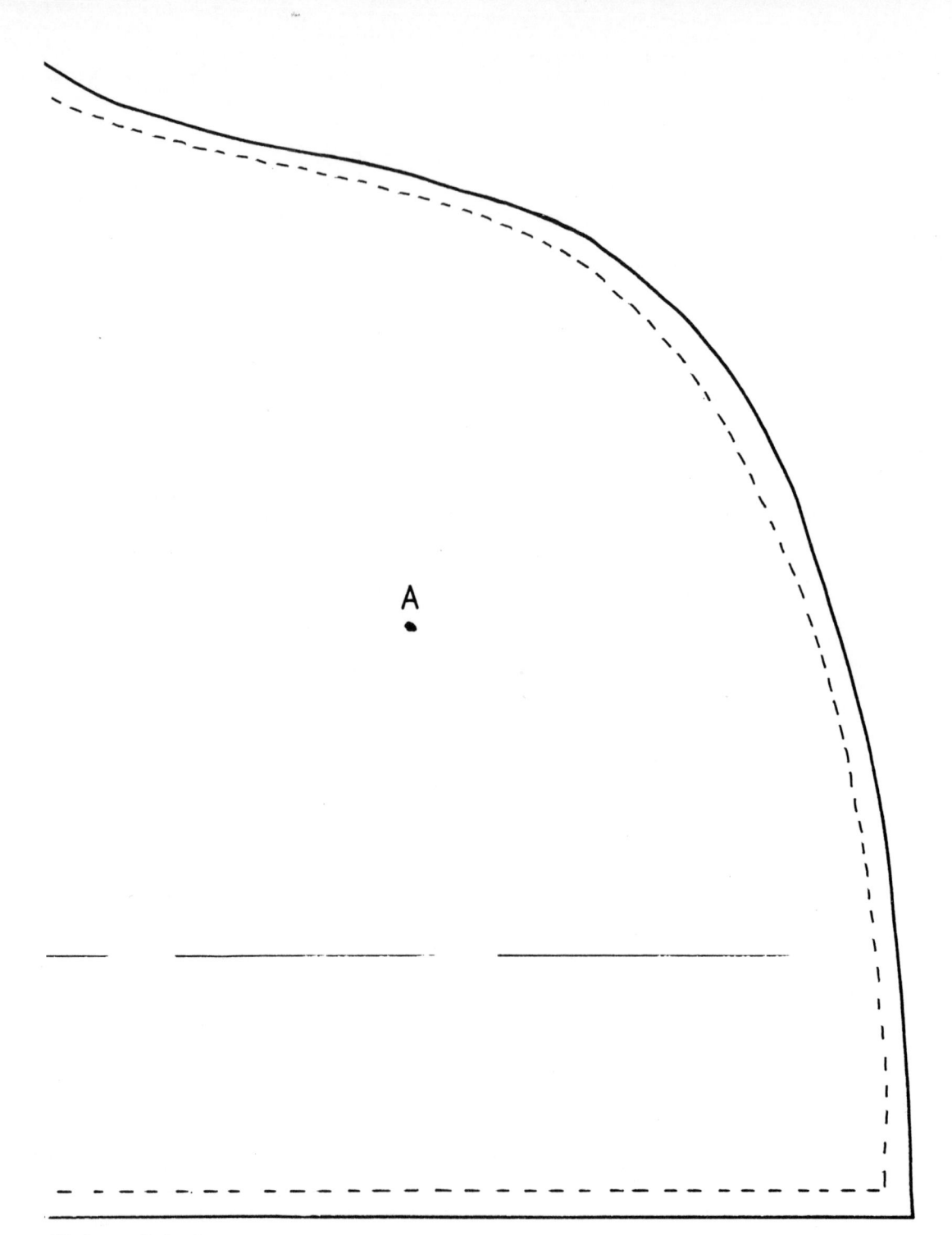

Tying of design

Make a large spot design at point A of pattern. To do this pick up a point of cloth (at A) and smooth it with the left hand and wrap round binding thread about 1 in. (2·5 cm) from tip, and tie lightly, Fig. 89, page 58.

Make a second tie ½ in. (1·5 cm) from the tip.
The eyes are small spot designs tied only once, ¼ in. (0·75 cm) from pen mark.
Also tie small spot for nose.

Front of cat

Fold the fabric down the one side of the front by the pencil marks. Use a safety pin to pick up the double fabric. Start ½ in. (1·5 cm) towards right of dot and pick up fabric as in Fig. 91, page 58. Bind thread tightly round fabric under the pin. Tie tightly and remove pin. Repeat this to form a row of three ties.
Make a second row by folding the fabric downwards on the spots.
For the back of the cat make one large spot design tied in two or three places.
Dye the fabric a bright colour.
Add further binding to each design, wrapping more round the eyes than the nose, and also binding the circle A to make it larger.
Re-dye a dark colour.
When untied, press the fabric to remove all creases and cut out the cat shapes.

To make up

Place the two right sides of fabric together (brighter side). Machine round carefully, Fig. 116(a). Snip turnings at curves, Fig. 116(b).
Turn right side out and stuff firmly. Oversew the edges together as in Fig. 117(a).
Bring the sides over to form a square end (box end), Fig. 117(b) and stitch in place.

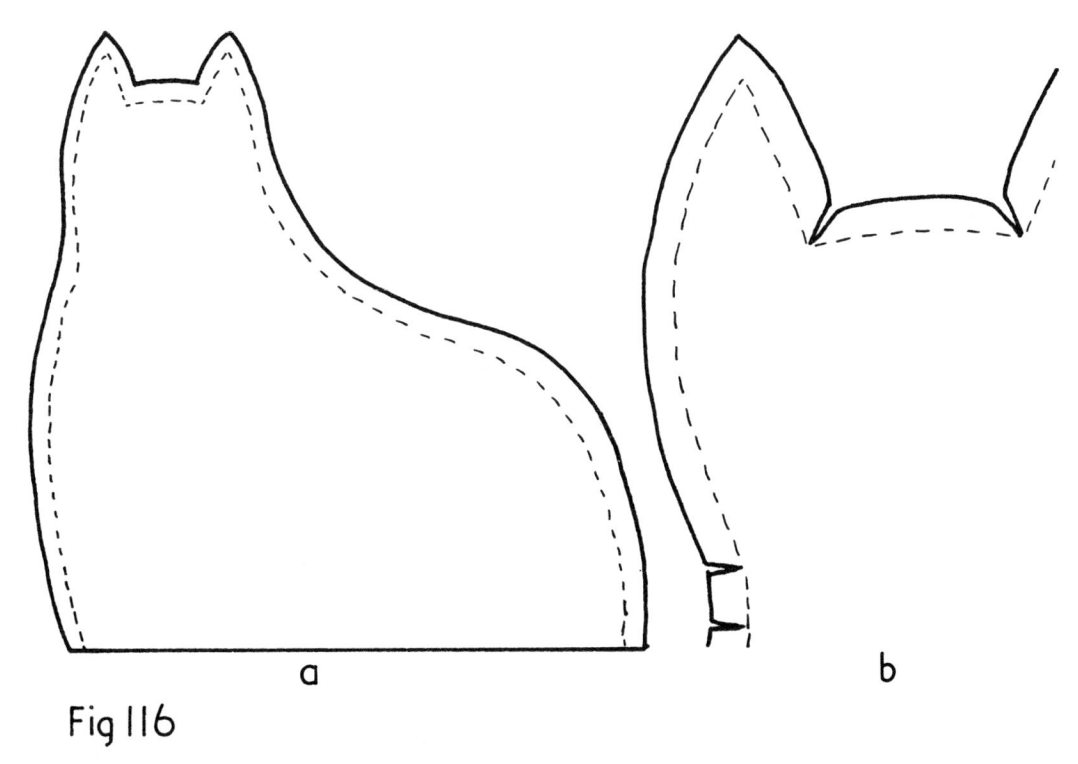

Fig 116

Fig 117

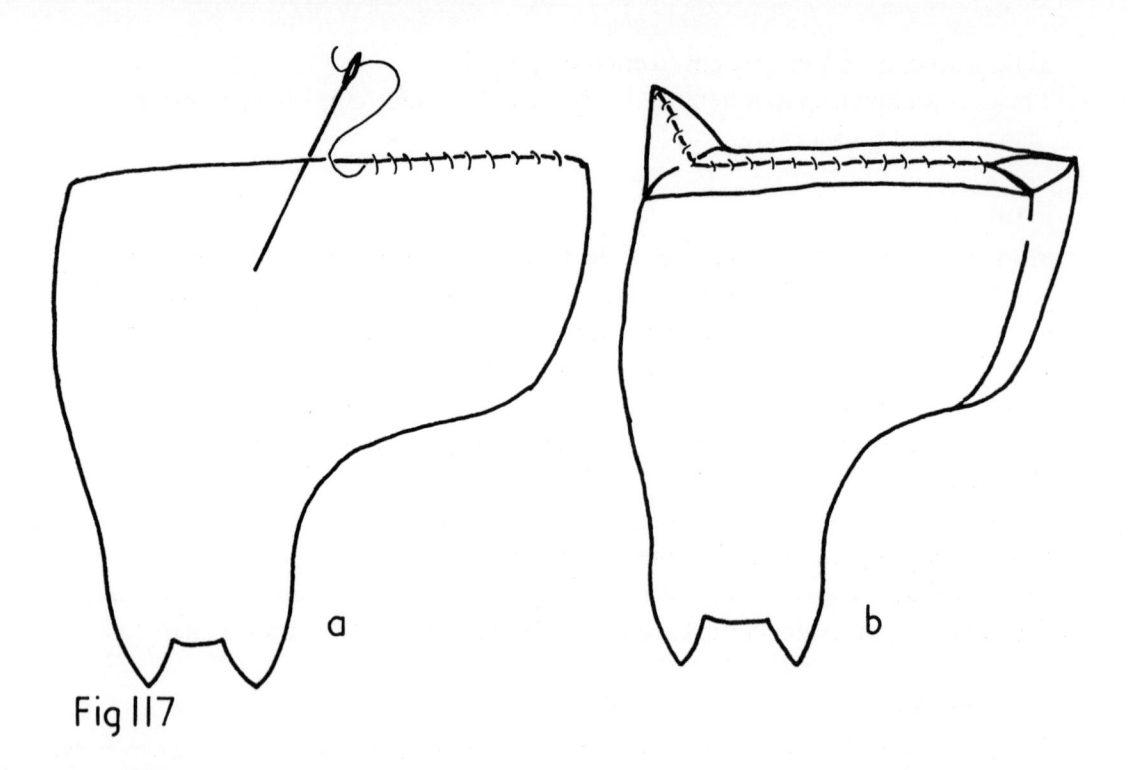

REPTILE

Materials required

19 × 14½ in. (48 × 37 cm) plain cotton (twill weave is good).
6 × 4 in. (15 × 10 cm) felt, colour of the orange dye.
6½ × 4 in. (17 × 10 cm) dark-coloured nylon jersey material, or any smooth non-fray fabric.
Two dyes, orange and blue.
Kapok (small quantity).

To dye the fabric

1. Pleat the fabric lengthwise and put the ties close together at one end. This is for the head, Fig. 118. Make all the binding cover a very small amount of fabric.
2. Dye in bright coloured dye, and dry.
3. Dye in blue coloured dye. Untie and press between layers of paper.

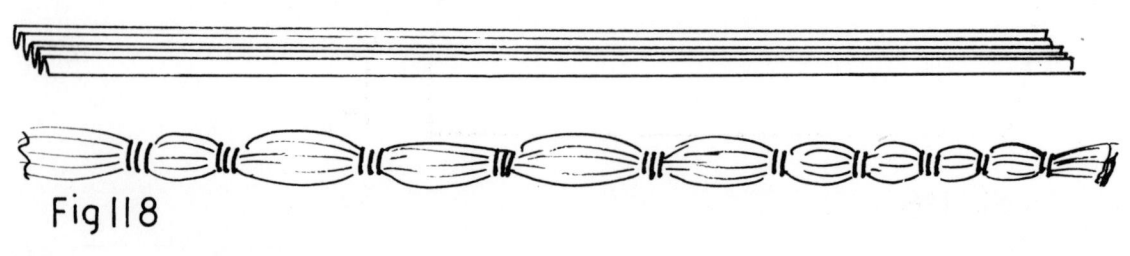

Fig 118

To cut out

1. Make pattern from Fig. 119.
2. Cut out as in Fig. 120 two body pieces, four legs. (These are made of fabric left over.)
3. Cut out four feet and one tongue in felt, Fig. 121. The tongue is only a straight piece with a double-pointed section.

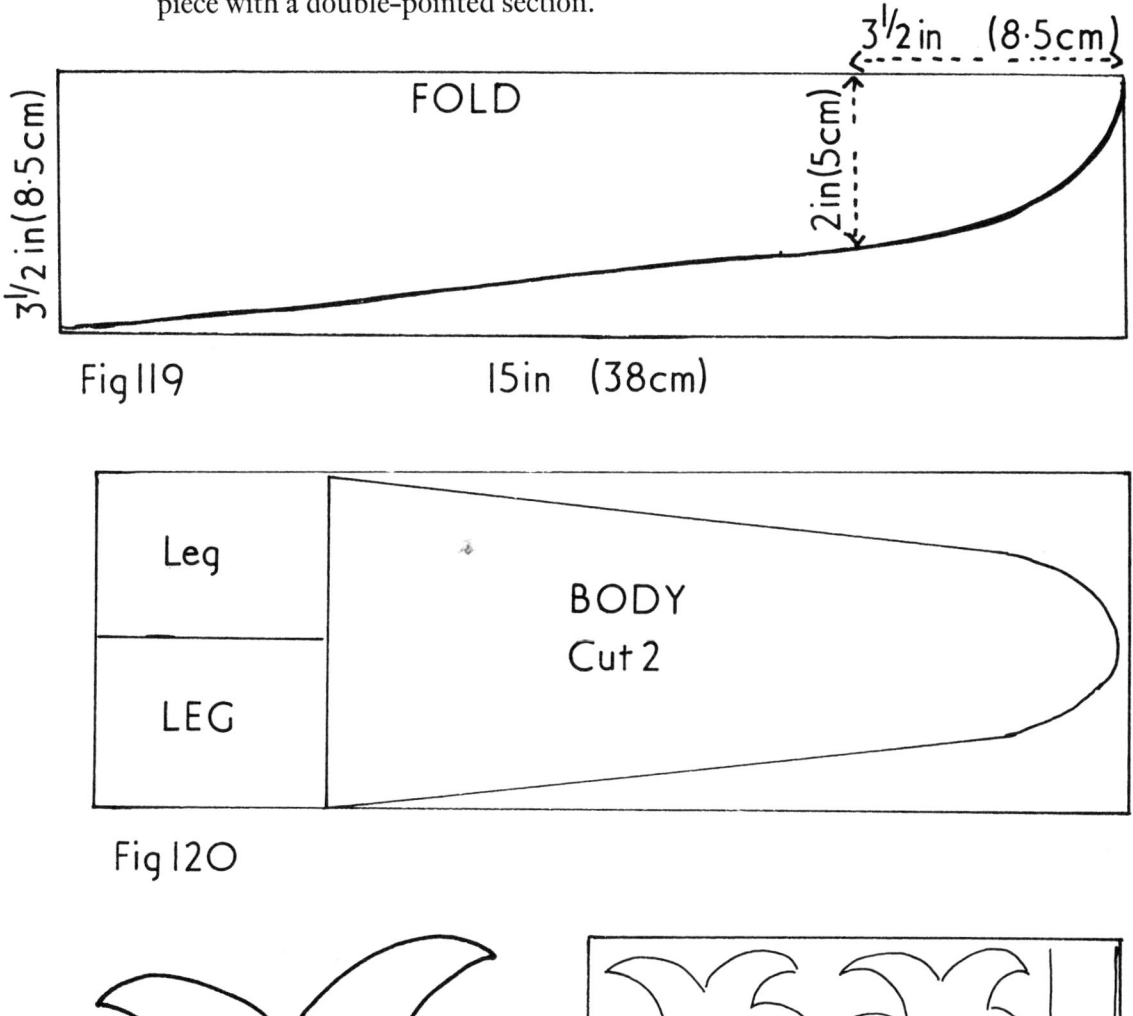

Fig 119 — 3½ in (8.5 cm), FOLD, 15 in (38 cm), 3½ in (8.5 cm), 2 in (5 cm)

Fig 120 — Leg, LEG, BODY Cut 2

Fig 121

To make

1. Join the two body pieces together, Fig. 122.
2. Turn to the right side and turn in the raw edge of mouth on to wrong side and run-stitch round, Fig. 123.
3. Cut out the nylon jersey fabric to shape of mouth, Fig. 124.
4. Pin mouthpiece into position and hold in place with running-stitches.
5. Stitch tongue to back of mouth.
6. Use strip of white felt to form teeth and stitch to front part of mouth, both top and bottom.
7. Eyes can be made of beads, stitched on, see Colour Plate 5.
8. Join each leg piece, Fig. 125, and turn right side out and stitch on to felt foot, Fig. 126.
9. Turn top part of leg inside for about ¾ in. (1·75 cm) and stuff each leg firmly with kapok, Fig. 127.
10. Stitch the legs on to the underside of the body.

A resist pattern can also be carried out with wax. If a pattern is drawn on to paper, using a wax crayon, and a wash of paint is added, then the areas which have been waxed will resist the paint. This idea can be carried out on fabric. The wax is melted in a double boiler (a can inside a saucepan of hot water makes a good double boiler). The heat should be constant although it may be low, just sufficient to keep the wax warm.

A design may be added to the fabric with a brush. Have plenty of papers underneath the fabric, submerge the fabric into a cold dye bath for about thirty minutes, rinse and dry. More design may be added. The fabric must be pressed with a hot iron between layers of paper in order to remove the wax, and finally washed. Hot candle wax may be dripped on to a fabric to form a pattern. Do not use newspaper – the ink may dirty the fabric.

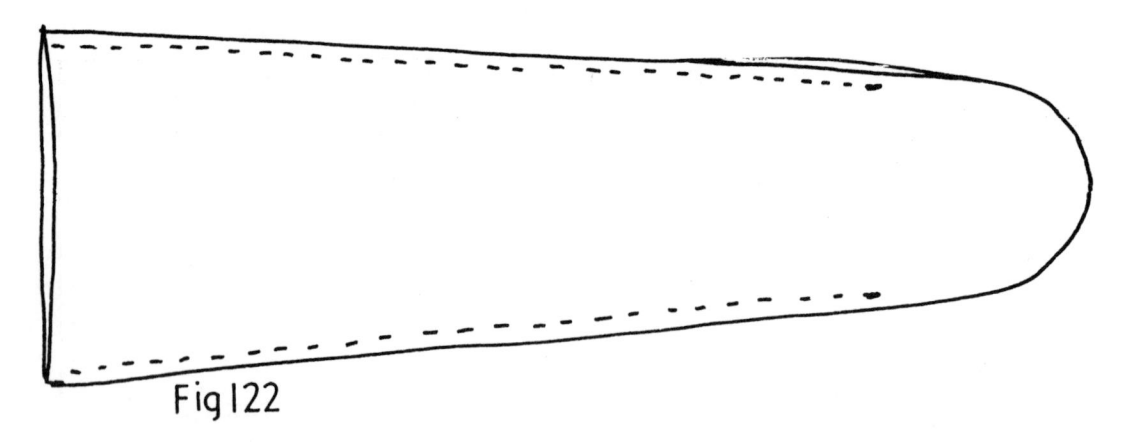

Fig 122

Fig 123

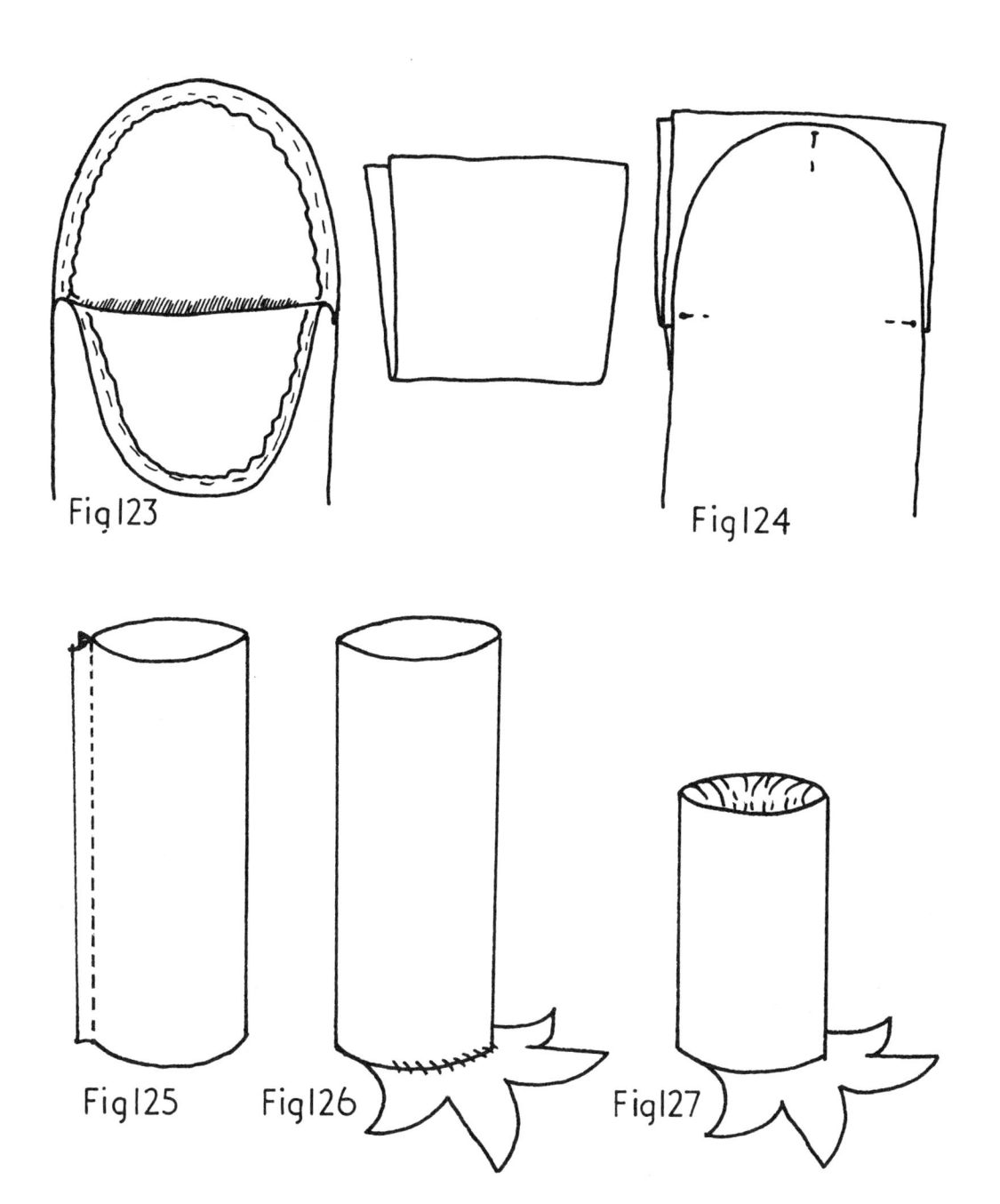

Fig 124

Fig 125

Fig 126

Fig 127

Fabric printing

The clothing we wear is often patterned, and this may be printed, i.e. the design shows best on the right side, and often there are many colours used in the design. A woven design is usually of a geometric pattern and can be seen on both sides of the fabric. If uncertain, then pull out a few threads and you will find that a colour may only show in parts on the right side of the fabric, but the threads go full length.

There are elaborate damask-effect patterns which are woven, the weave of the fabric showing up the different tones of the same colour in the pattern. These fabrics are expensive and are generally used for evening wear or special occasion dresses.

Knitted fabrics (jersey) may be printed but generally the pattern is obtained during the knitting stage, and again the design is generally geometric.

Designs can be printed on both cotton or jersey fabric and the dyes readily available are suitable for cotton fabrics, that is, if the material is to be washed then these dyes can be made fast. One can also print with paints, but these will not be colour-fast, i.e. the colour will wash off.

Fabric printing can be carried out for many purposes and need not be carried out with printing dyes unless the fabric is to be washed. Curtains for a Wendy House or puppet clothes can be printed easily. The basic equipment is as follows:

1. A piece of thin foam rubber, about 5×5 in. (13×13 cm).
2. A paint-brush.
3. A jar of ordinary ink.
4. A thick pad of newspaper.

For printing blocks you can use a wide range of materials, which may have a textured surface, i.e. a cork, corrugated cardboard, cotton spools, pieces of polystyrene which may be cut to a given shape, etc.

Place the foam rubber on to the plate, tile or wood, to form a printing pad, Fig. 128. Spread a little ink on to the pad, then press the printing block on to the pad two or three times, to obtain an even distribution of ink, then press firmly on to newspaper. Use the columns of the paper to try to print evenly.

Fig 128

You may print on to plain paper and make patterned wallpaper for a doll's house. You can overprint, that is use perhaps a different-shaped block and a different coloured ink. The block, when printed partly on top of the other block, will give an interesting result.

Experiments can be made in designing blocks by mounting pieces of string of various thicknesses on to a strip of wood. The string must be held firmly in place with an adhesive such as Marvin Medium, Fig. 129(a). You could use curtain-rings, Fig. 129(b) and bottle-tops, and when printing, print the block as separate units, using the space which is left to form a design or combining the units to form an all-over pattern.

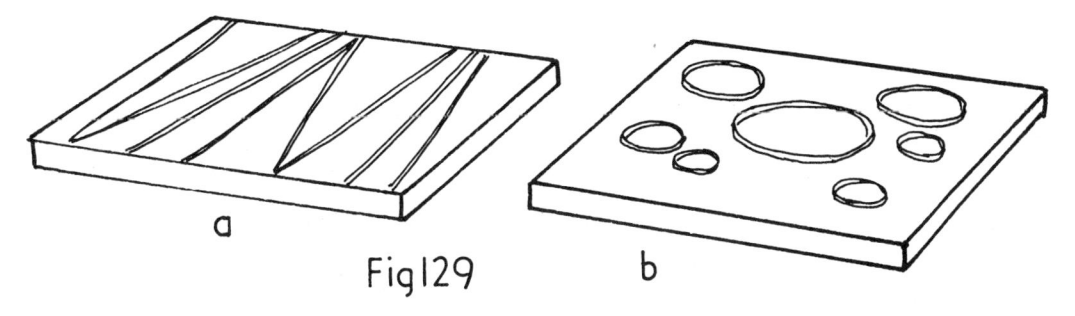

Fig 129 a b

Potatoes can be used for printing. First cut the potatoes in half and gouge out a design using a penholder with the nib placed in the reverse way round.

Polystyrene may have a design burned into it. Use a metal knitting-needle and heat it in the flame of a candle. The hot needle, when it touches the polystyrene, will leave a mark. The needle limits your design greatly to lines.

Powder paint may be mixed with a little water and used for printing both paper and fabric. (Remember it is not washable.)

Printing dye

Reeves make a water-bound printing dye. Mix the dye with water until it is like cream and spread on to the foam pad. Use as before, pressing the block two or three times on to the pad to obtain an even spread of the dye.

When completed the dye is made fast into the fabric by pressing with a hot iron for three minutes on the wrong side of the fabric. Have paper under fabric when pressing.

Note: Always have a pile of newspapers under the fabric when printing, but have plain paper between the fabric and the top sheet of newspaper.

Articles which can be printed

A pair of oven mitts may have a printed design on the backs, or a long oven-cloth which has turned back sections for the hands. You can also have printed designs on place mats, bags for pegs, gym-shoes, apron borders or doll's clothes, etc.

This subject leaves plenty of scope for design and build-up of colour reactions.

A little embroidery may be added to the printing when additional colour is required, or a design to look a little bolder.

PUPPET

Fig. 130   The patterns on these puppet dresses were printed using cotton spools and bottle-tops.

Materials required

Plain cotton fabric 14 × 18 in. (35 × 45 cm).
Felt for hands.
Reeves fabric printing dyes.

Trace off the pattern, Fig. 131.
Cut off a strip of fabric 5 × 18 in. (12 × 45 cm) for the bodice and print a design on it. The one used for the puppets in Fig. 130 was made up from rows of cotton-spool prints in yellow, and then blue. The skirt design was made up from two rows of cotton-spool prints and then bottle-top designs.

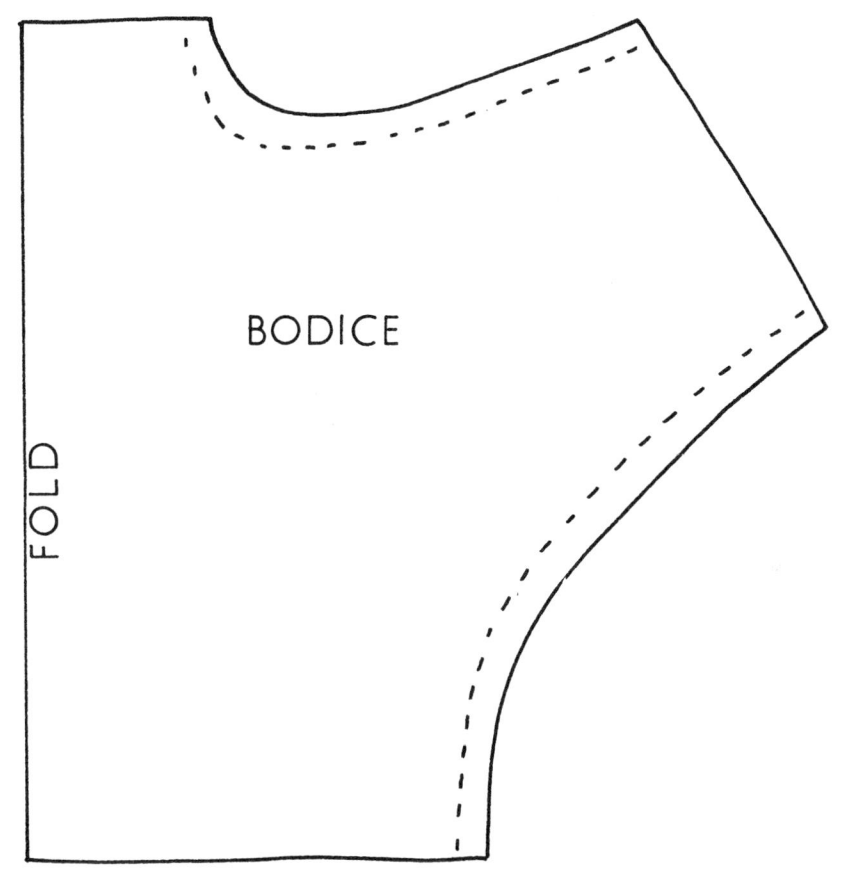

Fig 131

Cut out the bodice as Fig. 132 using the pattern, Fig. 131.

To make

1. Place the two right sides of bodices together and join. Snip the turnings at the seams, Fig. 133(*a*) and (*b*).
2. Trace off the hand pattern from Fig. 134, cut out as in Fig. 135 and make up as in Fig. 136.

Fig 132

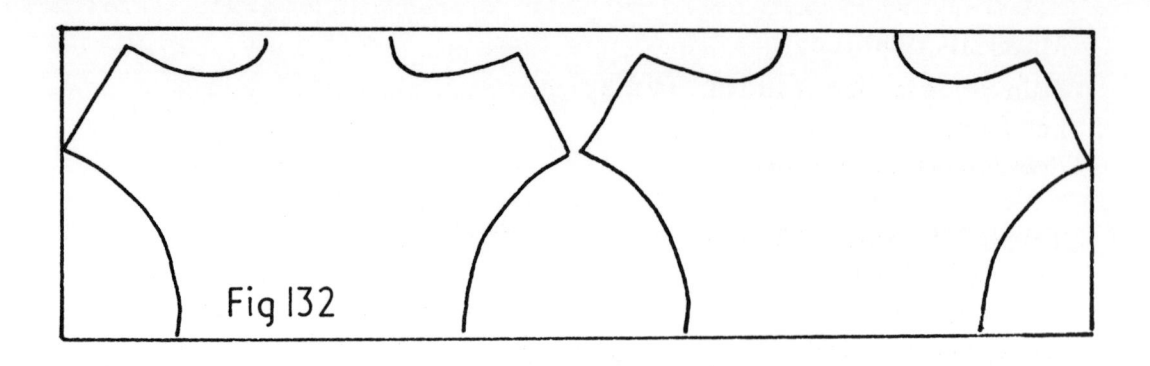

3. Place the hand inside the sleeve and stitch, Fig. 137(*a*). Do this to the other arm.
4. Turn right side out, Fig. 137(*b*).
5. Fold skirt piece in half, join the side seam and put a row of gathers at the top.
6. Place bodice inside skirt, and join, Fig. 138.
7. Turn right side out and make hem at bottom of skirt.

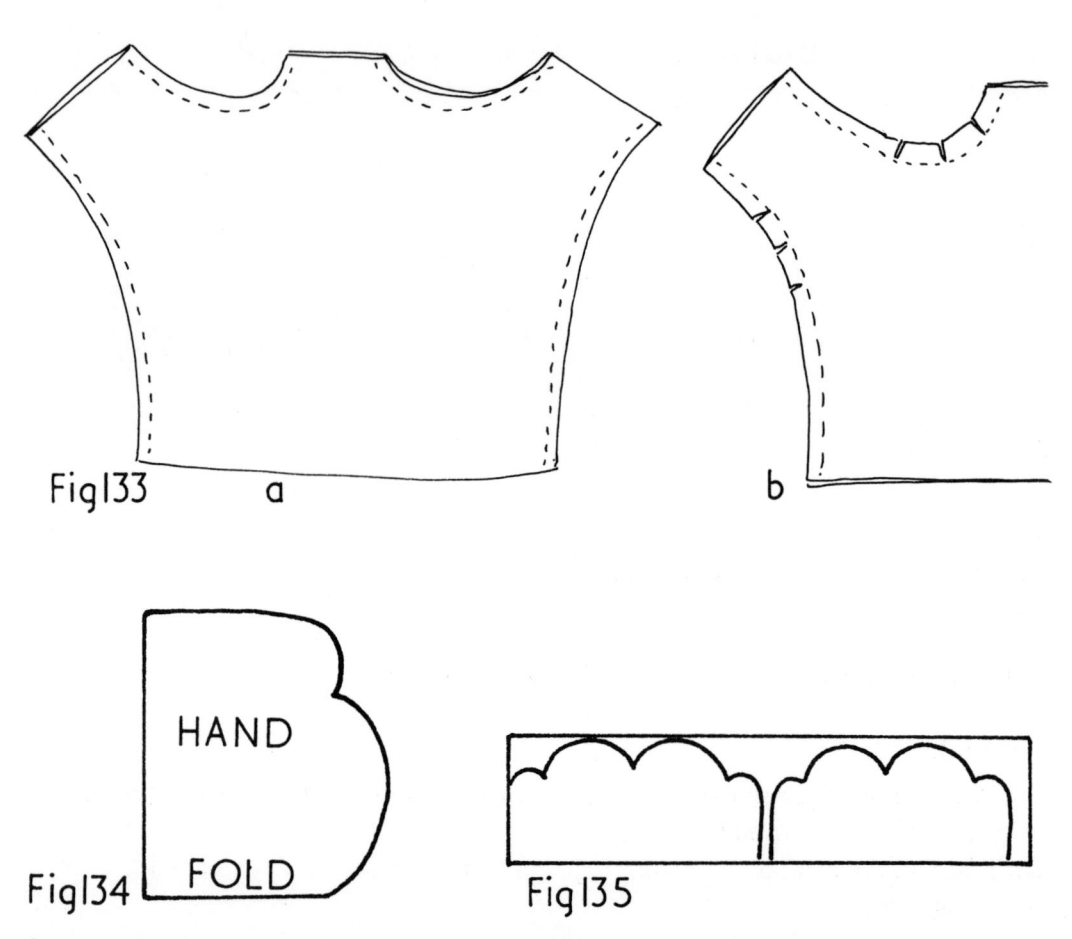

Fig 133 a   b

Fig 134 HAND FOLD

Fig 135

Fig 136

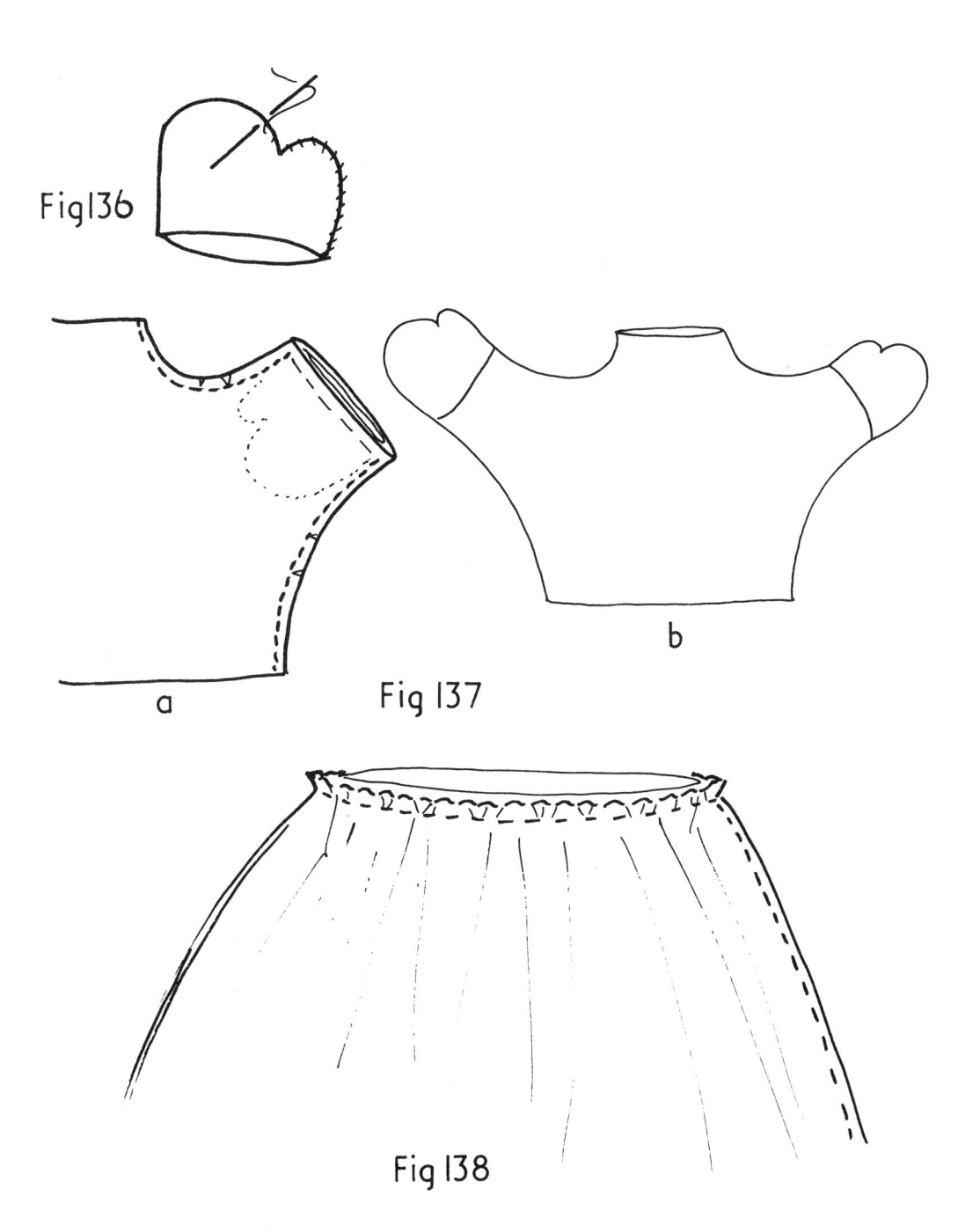

Fig 137 a   b

Fig 138

PUPPET HEAD

Materials required

Half a toilet-roll tube, or other tube of this size.
A tube (sweet tube) the width of a finger.
Wadding.
Old stocking.
Scraps of felt.

To make

1. Place the small tube inside toilet-roll tube, push wadding between the tubes to make rigid and use paste to make secure, Fig. 139(*a*), (*b*) and (*c*).
2. Cover the head with wadding, Fig. 139(*d*), then place several layers of stocking over the head and secure with a few stitches.
3. Make the features with scraps of felt, Fig. 139(*e*).
4. Stick or stitch on hair, made of knitting wool, sheep's wool, etc.
5. Place neck of head inside puppet dress and stitch.

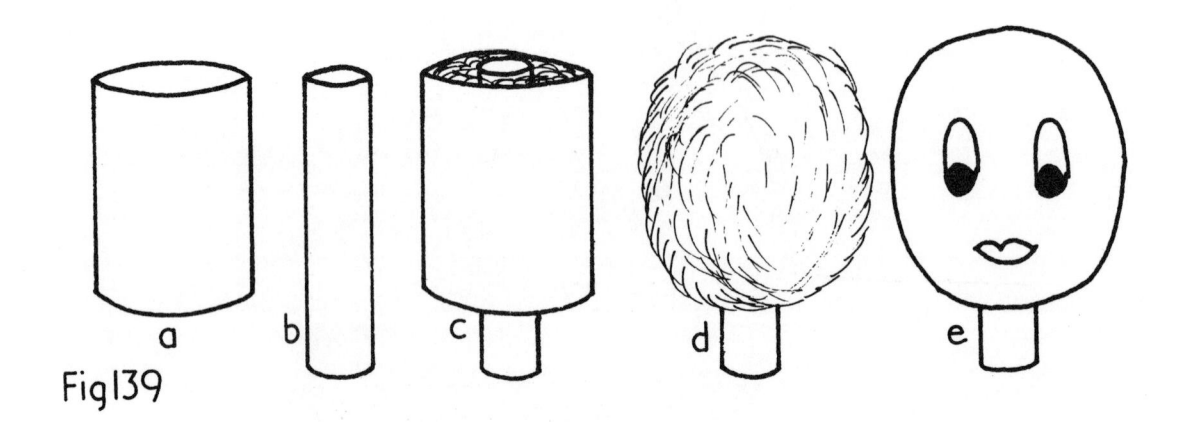

Fig 139

PRINTED DOLL

Materials required

18 × 14 in. (45 × 36 cm) plain cotton fabric.
Two pots of printing dyes (Reeves – water-bound).
14 × 3 in. (36 × 8 cm) yellow felt.
Scraps of black and red felt.
Kapok for stuffing.

Pattern

Trace off the pattern from Fig. 141, pages 87, 88, 89.

Cutting out

Fold the fabric and place on the pattern, Fig. 142, and cut out. Using the yellow felt cut out the hands, feet and hair, Fig. 143.

Fig. 140(a) This doll's clothes were printed with cotton spools, plastic bottle-tops and squeeze bottle-tops. The straight lines were made with the end of a ruler.

Fig. 140(b)   Pattern lay-out for the printed doll.

Printing the clothes

The design used in Fig. 140 was made up from using the following:

1. Cotton spool (large design at bottom of pants), Fig. 144(c).
2. Circles formed by using a plastic bottle-top, Fig. 144(a).
3. Straight lines made with the end of a ruler.
4. Small circles formed with the squeeze bottle-top, Fig. 144(b).

To make up

1. Working on the single fabric, machine from A–B of the opening, Fig. 145. Do this with both pieces.
2. Place the two right sides together, tack, then machine as in Fig. 146. Snip the turnings at the neck, leg section and tunic corners.
3. Turn right side out and stuff firmly with kapok. Sew up opening.
4. Join hair sections of felt together by oversewing, Fig. 147, and attach to head with a few stitches at lower edge of hair.
5. Cut out features from scraps of felt, Fig. 148(a), (b) and (c). The black centres of eyes are made by cutting circles of black felt, using a leather punch. Stitch features on to face.
6. Join two feet sections together and stuff slightly before finally completing the stitching. Make a second foot.

BACK OF HEAD
PATTERN OF HAIR
CUT 1

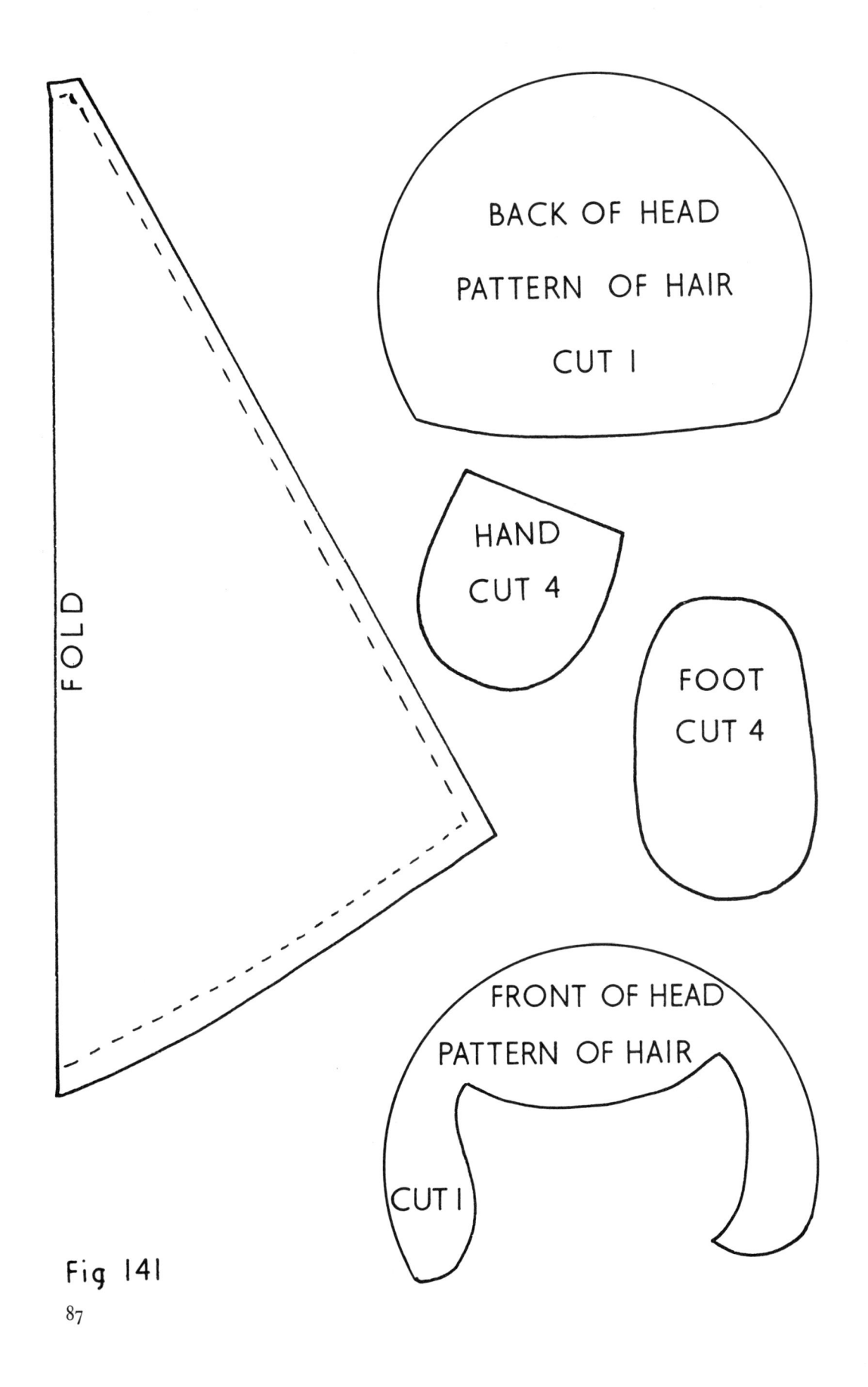

FOLD

HAND
CUT 4

FOOT
CUT 4

FRONT OF HEAD
PATTERN OF HAIR
CUT 1

Fig 141

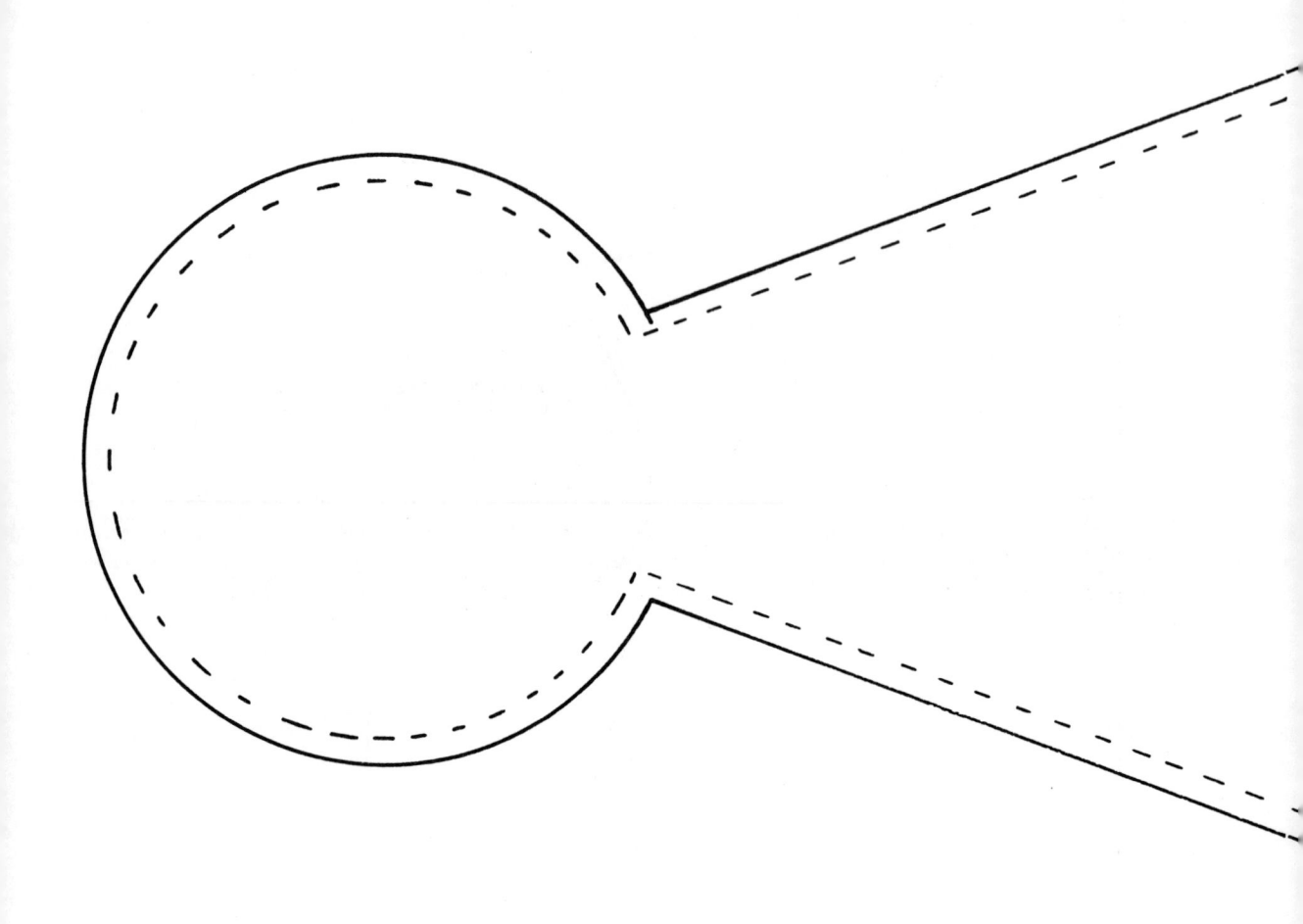

89

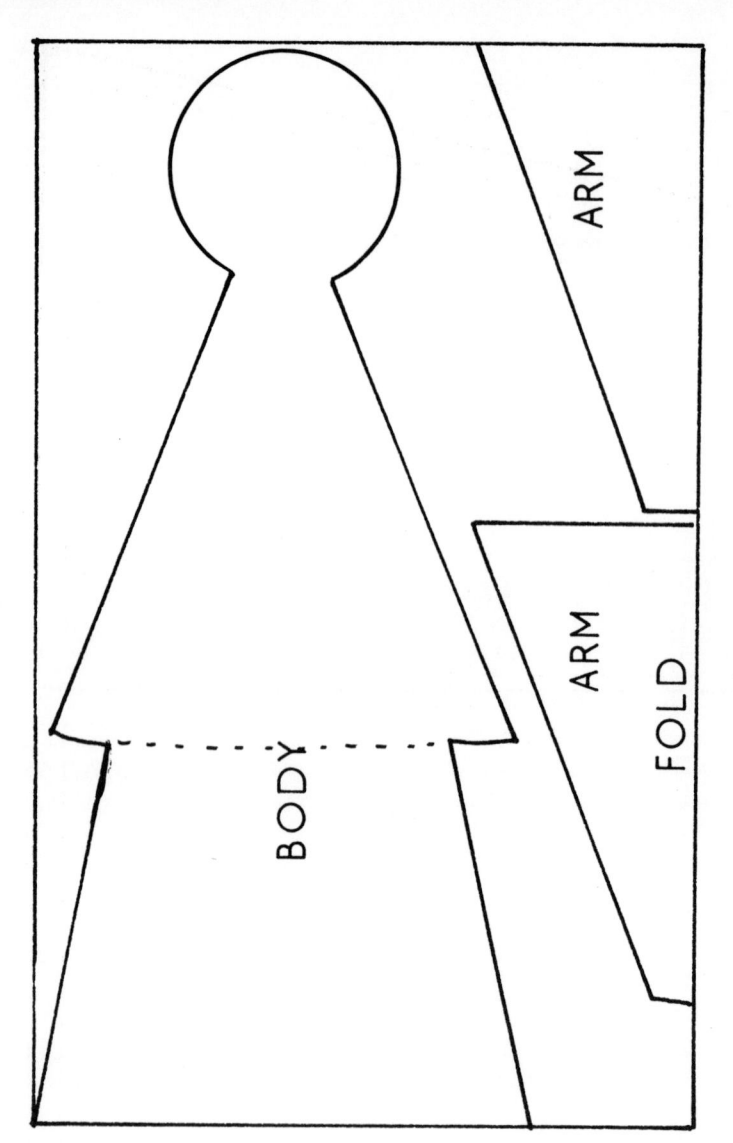

Fig 142

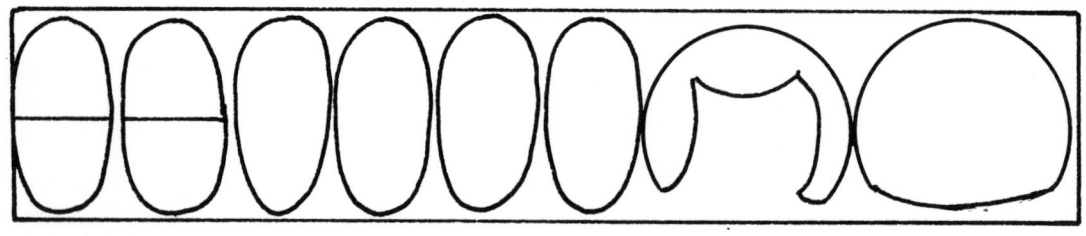

Fig 143

Fig 144

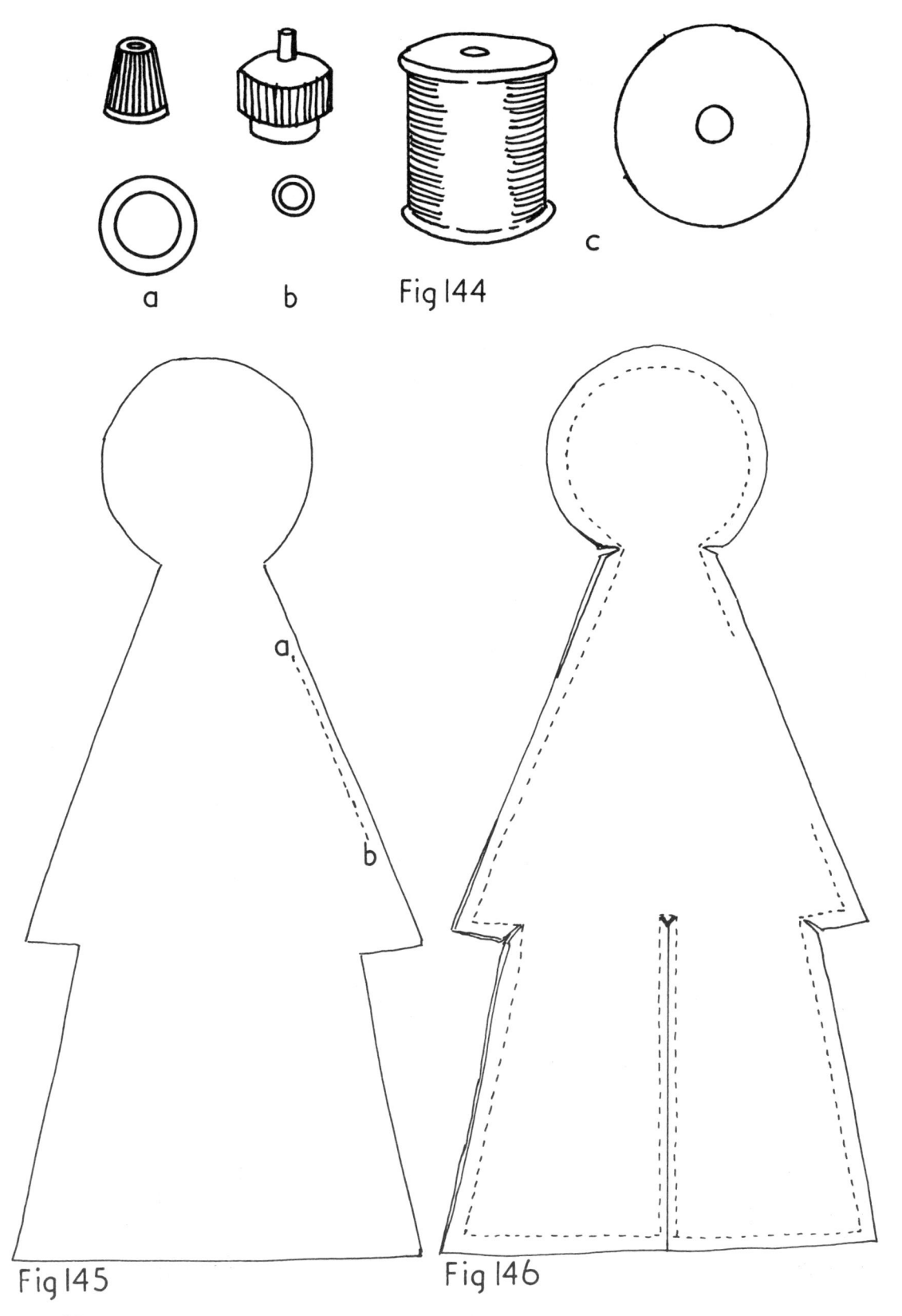

a b c

Fig 145

Fig 146

Fig 147   Fig 148

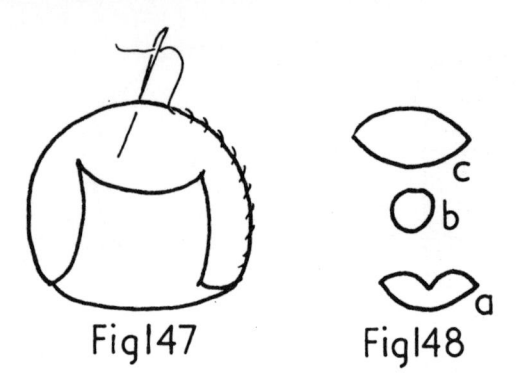

7. Attach the feet to the lower edge of trousers.
8. Fold arm-pieces as in Fig. 149(*a*) and stitch. Turn right side out by attaching a needle and double thread to top of arm and dropping the needle downwards inside the sleeve, Fig. 149(*b*), and then pulling through. Do this to both arms.
9. Make hands by oversewing two together, Fig. 150. Stuff and attach to arms, Fig. 151.
10. Attach arms to neck of body.

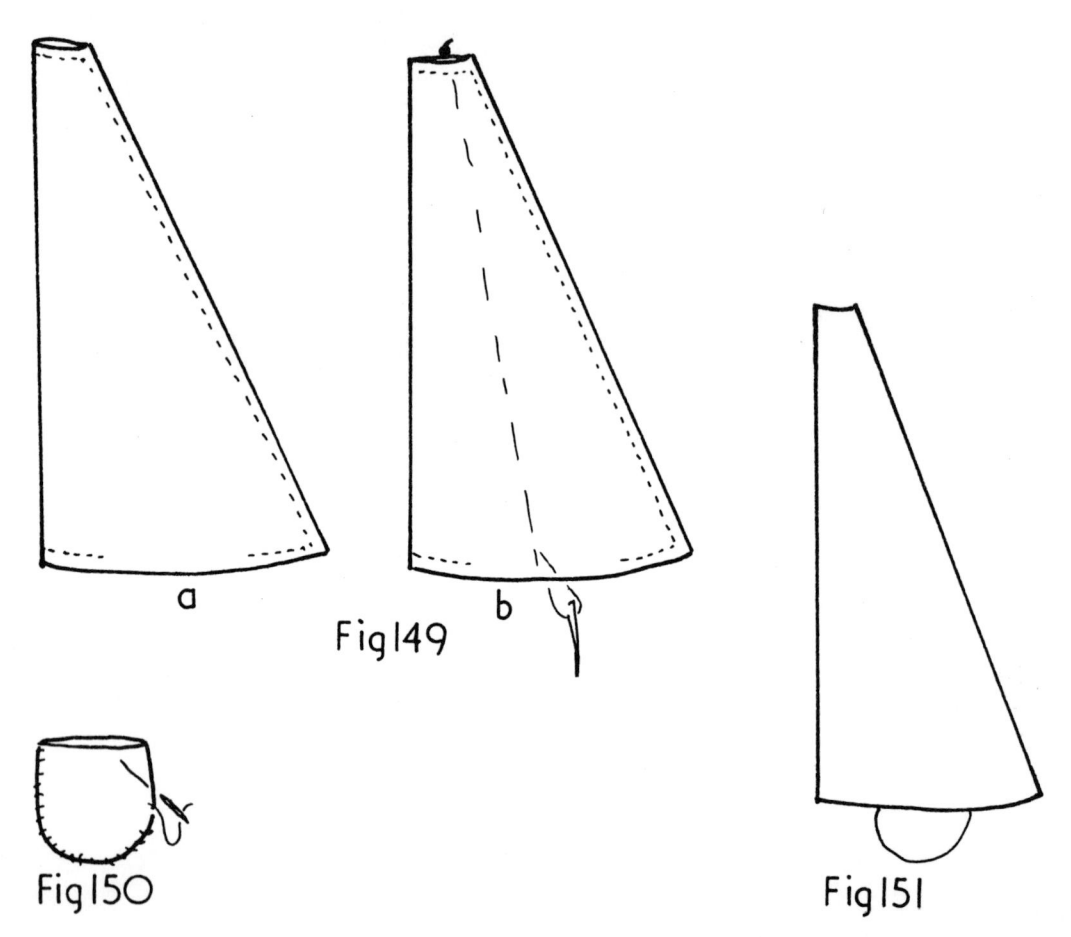

Fig 149

Fig 150   Fig 151

PRINTED DOG

Fig. 152 Printed dog made out of star-printed fabric. The collar and eyes were done with cotton-spool prints and the beads were sewn on when the dog had been made up. Scraps of wood were used to print the nose and mouth.

B BASE CUT 1 A

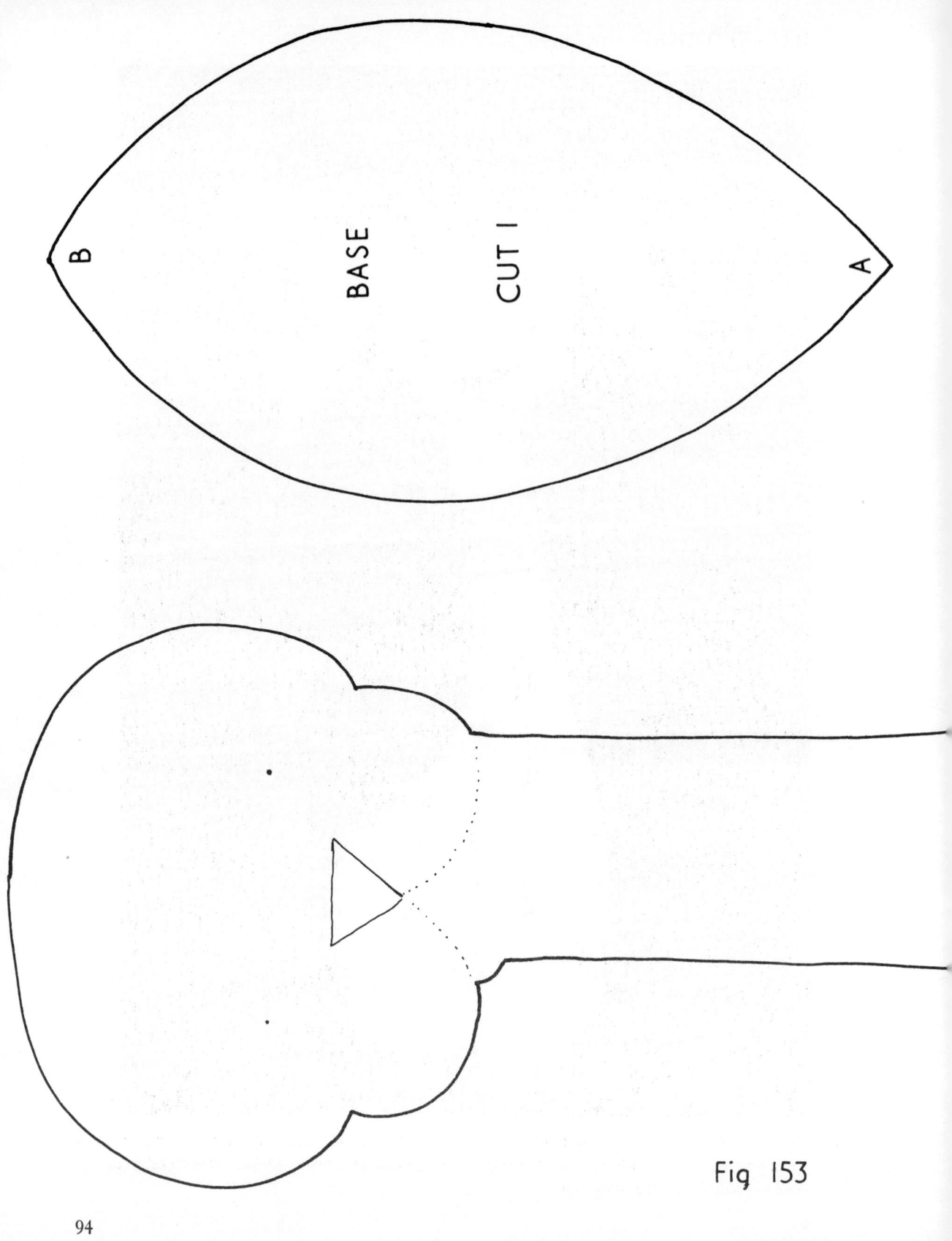

Fig 153

FOLD

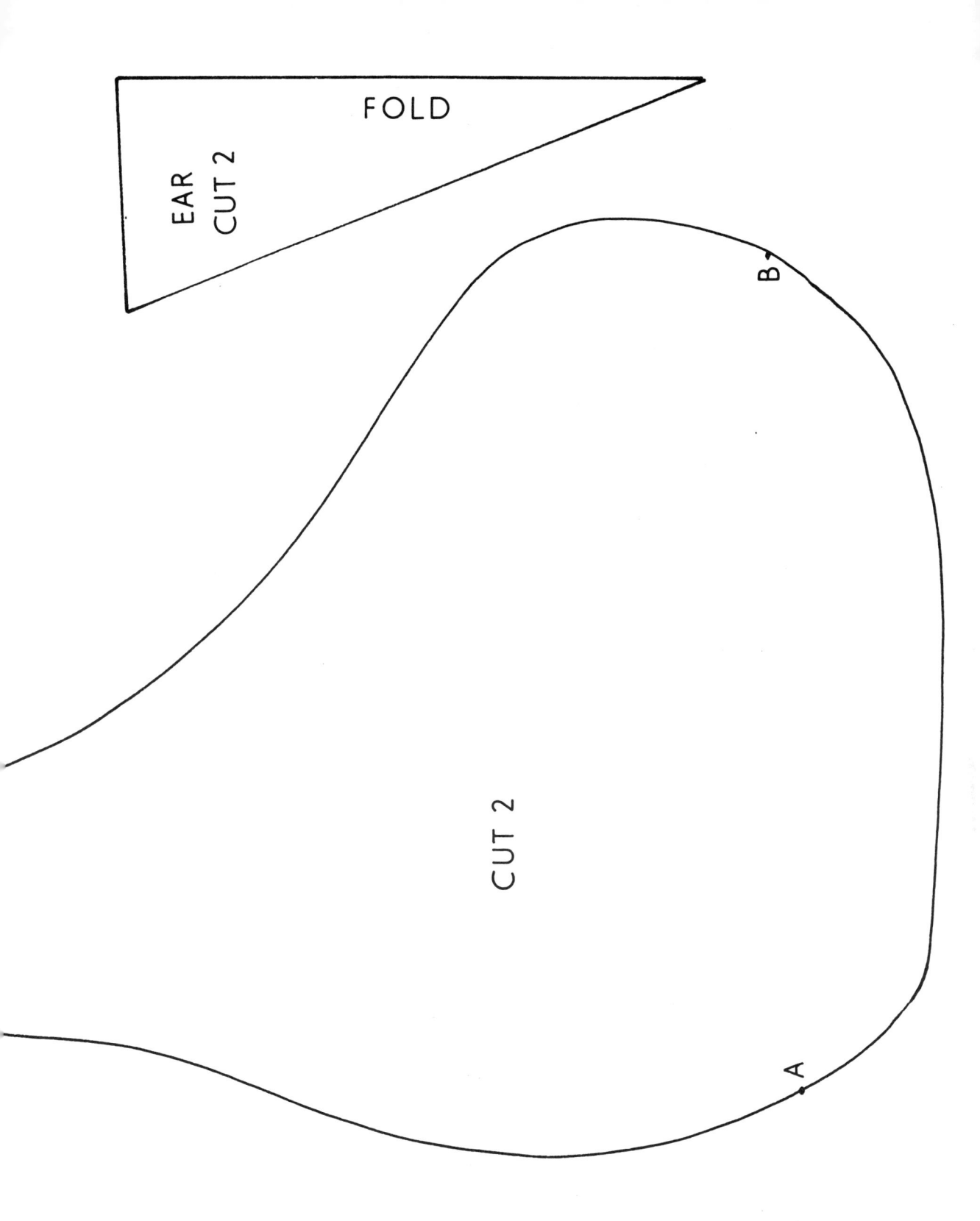

EAR
CUT 2

CUT 2

B

A

NO TURNINGS ALLOWED

Materials required

15 × 16 in. (38 × 41 cm) plain cotton fabric.
Vilene – 3 × 4 in. (8 × 10 cm).
Reeves printing inks.
Few beads for collar decoration.
Kapok for stuffing.

To print

1. Trace off the pattern, Fig. 153, and draw on to fabric, Fig. 154.
2. Print on a design for the body; in Fig. 152 a star pattern was printed and straight stitches added.
3. The design of the dog's collar was based on bottle-tops and beads, stitched on later.
4. Eyes were printed with a cotton spool and bottle-tops, and nose and curve of mouth were obtained from scraps of wood.

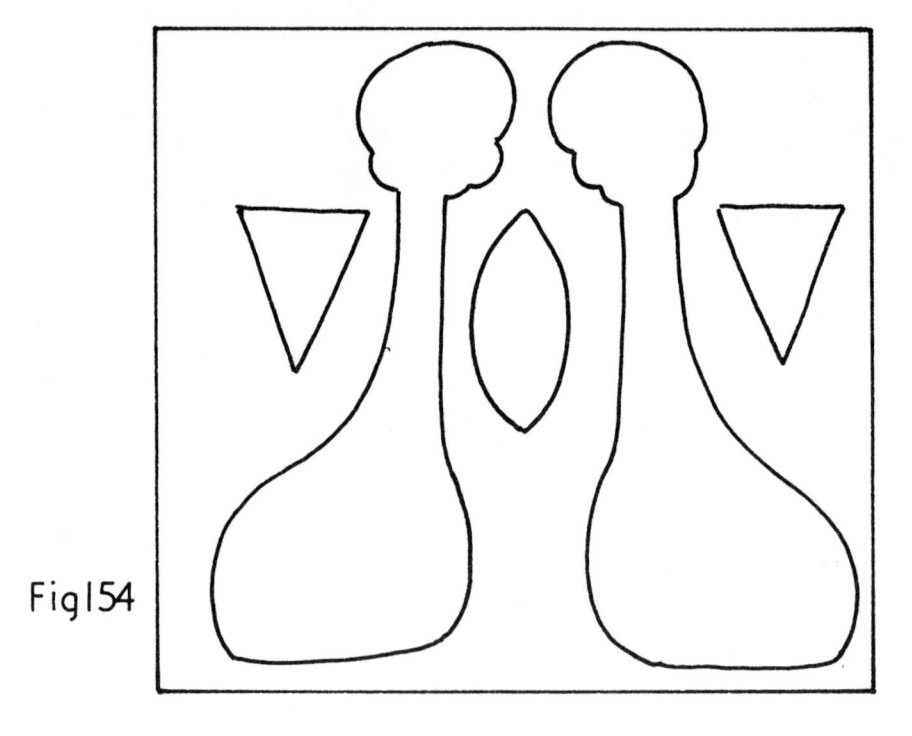

Fig 154

After printing, press the fabric on the wrong side to set the dye.

To make up

1. Cut out the various parts, allowing ¼-in. (1-cm) turnings.
2. Work any embroidery or stitch on beads to the body sections.
3. Place right sides of body together and machine, leaving a gap open at the base, Fig. 155.

4. Attach the base gusset from A to B of body (front section).
5. Snip the turnings, as in Fig. 155, then turn right side out.
6. Stuff firmly with kapok and stitch up the opening.
7. Cut out the Vilene to the shape of ear pattern. Place Vilene on to the fabric and tack, Fig. 156(a). Turn under the raw edges and oversew, Fig. 156(b). Attach ears to the dog, see Fig. 152.

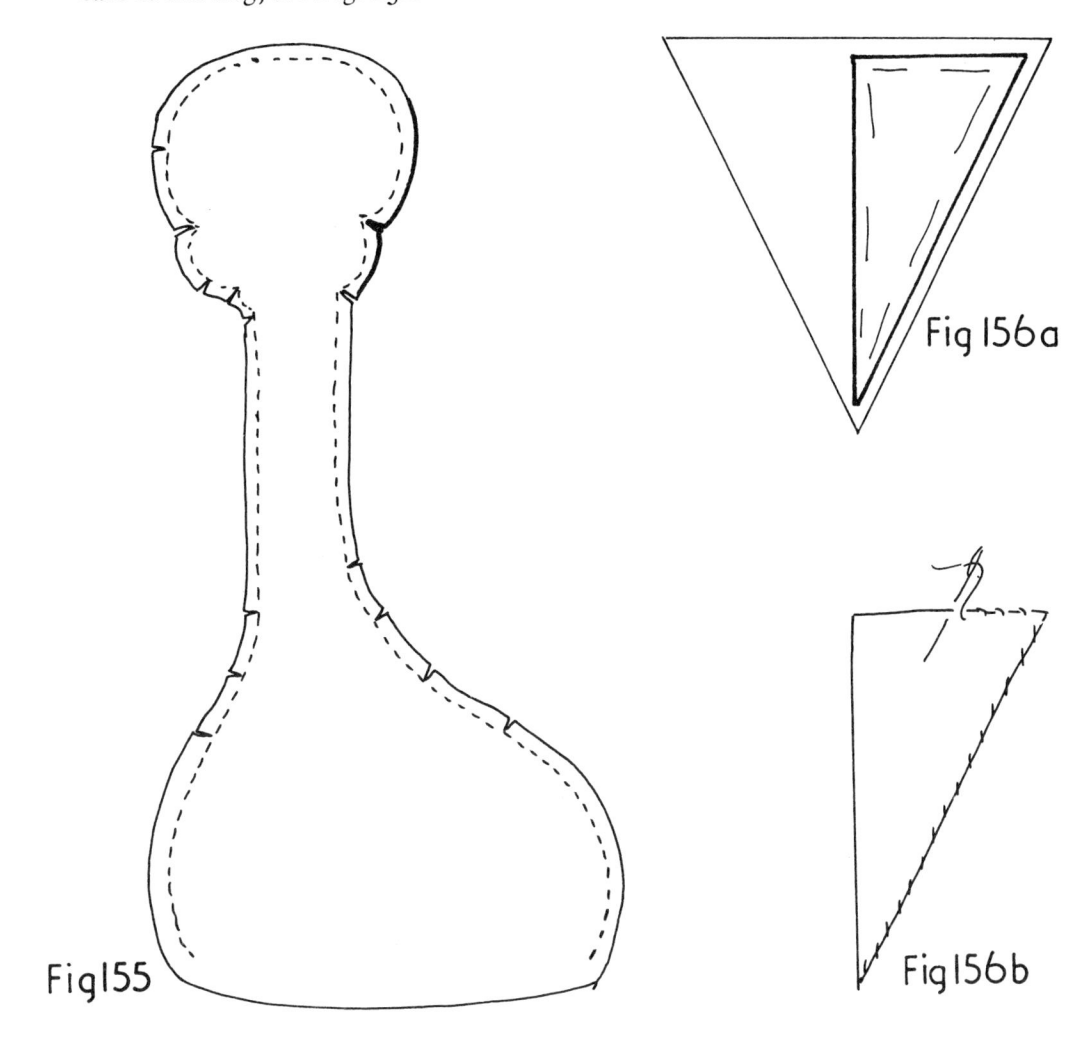

Fig 155

Fig 156a

Fig 156b

Books for reference

Fun with Fabric Printing, Kathleen Monk (Mills & Boon)
Introducing Textile Printing, Nora Proud (Batsford)
Textile Printing and Dyeing, Nora Proud (Batsford)

Embroidery

Fabrics may be enriched with stitchery carried out in various types of threads, or fabrics may be applied to a background, as in collage, and this also is called "embroidery".

In this particular section I have tried to introduce a finer type of fabric for counted-thread design, and this is called Java canvas. This fabric can be made up into a variety of articles. The two included are a mat which could form a set of mats for a dining-table, and a tissue-box cover, which would make a delightful gift for anyone. The cover may be made up in other fabrics such as linen, Crimplene, or any bonded jersey fabric. If a fine jersey material is desired because it is the right colour and thickness, then it may be backed with iron-on Vilene.

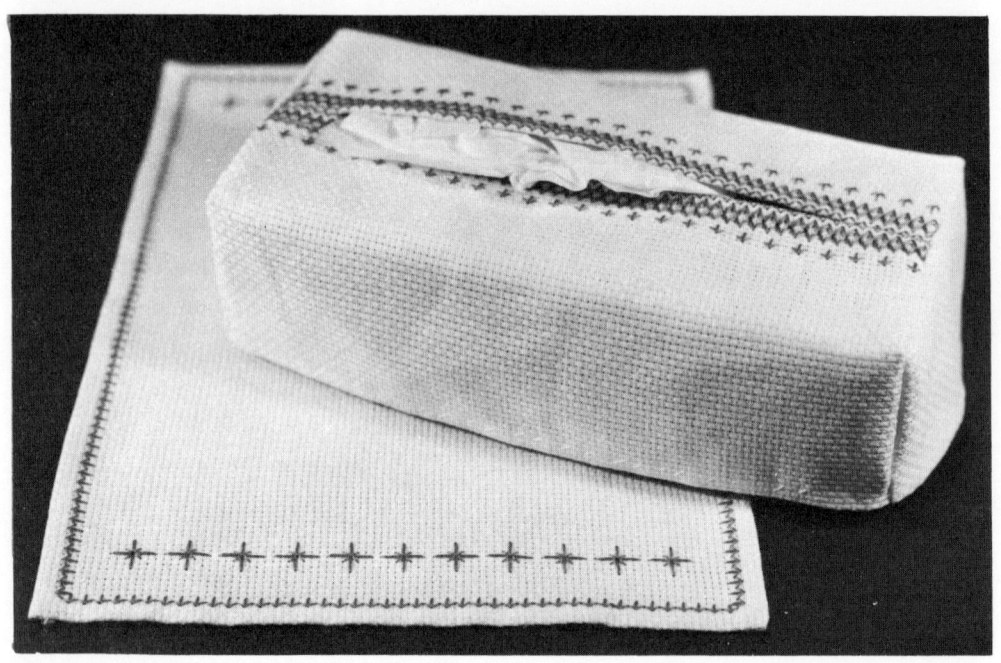

Fig. 157 Mat and tissue box cover made from embroidered Java canvas.

The toys made in the latter part of this section are made in felt, but bonded jersey fabrics would be just as nice. The one problem with bonded fabrics is that they are sometimes rather difficult to stitch due to the thickness of the backing fabric. Try using a thinner needle and finer thread. Embroidery may be too difficult but the fabric may be decorated with a pattern of threads and sequins, which could be stuck on. A printed design could also be applied and perhaps threads added to give extra finish and colour. Thin jersey fabrics may be used but should be backed with iron-on Vilene, otherwise the toys are liable to stretch out of shape.

A MAT

Materials required

15 × 11 in. (37 × 28 cm) Java canvas.
Embroidery cotton.

To make

1. Work a row of zigzag stitch, see page 47, 1 in. (2·5 cm) in from the raw edge. Turn the corner and add a row of straight stitches, Fig. 158.

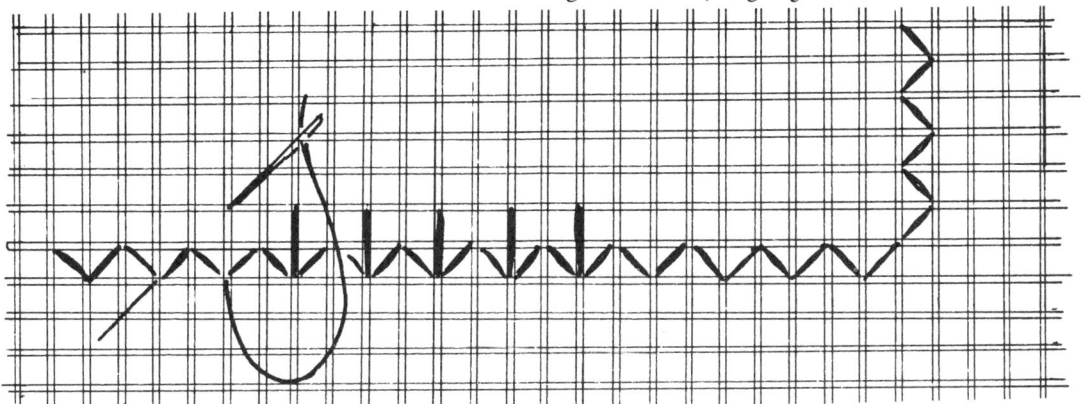

Fig 158

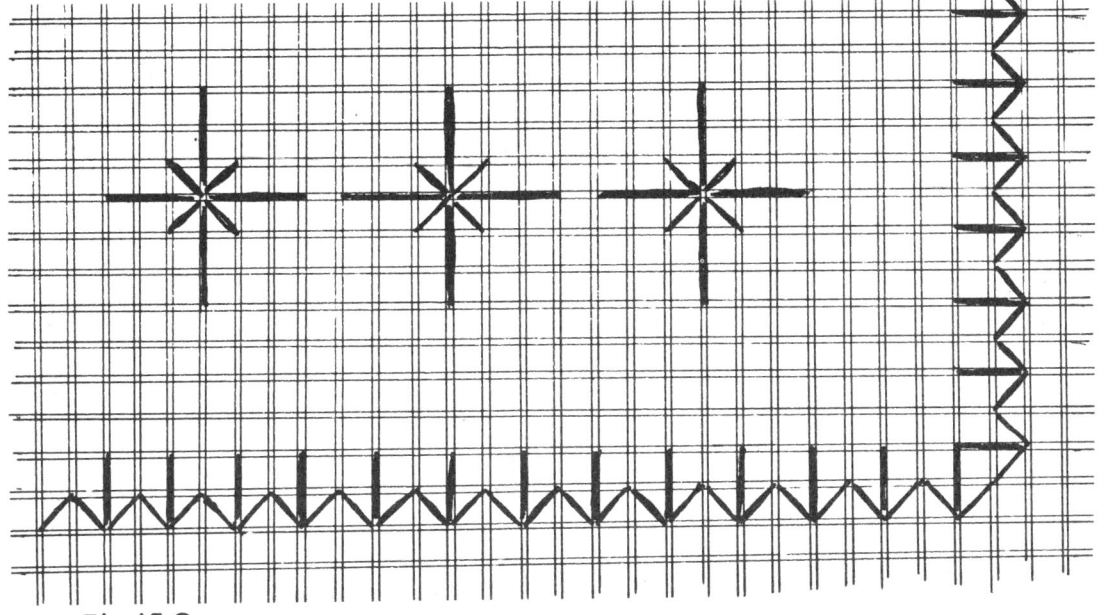

Fig 159

2. The large design is built up from eye-stitch, with four of the stitches being made longer, Fig. 159.
3. Turn under the raw edge and make a hem $\frac{1}{4}$ in. (5 mm) in depth all round hem using matching cotton.

TISSUE BOX COVER

(For box size 10 × $4\frac{3}{4}$ in., depth 3 in. 25·5 × 12 × 7·5 cm)

Materials required

$14\frac{1}{2}$ × 13 in. (36 × 32 cm) Java canvas.
Embroidery cotton.

Cutting out (Fig. 160).

Cut two pieces of fabric each 11 × $6\frac{1}{2}$ in. (27 × 16 cm).
Cut two pieces of fabric each $3\frac{1}{2}$ × $5\frac{1}{4}$ in. (8·5 × 13 cm)

To embroider

1. Embroider along one long side. Commence stitching $\frac{3}{4}$ in. (2 cm) from the raw edge. Try working zigzag stitch over two squares. If two rows are worked they can form large diamonds, Fig. 160(a).
2. Using a contrasting colour of thread work two rows of zigzag stitch inside the large diamonds, Fig. 160(b).
3. Work a row of zigzag stitch just above the large diamonds (or side nearest to raw edge), Fig. 160(b).
4. The border may be made larger by adding a further row of stitching as in Fig. 161.
5. Repeat the embroidery on to the other long strip.

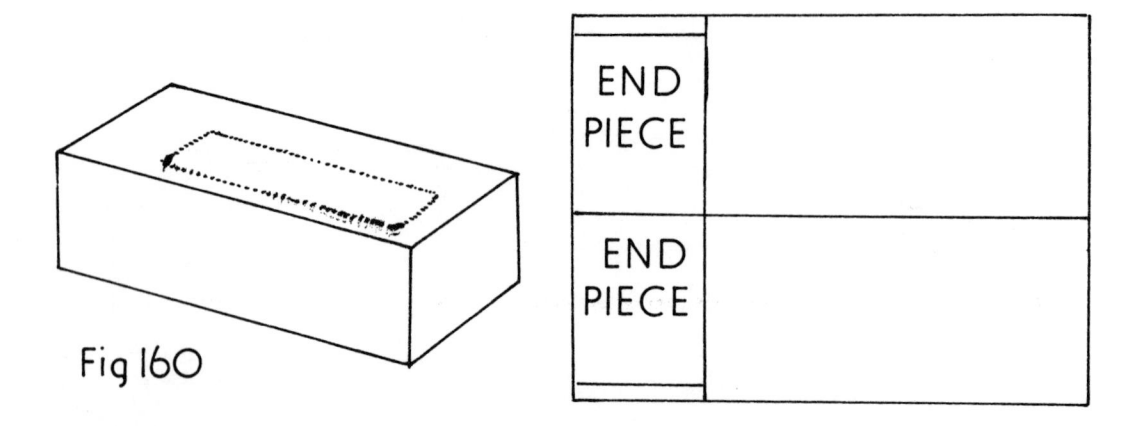

Fig 160

Fig 160b   Fig 160a

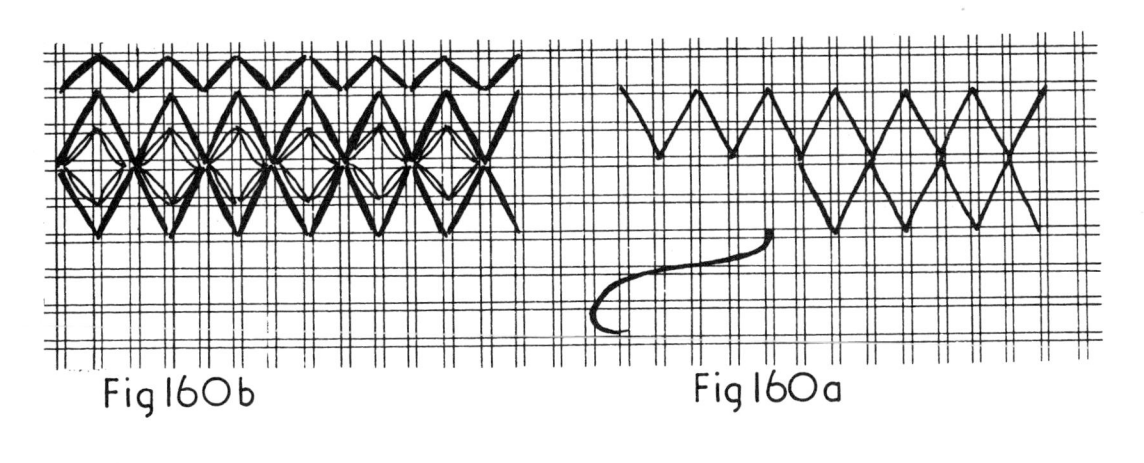

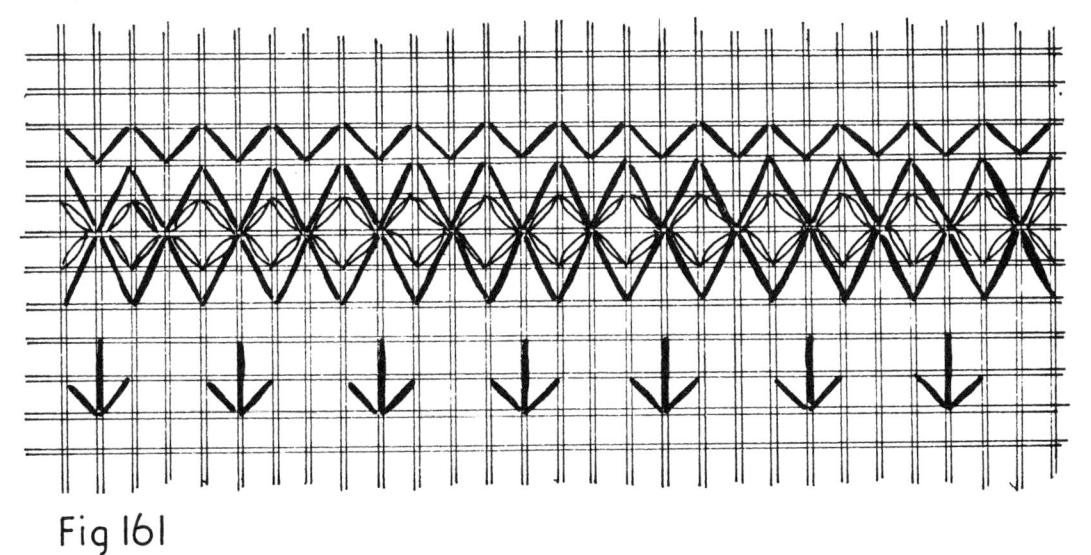

Fig 161

To make up

1. Turn under ¼ in. (5 mm) on to the wrong side and hem, Fig. 162(a). Do this for both pieces.
2. Place the two right sides together and join by oversewing for 1 in. (2·5 cm), Fig. 162(b), at the two ends only, then open out.

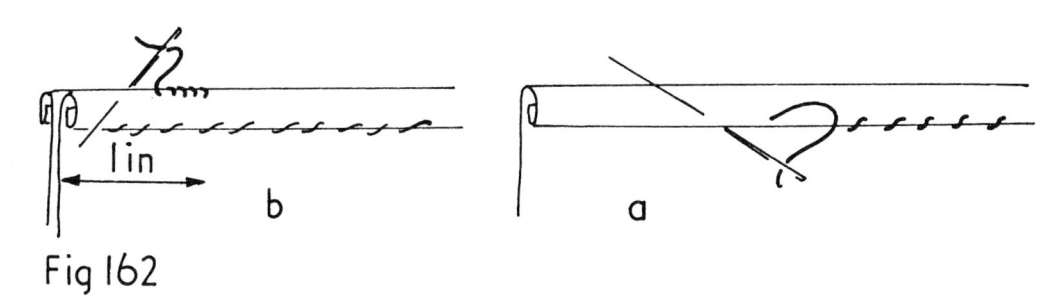

Fig 162

Fig 163

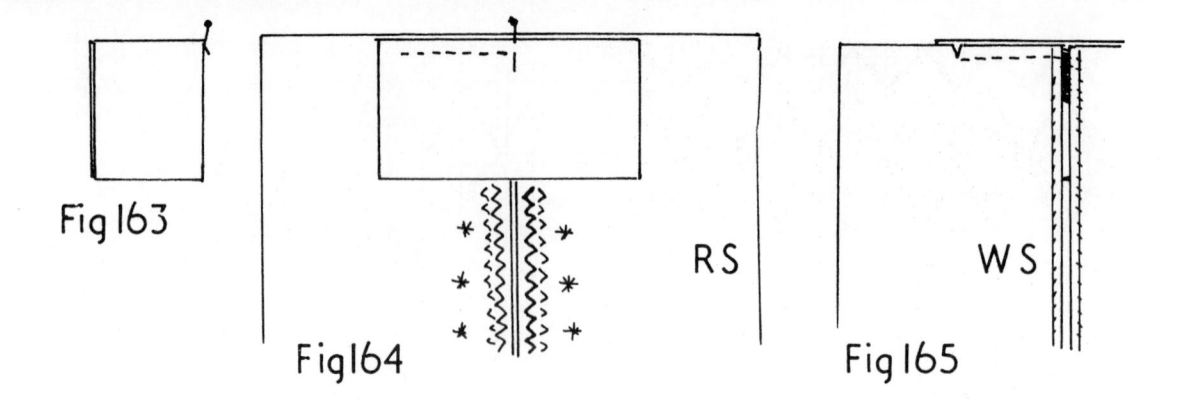

Fig 164   RS

Fig 165   WS

3. Fold the end piece in half and mark with a pin, Fig. 163. Place the pin mark to the join of the previous piece, pin into position and join with back-stitch, Fig. 164. Stitch to within ¼ in. (5 mm) of end of piece. Snip turning, Fig. 165, and continue stitching. Join on the remainder of the end piece and also the opposite end, so that it looks like a box.
4. Oversew the raw edges and make a ¼-in. (5-mm) hem on to the wrong side all round the lower edge.

Once you have got the "feel" of the fabric, you can experiment with other borders of your own invention.

A PENCIL MAN
(Take his hat off and put pencils in)

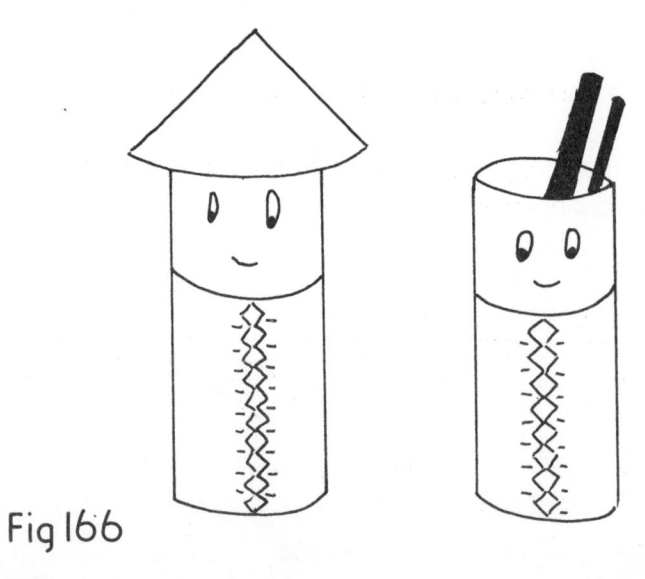

Fig 166

Materials required

Felt $7\frac{1}{2} \times 5\frac{1}{2}$ in. (19 × 14 cm) for body and hat.
Felt $5\frac{1}{2} \times 2$ in. (14 × 5 cm) for face.
Vilene $5\frac{1}{2} \times 3\frac{1}{2}$ in. (14 × 9 cm).
Toilet-roll tube.
Embroidery threads.

Trace off hat pattern, Fig. 167.

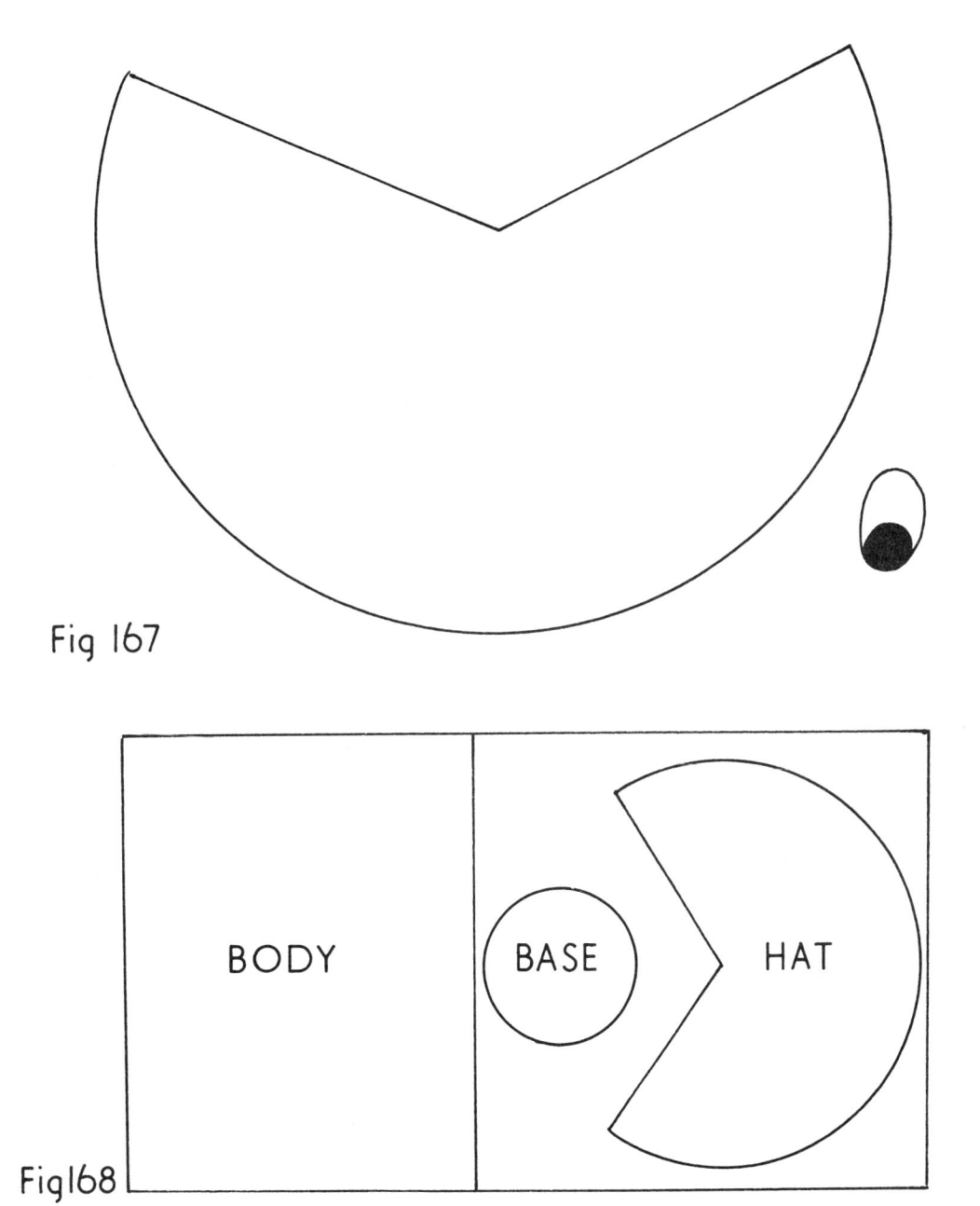

Fig 167

Fig 168

To cut out (Fig. 168)
1. Cut off a strip of felt 3 in. (8 cm) wide for body.
2. Place hat pattern on to felt and pin.
3. Cut out a circle of paper the size of base of toilet-roll tube and pin on to felt, then cut out both pieces.

To make
1. Fold the body piece of felt down the centre. Draw a line down it using white cotton and long stitches, so that when it is opened out it will show, Fig. 169(a) and (b).
2. Embroider down the front, Fig. 169(c).

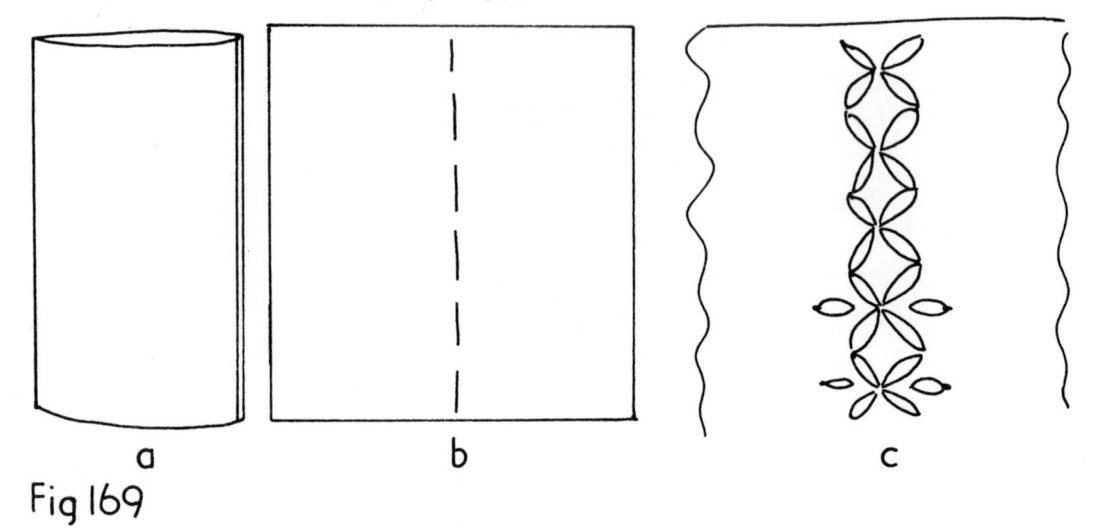

Fig 169

Here is one idea: Use zigzag chain-stitch. Work two rows to meet in the centre. Work detached chain-stitch in the spaces.
3. Join the body to head by oversewing the two pieces together, using cotton that matches either body or head, Fig. 170(a).

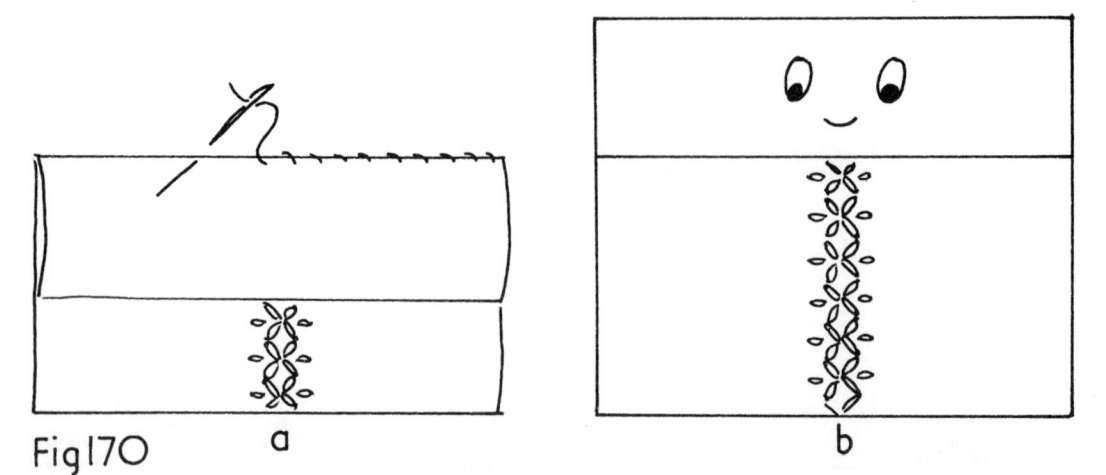

Fig 170

4. Open out and cut out the eyes in white and black felt. Place into position on to the face section and stitch, Fig. 170(b).
5. Mark the mouth and embroider in chain-stitch. (Make sure that the features are in line with the front of the body.)
6. Wrap the felt around the toilet-roll tube and stitch, Fig. 171(a).
7. Stitch base on to bottom of tube, Fig. 171(b).

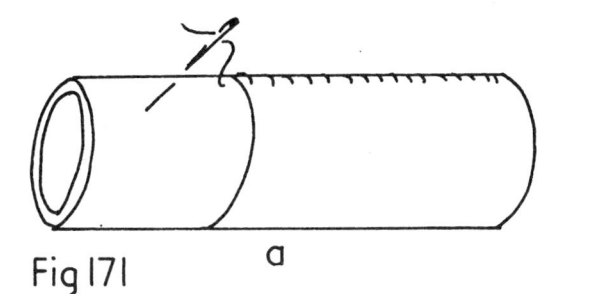

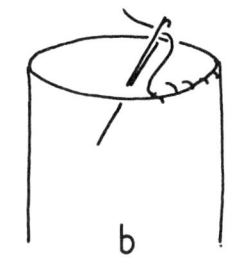

Fig 171

Make hat

1. Embroider around the outer edge of the hat. Use the same design as you used down the front of the body, Fig. 172(a).
2. Cut out the hat shape in Vilene. Tack the two together. Oversew round the outer edge, then down the join to form a cone, Fig. 172(b).

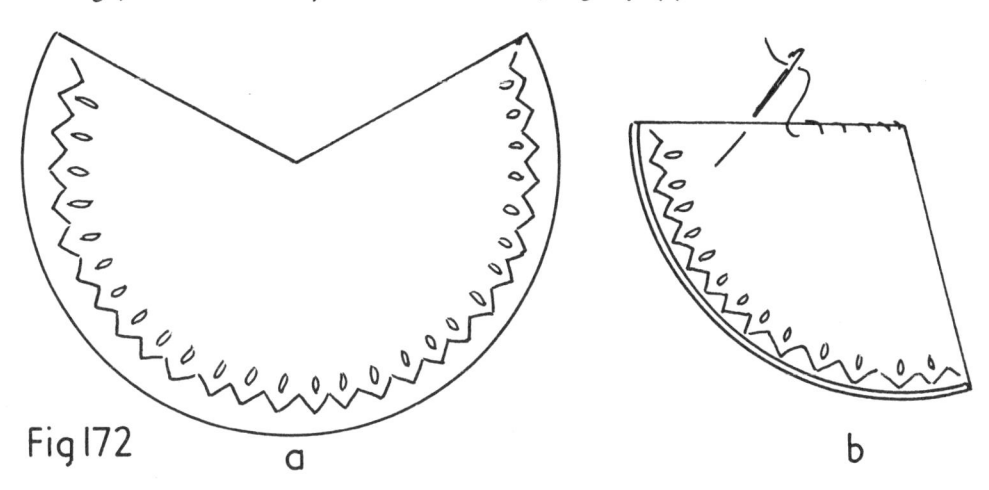

Fig 172

CUTE JANE

Materials required

Felt $4\frac{1}{2} \times 9$ in. (11 × 23 cm) for head.
Felt 3 × 10 in. (8 × 26 cm) for body and feet.
Scraps of red and white felt.
Kapok for stuffing.
Embroidery threads.

Trace off the pattern, Fig. 173.

CUT 2

BODY

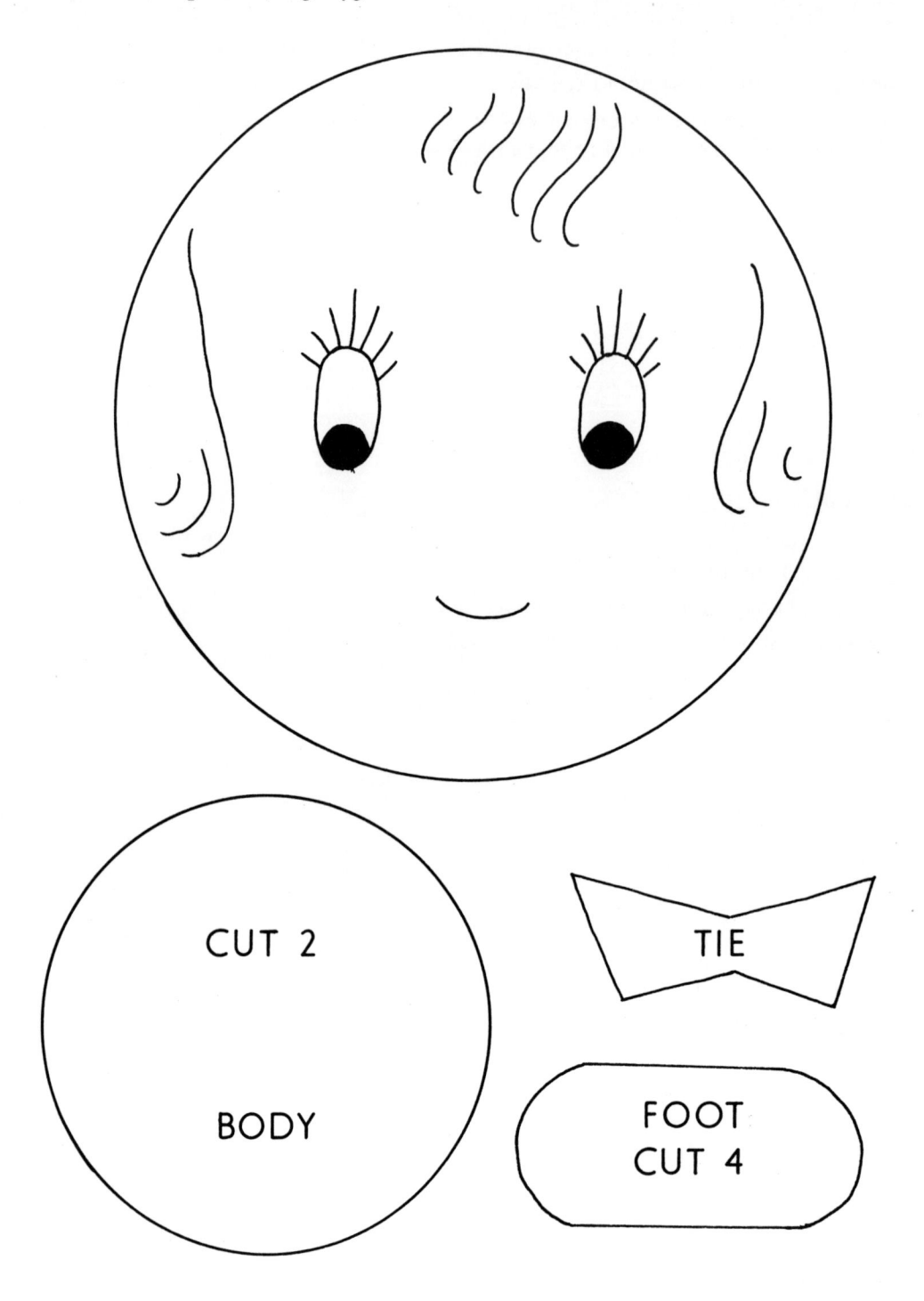

TIE

FOOT
CUT 4

Fig 173

To cut out

1. Cut out two circles for the head using the 4½ × 9 in. (11 × 23 cm) felt.
2. Draw round the body and foot pattern on to the other piece of felt, Fig. 174.
3. Trace off the eye pattern and cut out two white eyes and two black centres.

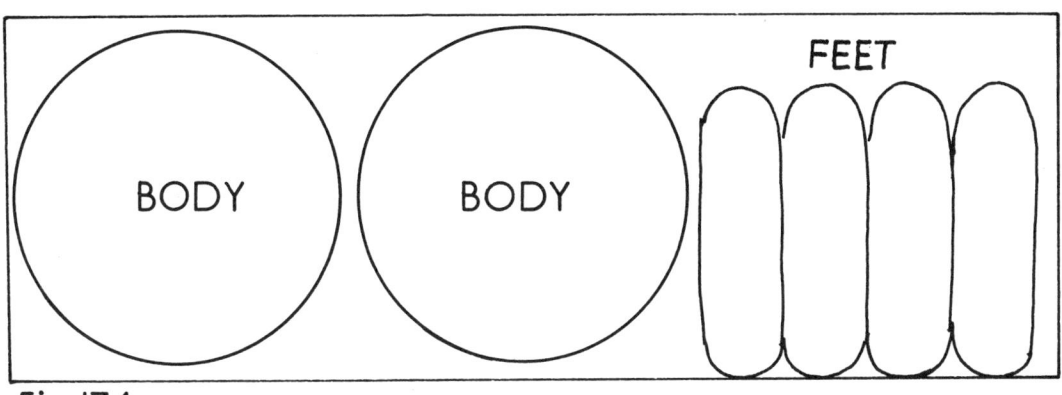

Fig 174

To make the face

1. Place the whites of eyes in position on the face and stitch with matching cotton. Place black parts of eyes into position and stitch, Fig. 175.
2. Use loop stitches of various sizes for the eyebrows.
3. Use chain-stitch for hair and mouth, Fig. 176.
4. Make nose with a fly-stitch.

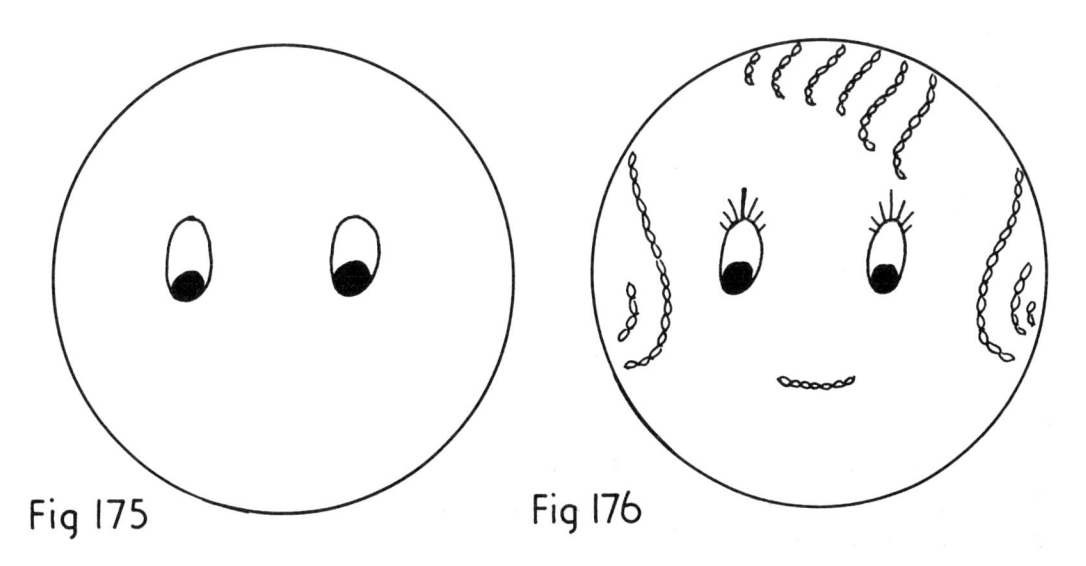

Fig 175   Fig 176

Body

1. Work fly-stitch down the centre of the body and a row on each side of the centre, Fig. 177.
2. Join head to body with small stitches, back and front, Fig. 178.
3. Place the front and back pieces together. Pin securely, then join together by oversewing, Fig. 179, starting at the base and continuing round the head. Before completing, stuff firmly.

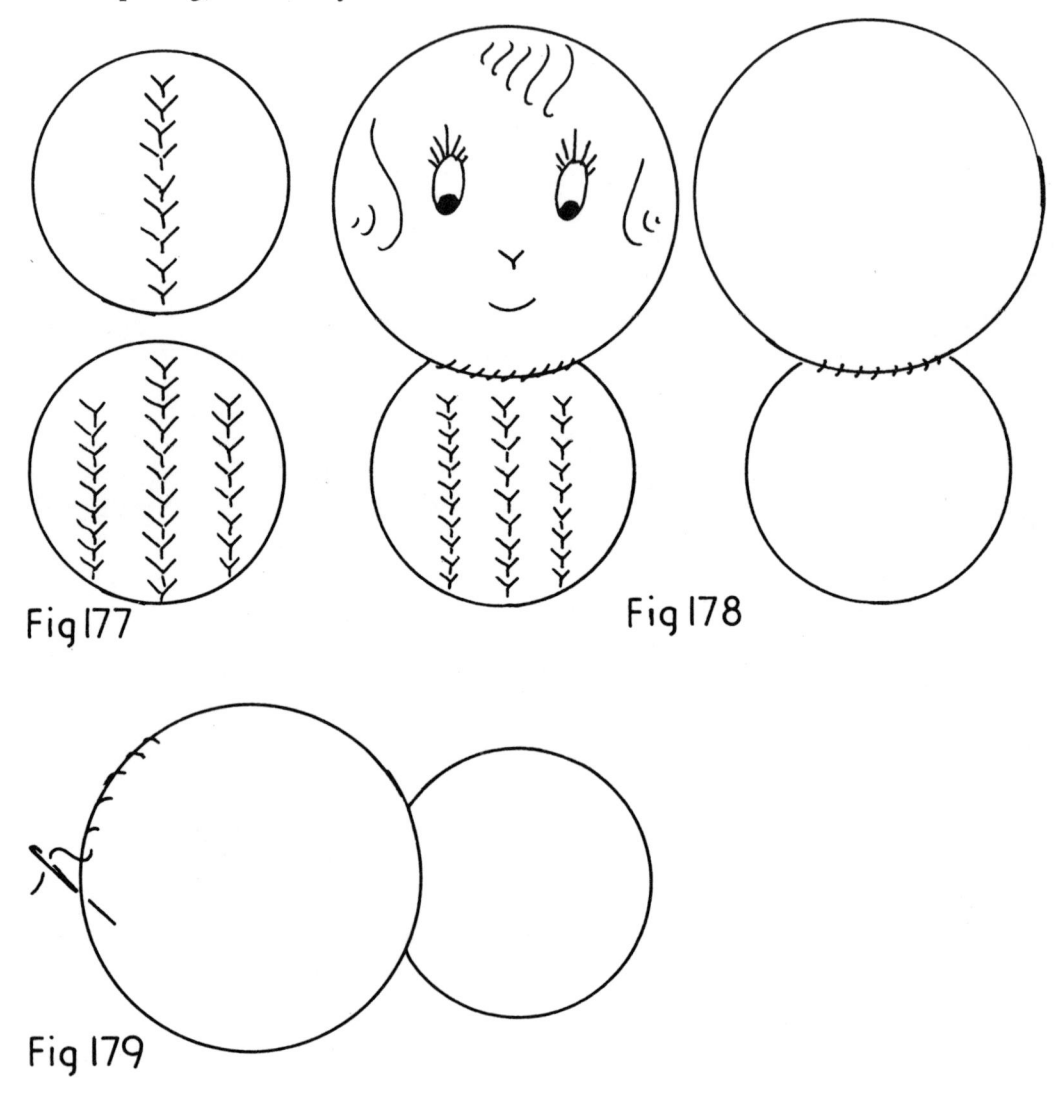

Fig 177

Fig 178

Fig 179

Feet

Embroider the top of each foot with french knots.
Place an embroidered foot on top of a plain one and join together with running-stitch. Stuff firmly before completing the stitching, Fig. 180.

Fig 180

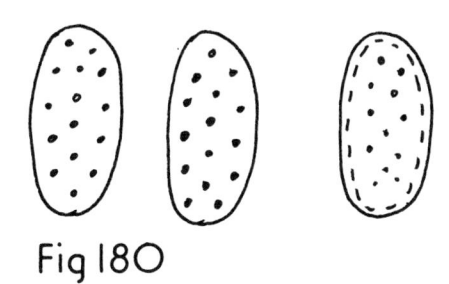

To complete

Stitch the feet on to the base of the body so that it looks like the illustration.
Make tie by putting a strip of felt over the centre and round the tie, Fig. 181.
Stitch on.
To make it move about attach a piece of shirring elastic to the top of head, Fig. 182.

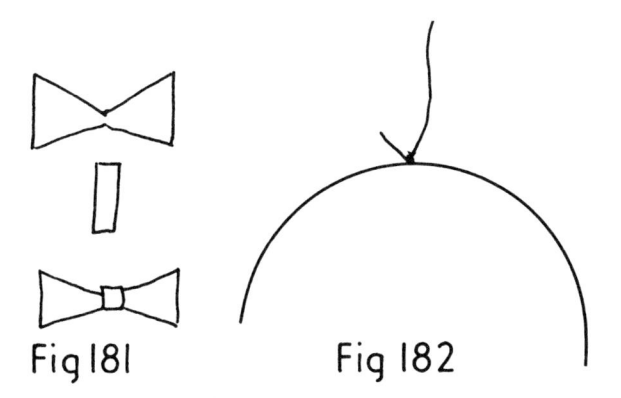

Fig 181   Fig 182

Books for reference

Primary Embroidery Stitches and Designs, A. V. White (Routledge & Kegan Paul)
Toys for your Delight, Winsome Douglass (Mills & Boon)
Performing Toys, A. V. White (Mills & Boon)
Embroidery Design, Enid Mason (Mills & Boon)

Flat maths

The designs in this section are all based on the idea of creating interesting patterns from the use of a circle divided into a number of directions, maybe 6 or even 40.

Materials required

Compass.
Protractor.
Ruler.
Plain paper.
Cardboard or stiff card.
Fabrics for covering the card.
Embroidery cotton.
Thick needle, such as a darning needle.
Leather punch.
Transparent paper or fabric, net or bonded fabric, e.g. Vilene. The designs can be carried out on paper first or direct on to card. It is best to cut the card at least 1 in. (2·5 cm) larger than the design because this gives an attractive border.
The card may be covered in fabric before the design is carried out. This helps to give an interesting background.

To cover a circle

Cut the fabric $\frac{1}{2}$ in. (1 cm) larger than the card.
Put a running-stitch round the outer edge of fabric (Fig. 183(a)).
Place cardboard on to fabric and pull up the thread so that the raw edge curls over the card (Fig. 183(b)). Glue raw edges.

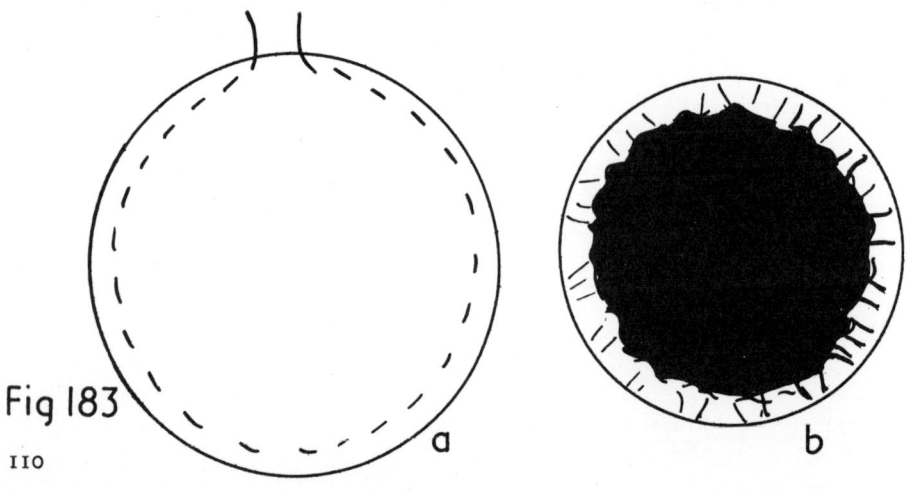

Fig 183

To cover square or oblong

Cut fabric by the straight thread ¼ in. (5 mm) larger all round than the card. Place card on to the fabric and bring over raw edge of each side down on to the card and stick with adhesive, Fig. 184(*a*) and (*b*).

Fig 184

To mark design

Pierce all the holes for the design through from the wrong side, using a thick needle.

SIX-POINTED STAR

Draw a circle on to stiff cardboard, using a compass.
Divide the circumference into six by marking off half the diameter of the circle with the compass, marked as in Fig. 185(*a*).
Join A, C and E to form a triangle, then join B, F and D as in Fig. 185(*b*).

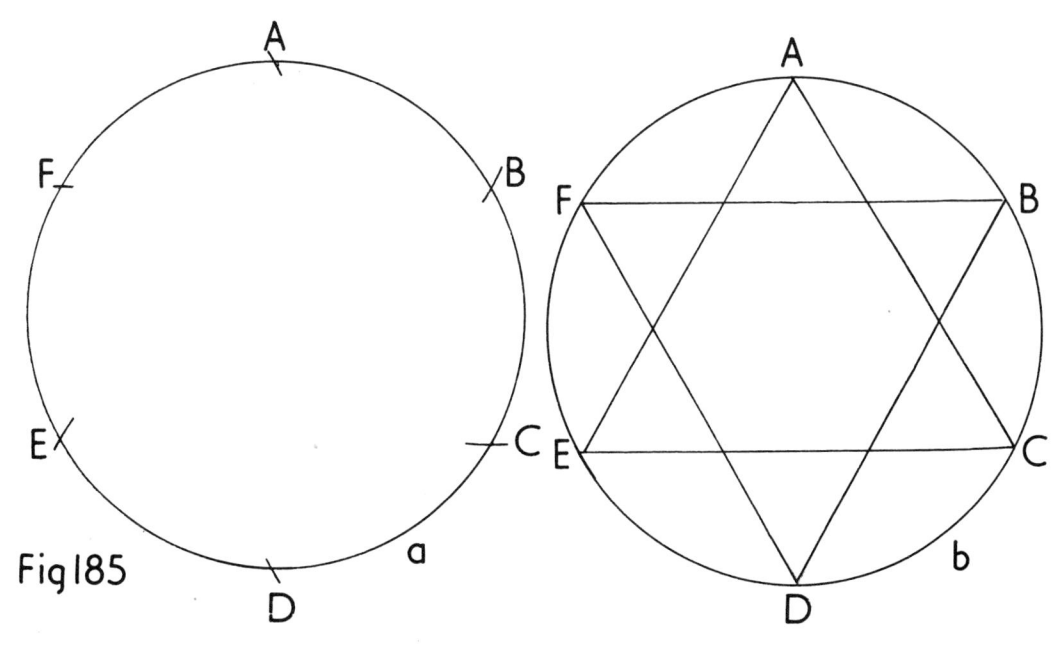

Fig 185

Carry out the design by covering the circle with fabric, page 110.
Pierce the points of the star by pushing a thick, sharp-pointed needle through the cardboard (from the wrong side). Thread a needle with embroidery cotton (put a knot on end) and push the needle through from Point A and back to Point C. (Point C can easily be found by inserting a pin through from the wrong side so that the point shows on the right side.)
Mark out the complete star on to the right side, using threads.
Colour may be added to the points of the stars by cutting out triangular shapes of felt. The shapes can be traced off from the wrong side of the card.
Cut the triangles slightly smaller than the original size, thus allowing for a border to show between the felt and thread, Fig. 186. A hole may be cut in the centre of each triangle using a leather punch, Fig. 187. To secure the pieces of felt firmly into position, use an adhesive.

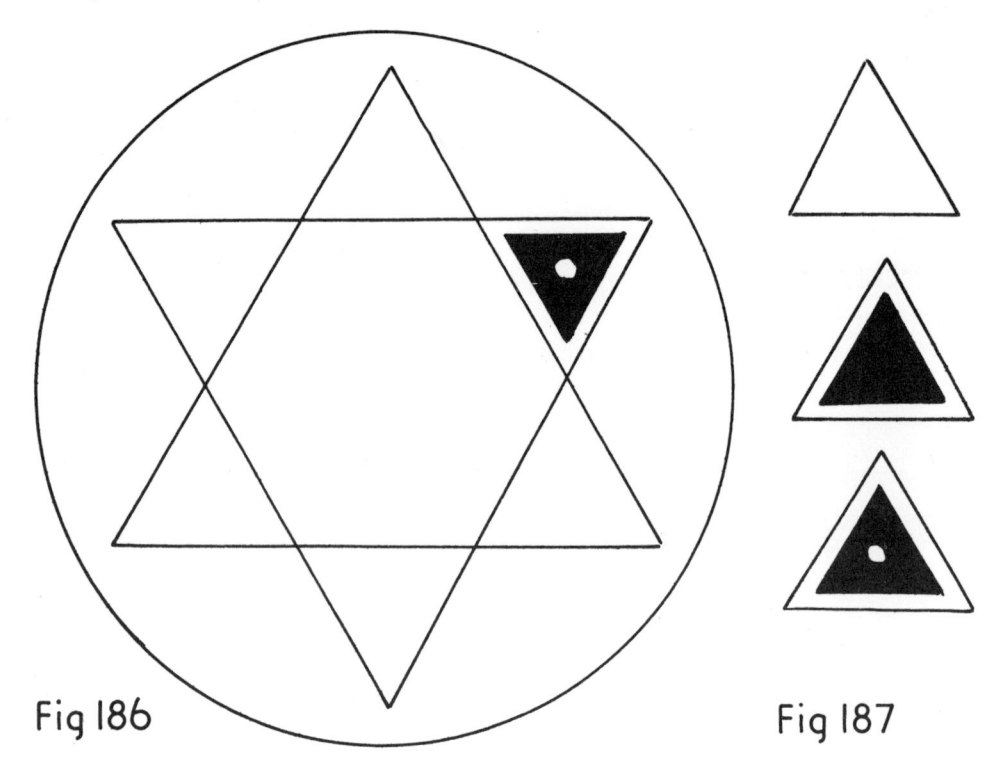

Fig 186   Fig 187

The centre of the design can be made interesting by piercing a hole in the centre, using a needle, and radiating long stitches from the centre to the straight sides at top and bottom of the hexagon. This design could also be built up from layers of thin paper or transparent fabrics.
The design, Fig. 188, is based on four circles which fit into a larger one. The larger circle of cardboard would be covered in fabric as in Fig. 183, page 110. The lines represent stitches that are threads which are brought through from the back of the cardboard. Sequins and beads are added and these are applied to the fabric with an adhesive.

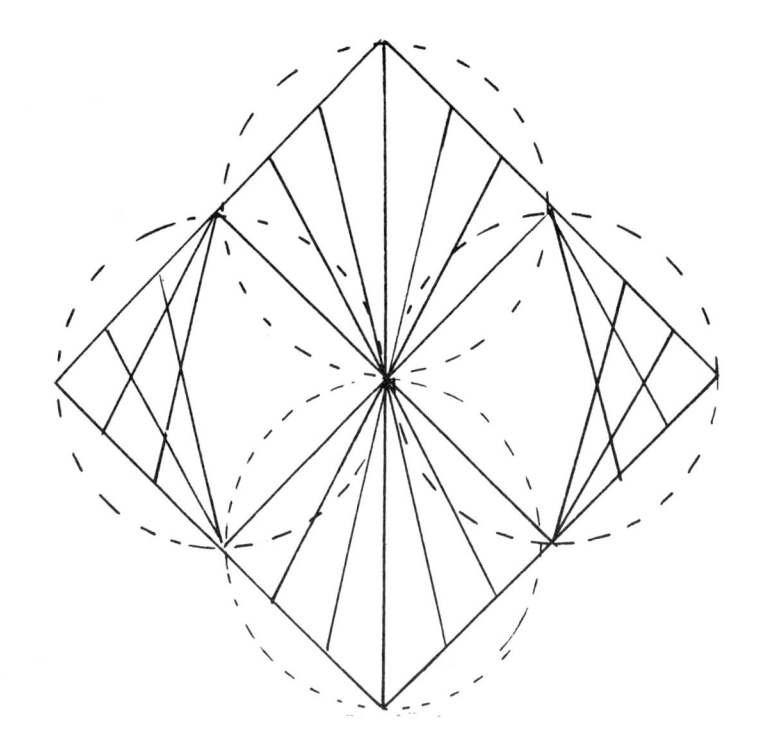

Fig 188

NINE-POINTED STAR

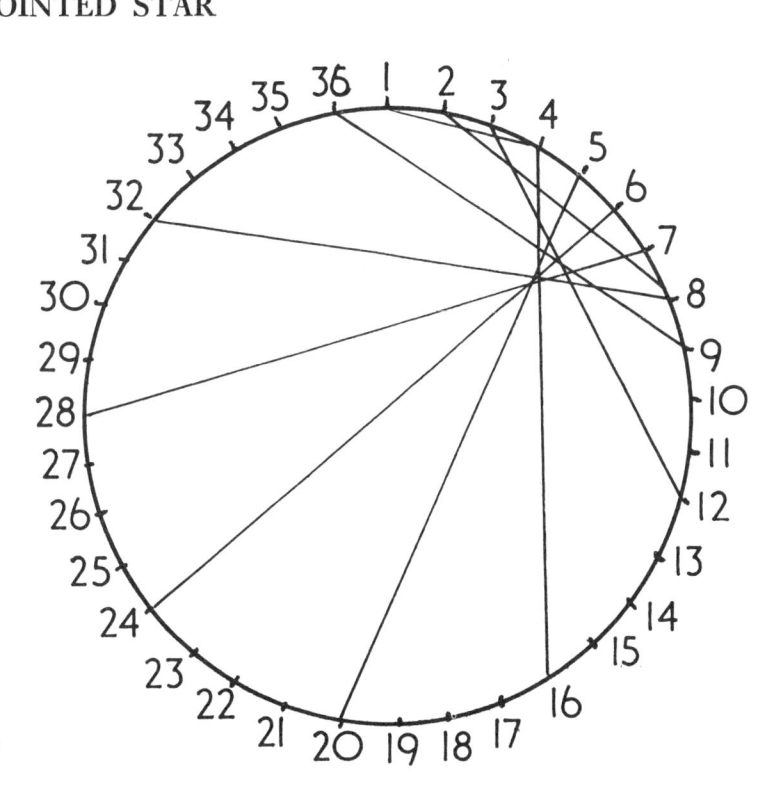

Fig 189

113

Draw a circle and divide the circumference into 36 (use a protractor) and number.
Mark off the story of four.
Rule from 1 to 4, 2 to 8, 3 to 12, continuing up to 36, Fig. 189.
Make the points of the star by joining 12, 24 and 36.

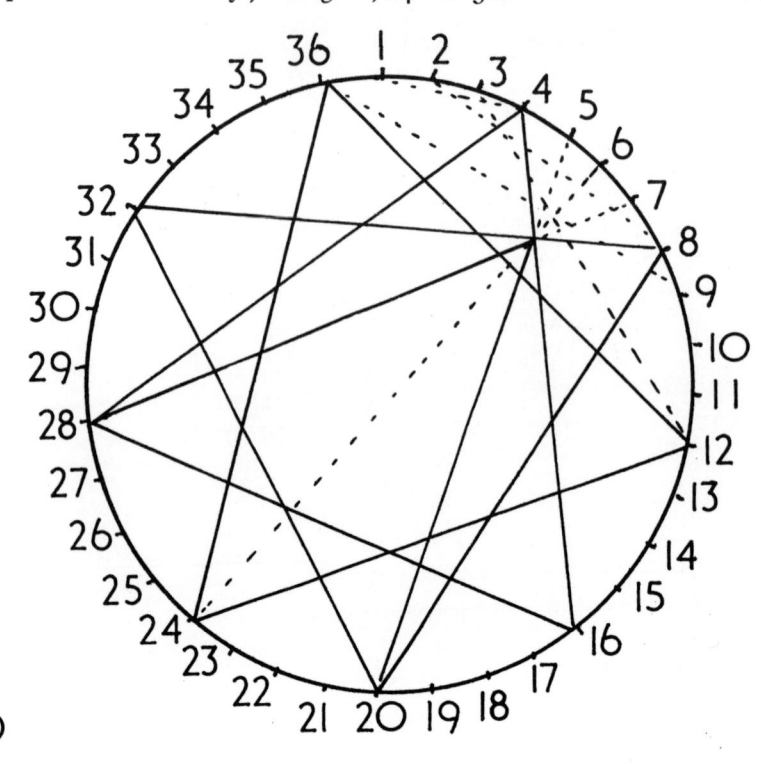

Fig 190

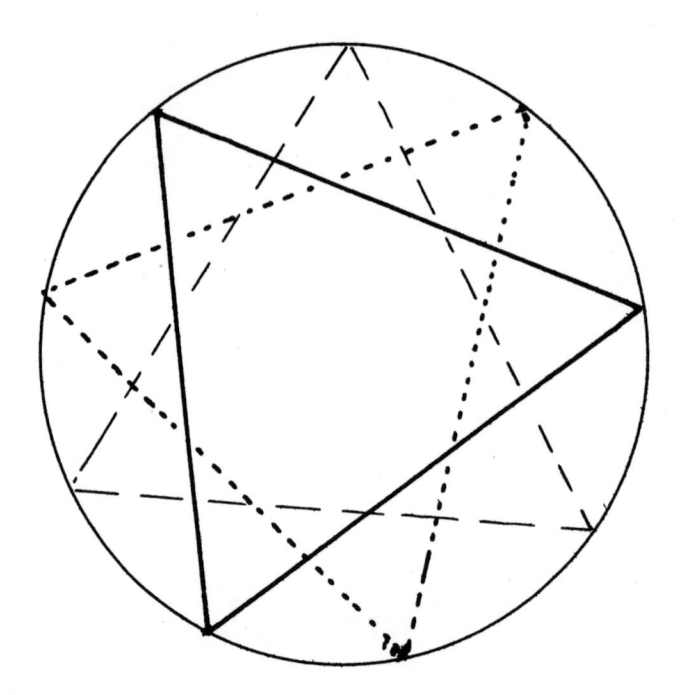

Fig 191

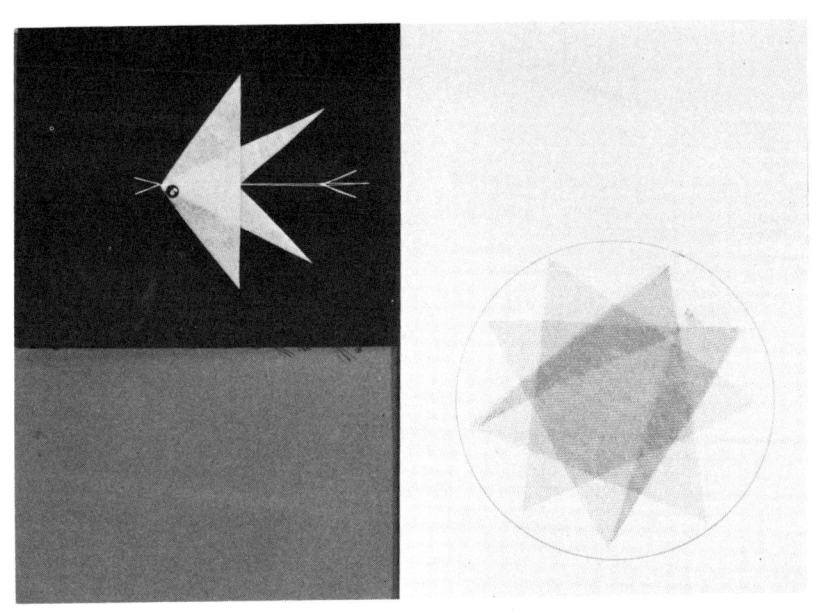

Fig. 192 Star and fish made of transparent fabric triangles. The eye for the fish was made from a bead and long and short stitches were used to make the tail and fins.

Next use point 8, add 12 = 20; 20, add 12 = 32.
Join points 8, 20 and 32 to complete the star, Fig. 190.
If you look carefully at the finished shape you will see that it is really made up from three triangles, Fig. 191.
Take a tracing of one triangle and cut out in thin paper or transparent fabric.
Do this for the three triangles. Arrange them so that they overlap each other to form a nine-pointed star.
The points of the star can be secured with a firm adhesive.
This design can also be carried out by using the lines of the design only, Fig. 192.

THE STORY OF FIVE

Use a compass and make a circle. The circle may be divided into four. Then each quarter subdivided into 10; for this use a protractor.
Number from 1 to 40.
Mark off the story of five.
Rule from 1 to 5; 2 to 10; 3 to 15; continue up to 40, Fig. 193.
From the pattern of lines an interesting design can be built up.
Rule from 15 to 35, thus forming a triangle.
Join 20 to the centre of the circle, also 30, Fig. 194.

Fig 193

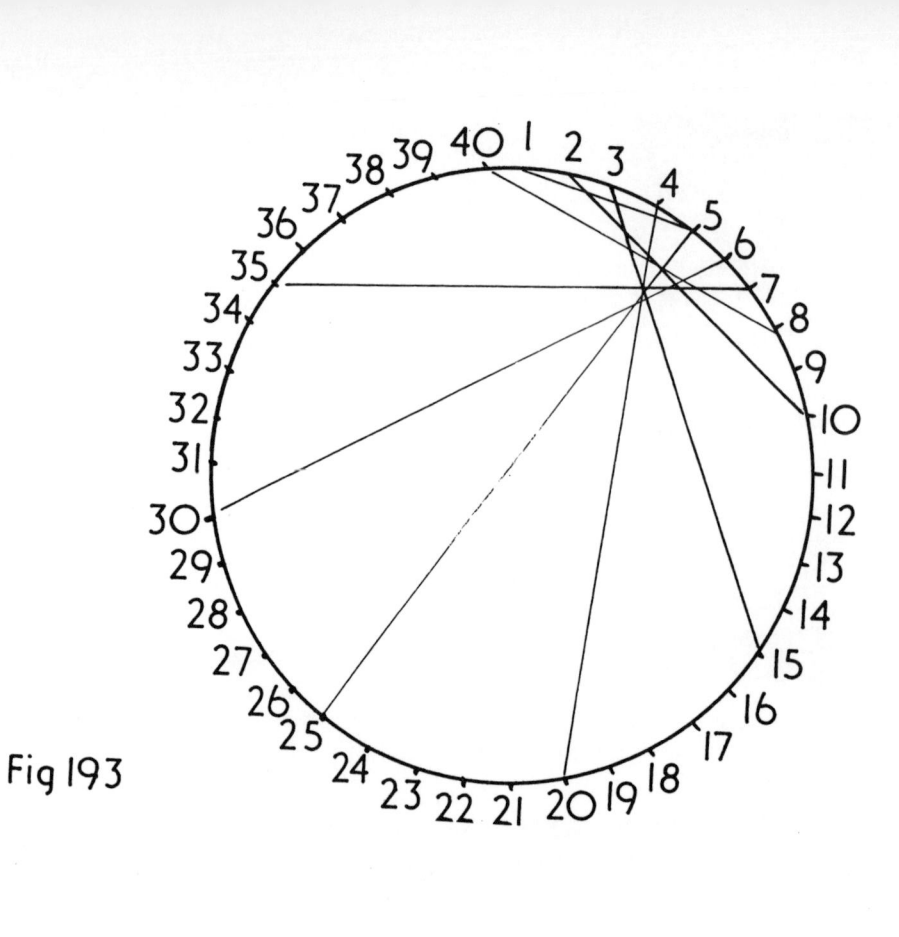

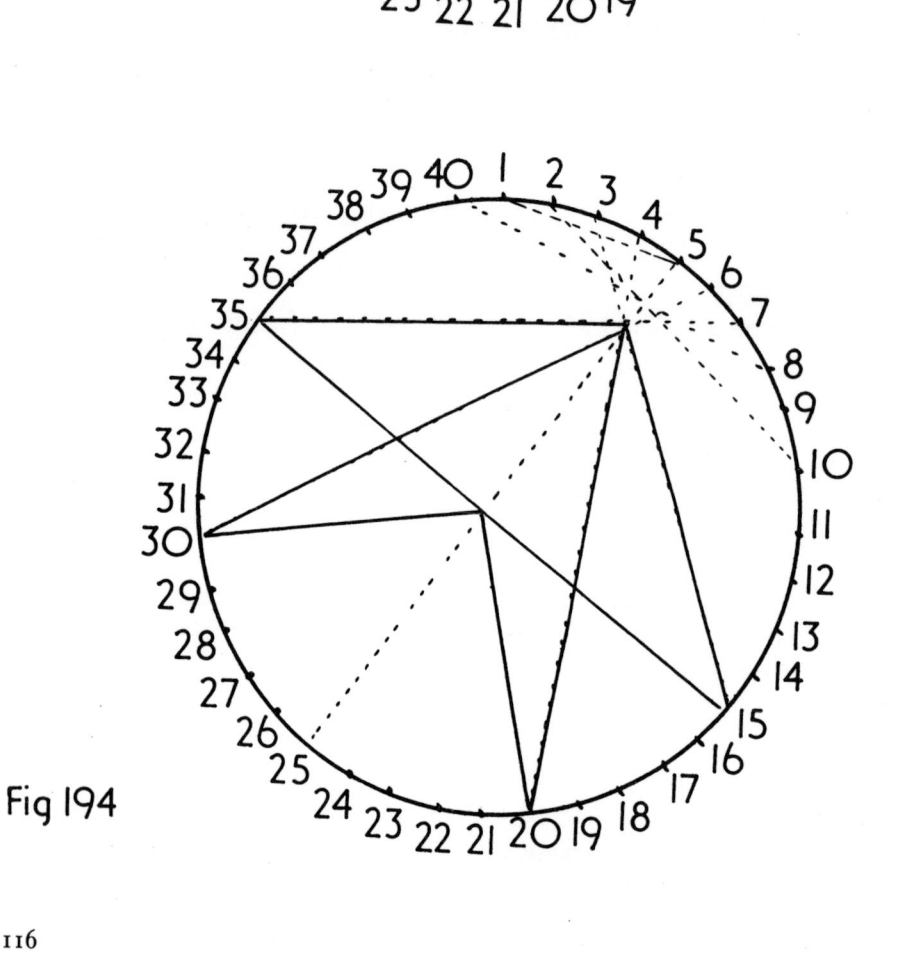

Fig 194

Fish

The pieces could be cut out of transparent fabric. Arrange so that the pieces overlap, stitch on a bead for an eye and put on a long stitch for the tail and two shorter stitches. See Fig. 192.

There are other patterns which can be built up from the story of five. Look at Fig. 195. This design is based on Fig. 194. Nos. 10, 25 and 40 have been joined together, but the lines have only been emphasised when they joined the triangular shape. The shapes could be cut out of transparent fabric and then other aspects of the design would appear through the variety of the strength of colour.

Turn the book round, look at the design. An attractive border could be built up from a row of these shapes.

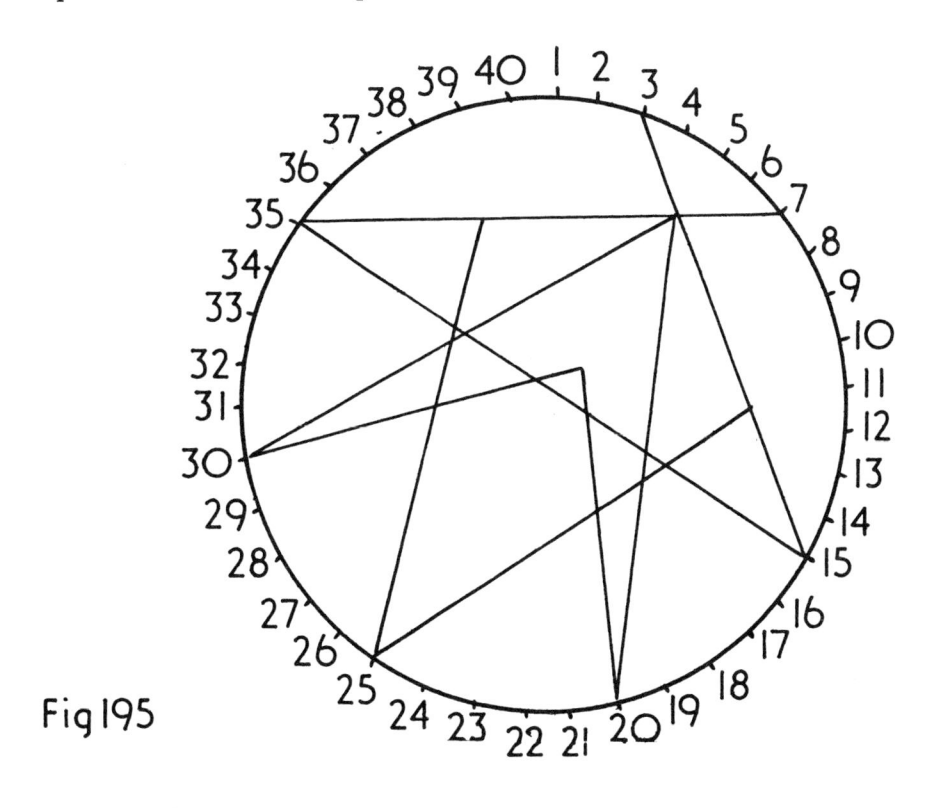

Fig 195

THE STORY OF FOUR

Using the previous division of a circle into 40, rule out the story of 4.
Rule from 1 to 4; 2 to 8; 3 to 12; and continue to 40, Fig. 196.

On this foundation try out the following:

Twice 16 is 32. Rule from 16 to 32.
32, add 4 = 36. Rule from 36 to 16.
Rule from 28 to 24.

Fig 196

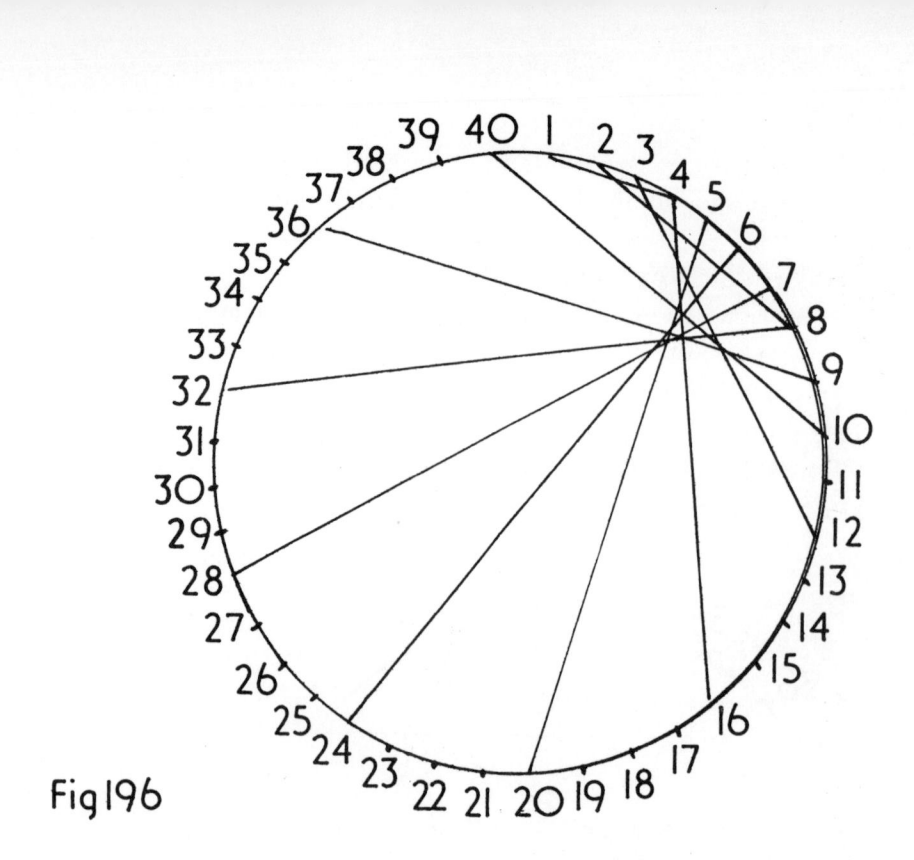

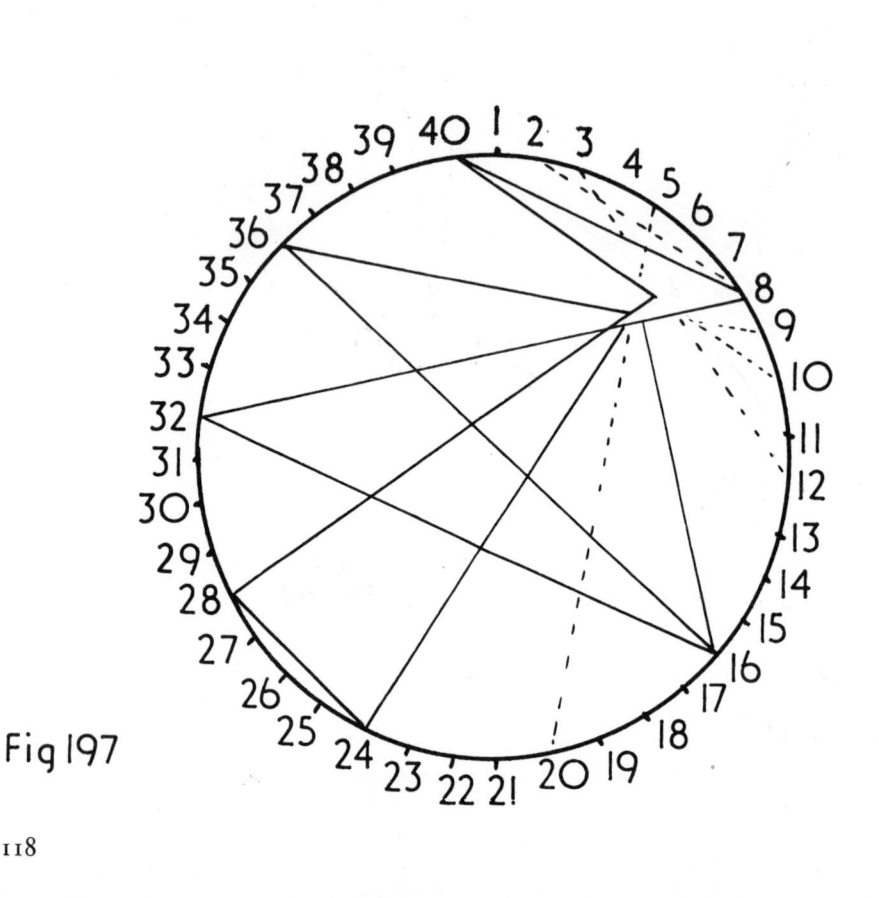

Fig 197

This gives an interesting design.
Look at it on its side.
We now have four major divisions on the lower half.
Try five divisions. Add 4 to 36 = 40. Five into 40 = 8.
Rule from 40 to 8. Make the line 32 to 8 heavy. Now look at the design.
Rule all the lines to be used for the design in heavy or contrasting colour, Fig. 197.
This design can be carried out with layers of transparent fabrics or net could also be added.

Making up of fabrics

Some fabrics are attractive in their own design, while others may be purchased plain and decorated by tie-and-dye or fabric printing.

In this section I have included the making of a simple smocked apron. Smocking is one of our oldest forms of embroidery and we should be very proud to be able to do it. In the old days it was used to decorate the peasant's smocks, which were made of linen and worn by the men. Some of the counties of England had designs of their own. If you use a fabric with a checked design, such as gingham, then it is very simple to carry out the actual embroidery stitches.

An apron, or a slip-over style of pinafore, are ideal for fabric printing or tie-and-dye. These fabrics can also be used for beach-bags, over-blouses, or even skirts. There is no need to make skirts with plackets; just use two straight widths of fabric with two rows of elastic to form a waistband.

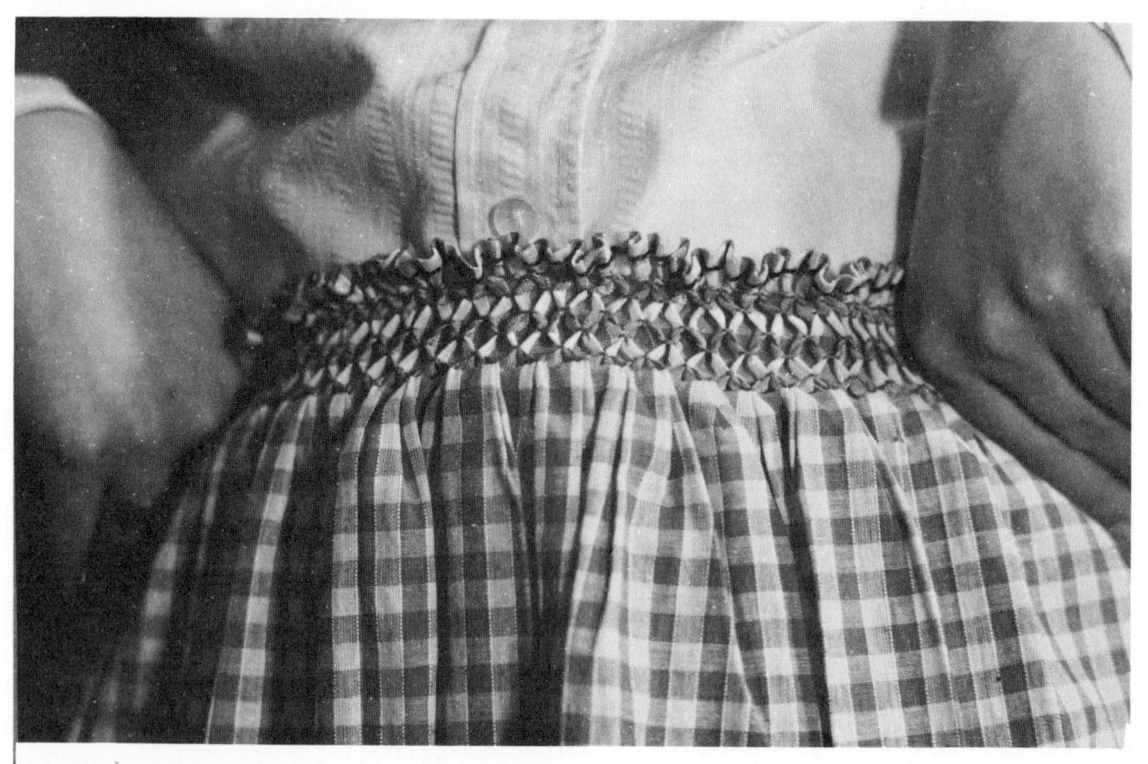

Fig. 198 Smocked apron.

SMOCKED APRON

Material required
22 × 36 in. (55 × 90 cm) $\frac{1}{4}$ in. (6 mm) checked gingham.

To make
1. Cut off a strip 2 × 36 in. (5 × 90 cm) for the ties.
2. Make a hem to equal the depth of one square along the one long edge. Hold in place with machine stitching or small running-stitches, with a contrasting colour of embroidery thread, threaded into the stitches. (This is the top of the apron.)
3. Make a hem to equal one and a half squares along the other long side and hold in place with machine-stitches, or decorative hem.

Preparation for smocking
1. Measure 3 in. (7·5 cm) from the side, and using a long length of cotton, put a knot on the end and also fasten on with a back-stitch. Pick up each alternate square, Fig. 199, and continue to within 3 in. (7·5 cm) of the end of the fabric. Do not fasten off, but leave end hanging.

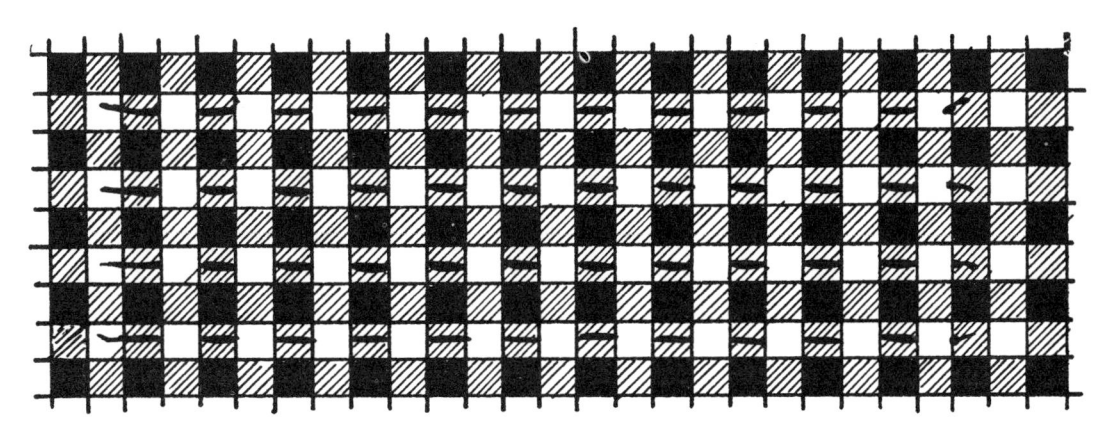

Fig 199

2. Put in several rows according to the depth of smocking required.
3. Draw up the threads so that the fabric is 1 in. (2·5 cm) less than the finished width of smocking. Tie the ends in twos, Fig. 200.

Fig 200

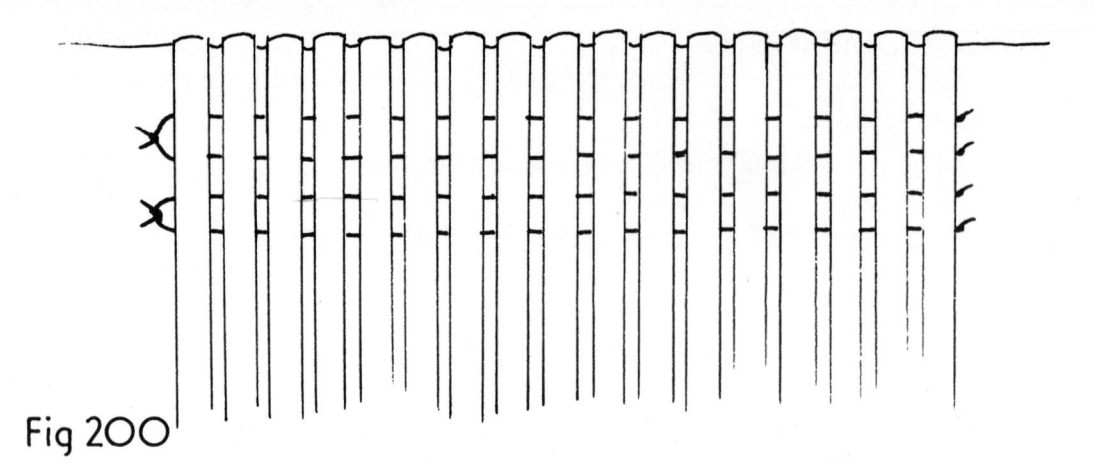

SMOCKING STITCHES

Always fasten on the embroidery thread securely on the wrong side.

Cable stitch (Fig. 201)

Work from the left to right. Pick up one pleat at a time and always keep the needle in the same straight line, with the thread alternately below and above the needle.

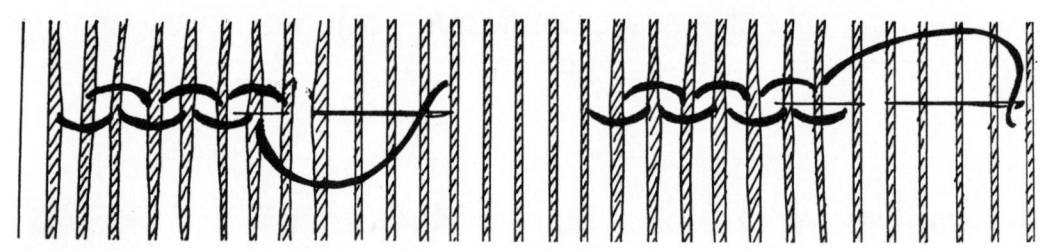

Fig 201

Vandyke stitch (Fig. 202)

Work from right to left. Commence by passing the needle through two pleats, Fig. 202(*a*), and repeat over the same pleats, Fig. 202(*b*).
Take one stitch through two pleats, Fig. 202(*c*) and repeat, Fig. 202(*d*).
Continue stitching the pleats together in twos to form vandykes.

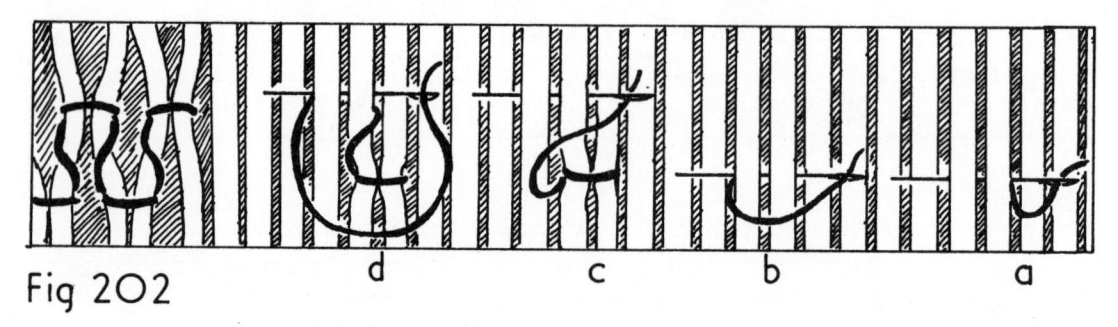

Fig 202

Several rows of stitches may be worked to form a pattern. When the required depth of smocking is complete, remove the threads used for the preparation.

A strip of cotton seam tape may be stitched along the top edge of the first row of smocking at the back of the apron, to prevent the smocking from stretching too much.

The ties – turn under a hem the depth of the squares and hold in place by either machine or decorative stitching. Do this to two long sides and one short. Attach the ties to the waist of apron.

PLAIN APRON
(Suitable for embroidery or printing)

There are many styles of aprons. Two examples are illustrated. Fig. 203 has a very large pocket, and Fig. 204 three deep pockets, and both of these aprons would be ideal for fabric-printed designs or tie-and-dye.

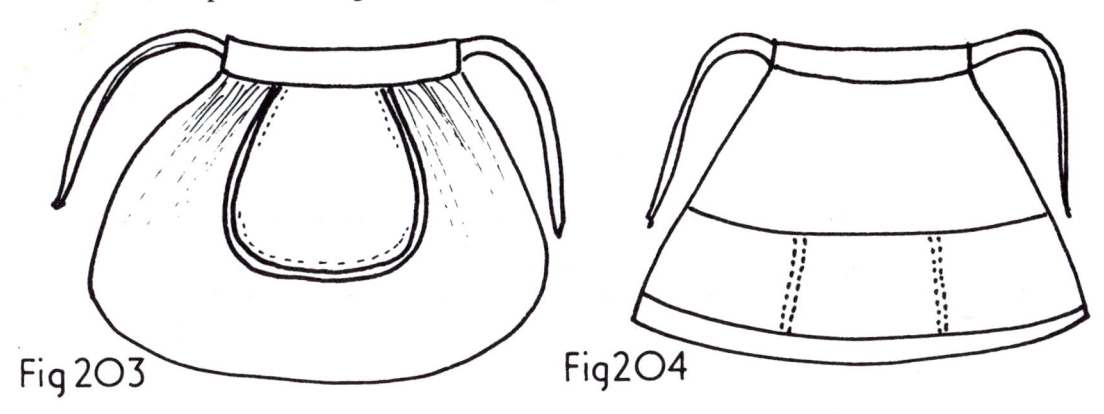

Fig 203   Fig 204

Material required
Piece of cotton fabric 36 × 36 in. (90 × 90 cm).

Cutting out
1. Cut off a length 24 × 36 in. (60 × 90 cm) for apron.
2. Cut two strips 3 × 18 in. (8 × 46 cm) for ties.
3. Cut a strip 4 × 18 in. (10 × 46 cm) for waistband.

To make
1. Neaten round two short sides and one long side by turning under a hem or attaching bias binding.
2. Gather the top edge by means of a row of running-stitch or large stitch on machine, and draw up ends until the apron measures 17 in. (42 cm).

3. Turn under ¼ in. (0·5 cm) turning on to wrong side of waistband, on two short sides and one long, Fig. 205.
4. Place right side of waistband to right side of apron, Fig. 206. Tack and machine.
5. Turn waistband half over on to back of apron and hem along lower edge, Fig. 207.

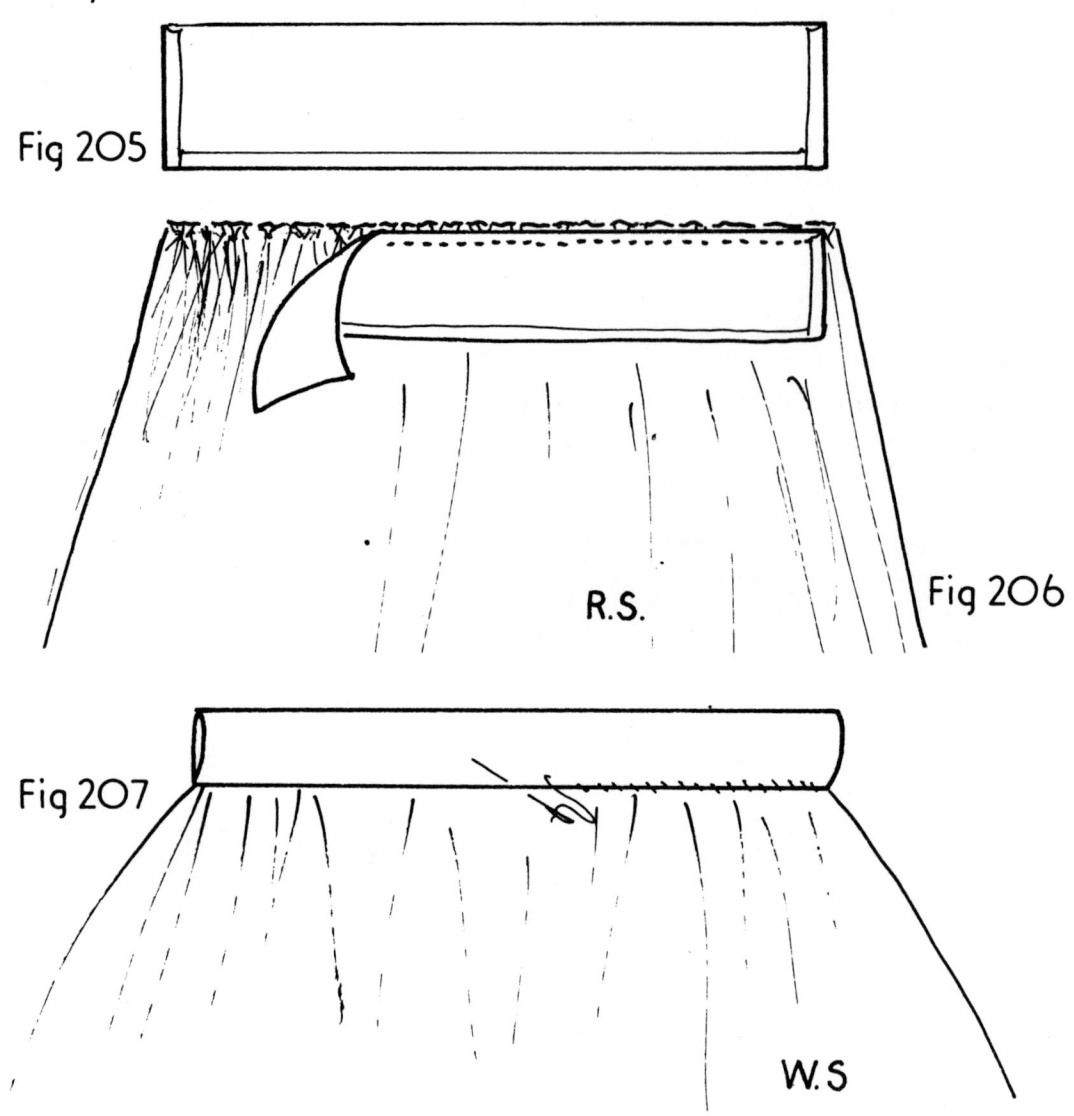

Fig 205

R.S.　　　　　Fig 206

Fig 207

W.S

6. Turn under the raw edge of the ties along two long sides and one short side, and machine.
7. Gather end of tie to fit inside waistband, Fig. 208, and machine.
8. A pocket could be made from the fabric left over. To do this, turn down a turning at top of pocket and machine, Fig. 209(a). Turn down again, and crease, Fig. 209(b). Make a turning all round the pocket, Fig. 209(c). Tack into position, and machine. Secure the corners firmly.

Fig 208

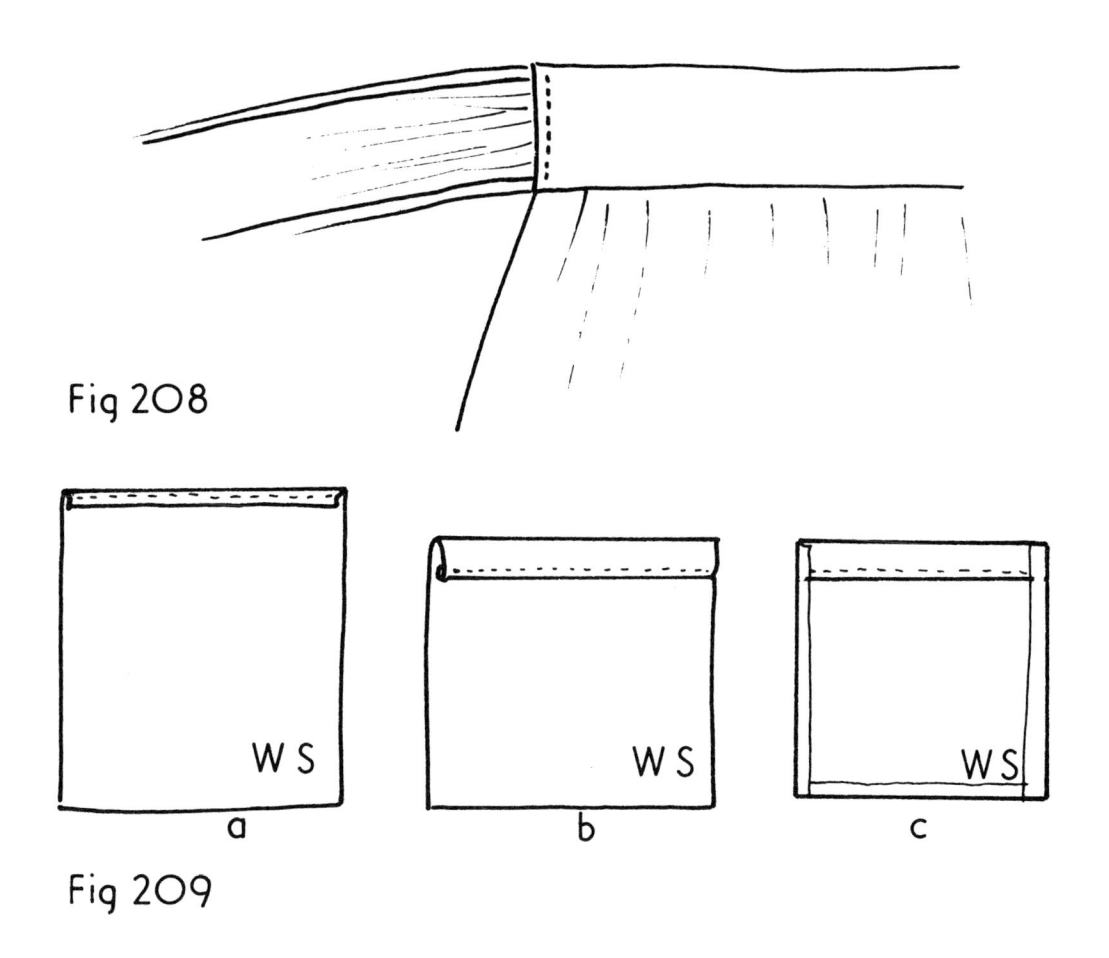

Fig 209

BEACH-BAG

Materials required

18 × 24½ in. (45 × 62 cm) towelling or sailcloth.
A circle 8½ in. (22 cm) diameter.
2 yards (2 metres) ¼ in. cord (0·5 cm) thick.

To make

1. Fold in half width ways and join down side, Fig. 210. Neaten raw edge with swing-needle machine, or oversewing.
2. Mark the four quarters of the circumference of circle, Fig. 211. Fold side of bag to mark each quarter section, Fig. 212.
3. Place the circle to the side of bag, matching the quarter marks. Tack and machine ½ in. (1 cm) from the edge, Fig. 213. Neaten raw edge.
4. Make a 2-in. (5-cm) hem on to the wrong side at top of bag and machine, Fig. 214. Make a second row of machining ½ in. (1 cm) from top edge.
5. Make two slits on right side in the hem, one at each side, and neaten.

6. Divide cord in half and thread a length through, and knot ends together. Thread the second length through the opposite way, and knot ends together. The bag may have a row of braid stitched 1 in. (3 cm) up from the base. It may also be decorated with appliqué or a printed design.

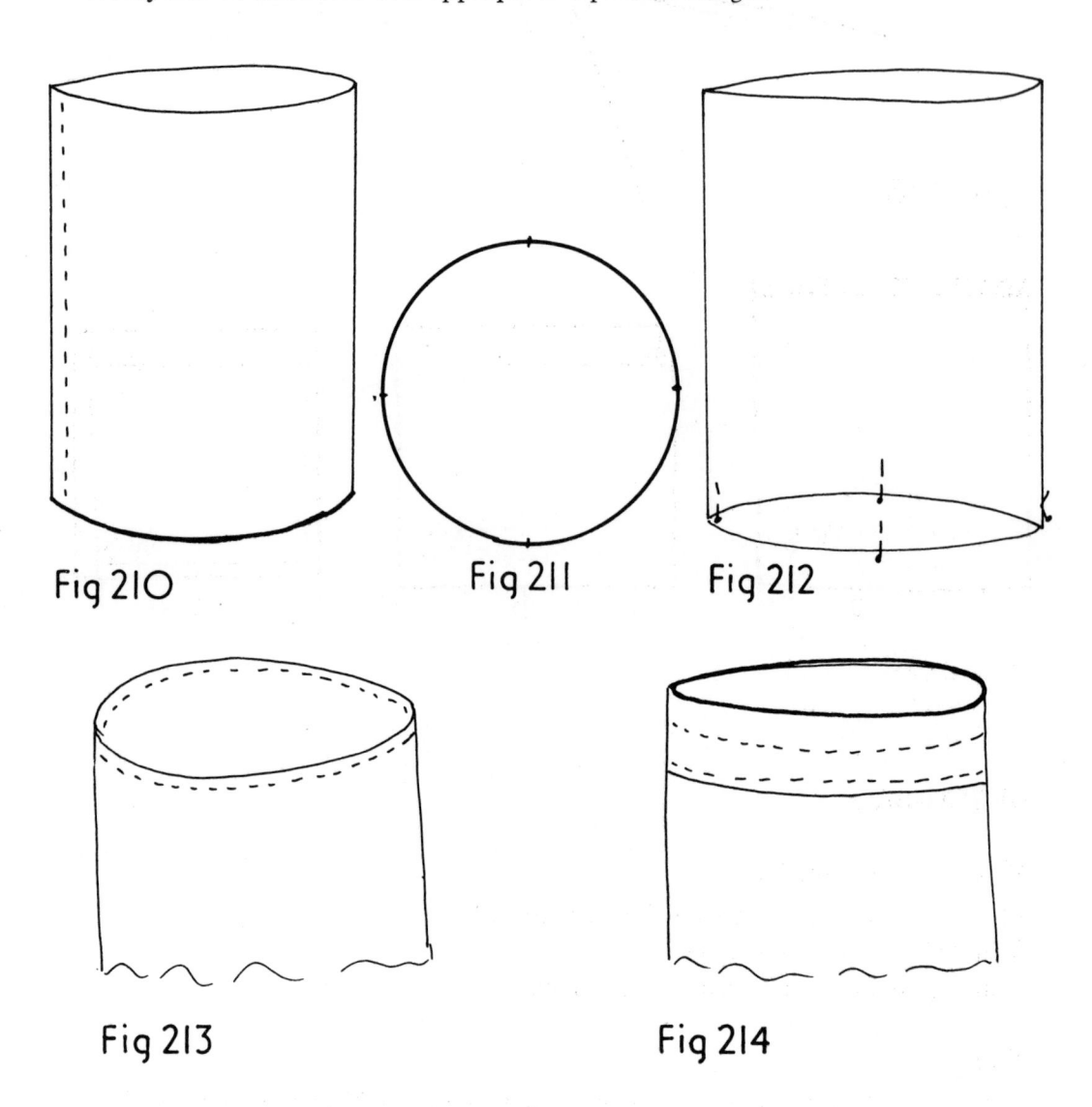

Fig 210   Fig 211   Fig 212

Fig 213   Fig 214

OVERBLOUSE (Fig. 215)

The pattern would fit a 32-in. (76-cm) bust measurement (turnings are allowed). Each square equals 1 in. (3 cm). Make pattern from Fig. 216.

Materials required

A piece of plain or printed cotton, 23 × 36 in. (57 × 90 cm).
50 in. (127 cm) of bias binding to match or in contrasting colour.

Fig 215

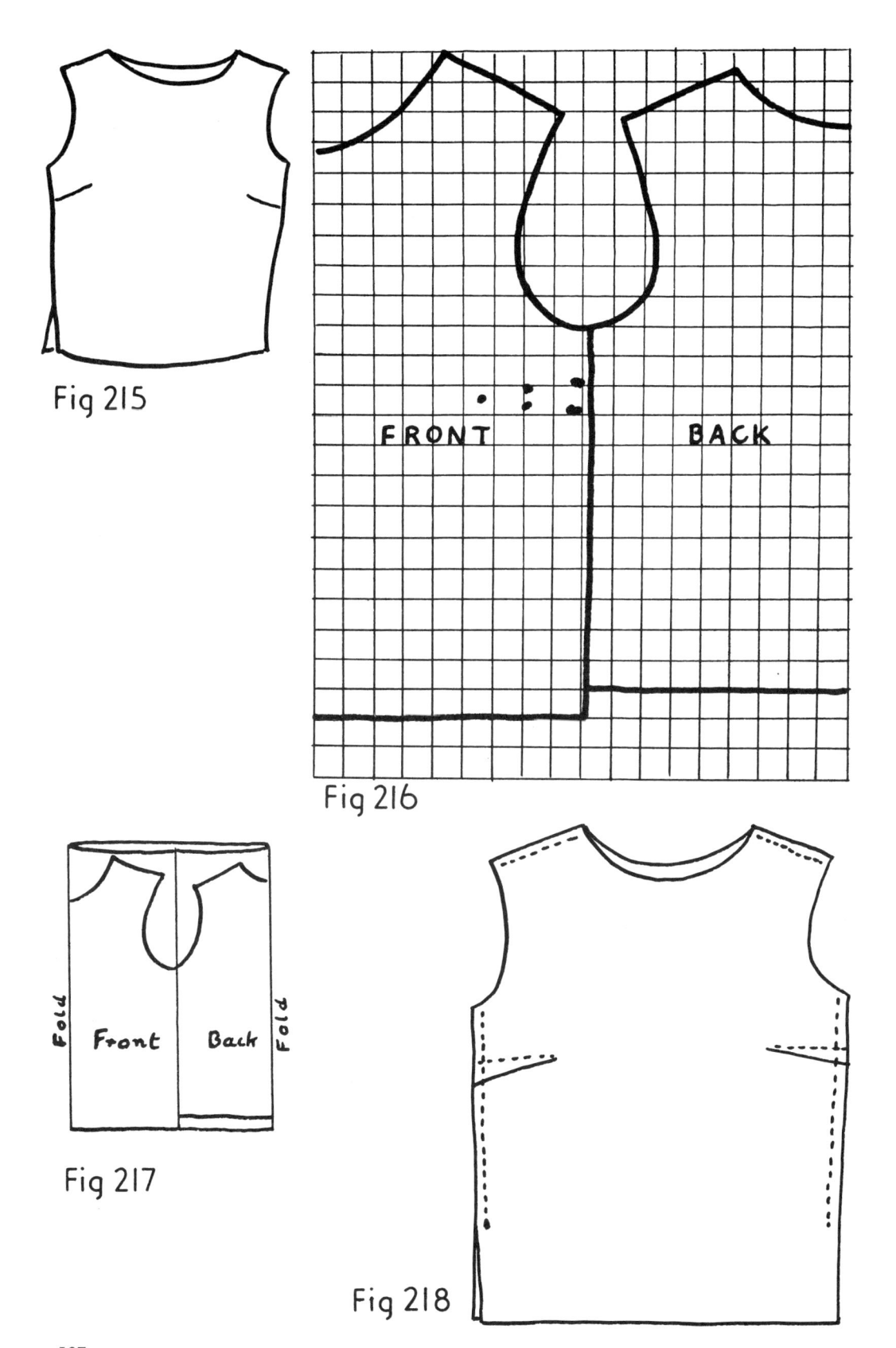

Fig 216

Fig 217

Fig 218

Fig 219 Fig 220 Fig 221

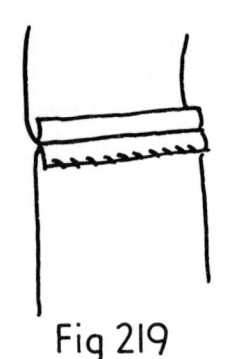

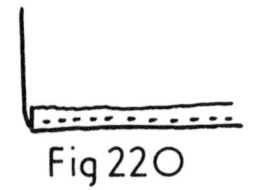

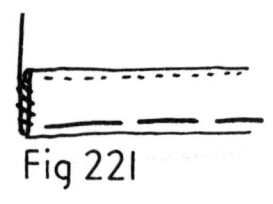

Cutting out

Refold the fabric so that the front of the pattern can be placed to a fold, also the back of the pattern, Fig. 217.
Pin carefully and cut out.

Making up

Mark the dart by marking through the rounded marks in the pattern. Fold each section of the bodice into two and stitch in the dart, keeping the right side of the fabric inside. Open out the back and front bodices and place together with right sides of fabric facing.
Join shoulder seam by machining $\frac{1}{2}$ in. (1 cm) from raw edge.
Do the same to the side seam but stop 5 in. (13 cm) from lower edge, Fig. 218.
Press seams open and oversew the raw edges singly, Fig. 219.
Turn up a single turning on lower edge of garment, Fig. 220 and machine. Turn up a $1\frac{1}{2}$-in. (4-cm) hem and tack, Fig. 221.
Neaten the armhole and neck with bias binding.

The slit openings on the sides of this overblouse should be secured at the end of the machine stitching of the seam. This will prevent the seam from splitting open.

A SLIP-OVER PINAFORE (Fig. 222)

This is an attractive design and quick to put on, because there is only a button and loop fastening at the back of neck.
The design may have a deep pocket at the front. The material may be plain or patterned, or even printed by making your own printed design.
Make pattern from Fig. 223; each square equals 1 in. (3 cm).

Materials required

A piece of firm cotton material 27 × 36 in. (69 × 90 cm).
A card of bias binding.

Cutting out

Place the front of the pattern to the fold of fabric, pin carefully and cut out.

Making up

Place one front and one back shoulder together and join with a french seam (see page 132).

Stitch bias binding (see page 132) all round the edge of pinafore and armholes. At the back neck, work a loop and stitch on a button on the opposite half of the garment, Fig. 224.

Pocket (see page 125)

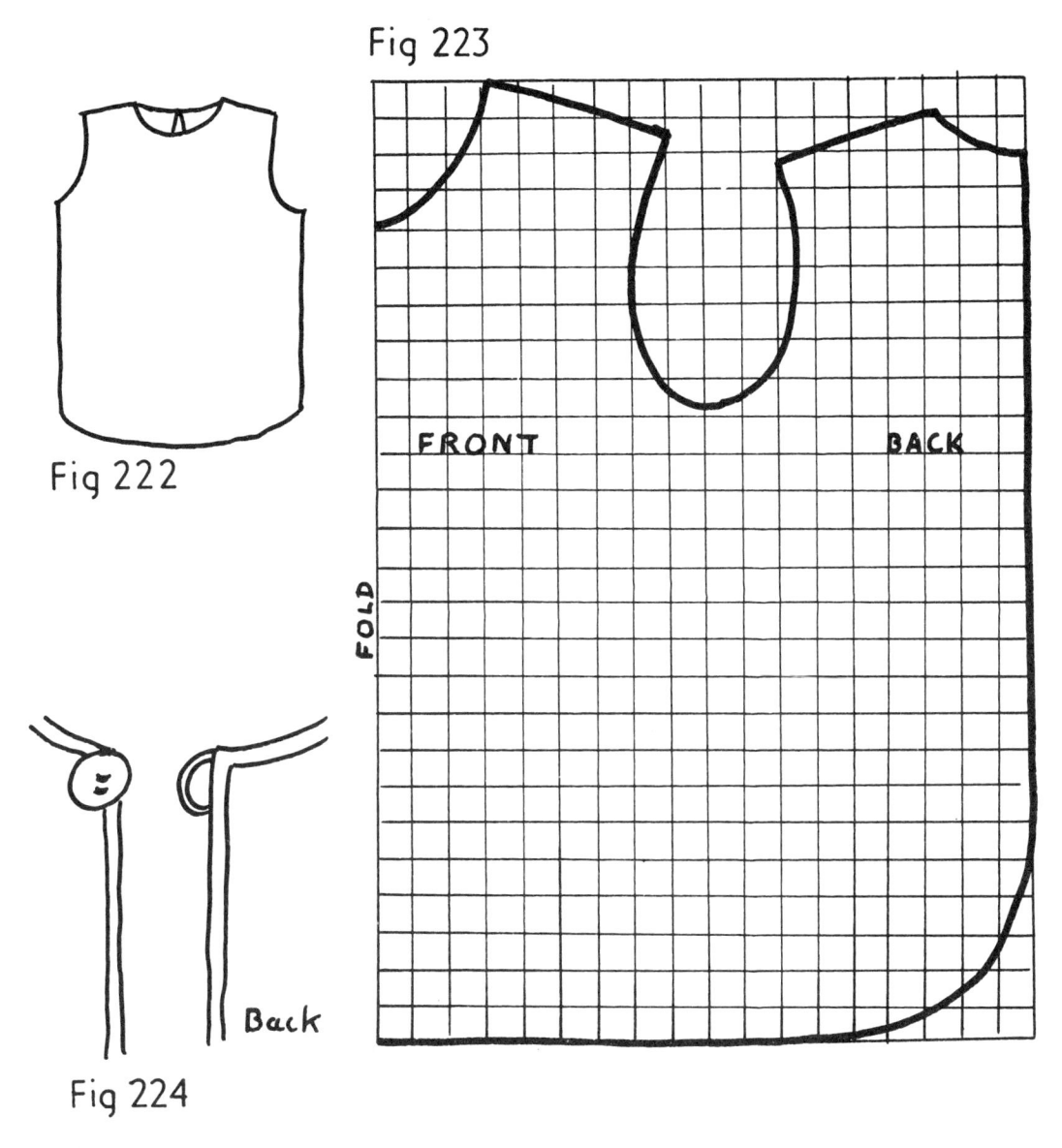

Fig 222

Fig 223

Fig 224

GENERAL INFORMATION ON STITCHES AND PROCESSES

This is only a brief section on some useful knowledge on stitches and processes which may be required to achieve some of the work described on earlier pages.

LONG-EYED EYE-STITCH, Fig. 159, page 99
This is worked with four long stitches and four short.

RUNNING-STITCH, BACK-STITCH
Fasten on by working a single back-stitch, then another stitch over the previous one.
Fasten off in the same way. Do all this on the wrong side of fabric.

RUNNING-STITCH
This is a stitch where the size of the stitch should be equal to the space left. It may be used to hold a hem in position if it is to be decorated with further stitchery, Fig. 225.

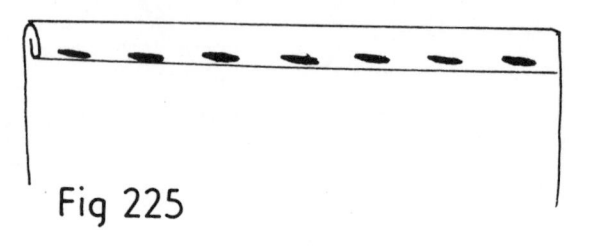

Fig 225

DECORATED RUNNING-STITCH
1. **Snails trail.** This is a contrasting coloured thread which is worked as in Fig. 226(*a*).
2. **Double threading.** Work one row as in Fig. 226(*b*) and a second row as Fig. 226(*c*).

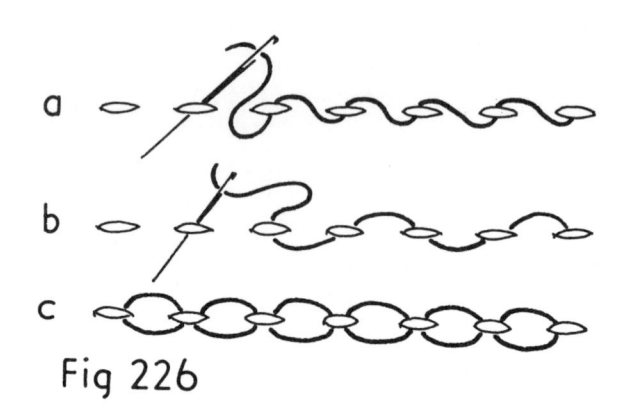

Fig 226

BACK-STITCH, Fig. 227
This is used to join two pieces of material together, instead of machine stitching.

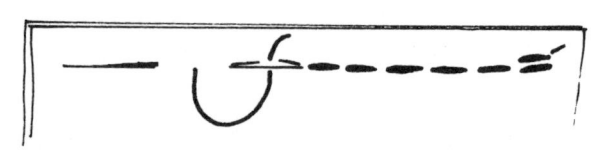

Fig 227

OVERSEWING, Fig. 228
This is used to prevent raw edges from fraying or to join two pieces of fabric together, which do not fray, i.e. felt.

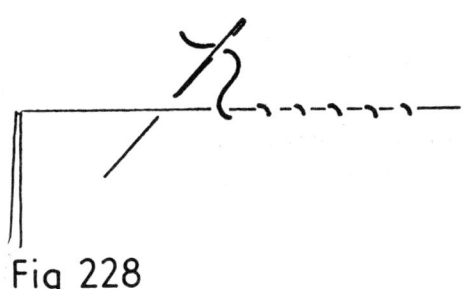

Fig 228

HEMMING, Fig. 229
This is used for holding hems, bindings, etc. in position.

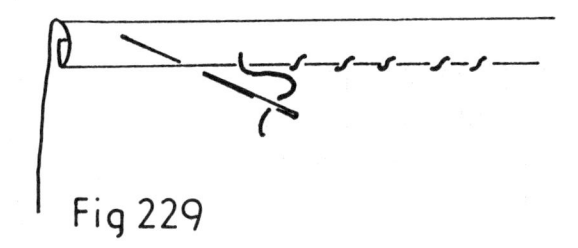

Fig 229

FLY-STITCH
Work, as Fig. 74, page 50.

LOOP-STITCH, Fig. 230
May be used for a decorative edge.

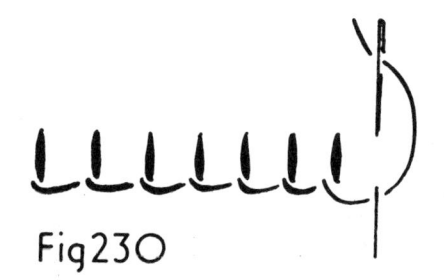

Fig 230

CHAIN-STITCH, Fig. 231
Worked in two stages and forms a continuous line. May be used for outline of embroidery, or stems.

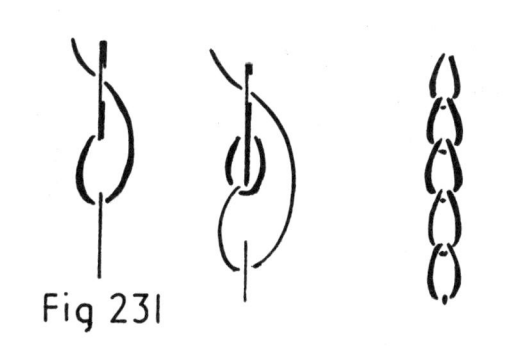

Fig 231

DETACHED CHAIN-STITCH, Fig. 232
Work as in Fig. 232(*a*) and then pass the needle to back of fabric, Fig. 232(*b*).

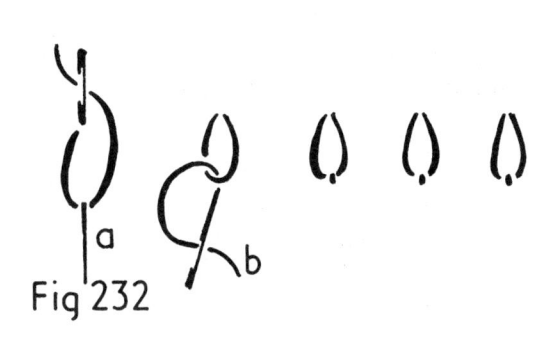

Fig 232

FLOWERS, Fig. 233
These may be worked as in Fig. 233(a) and (b). For the six petals six dots should be marked.

Fig 233

EYE-STITCH, Fig. 234
This stitch is usually worked on a fabric with an even weave. All stitches radiate from the centre.

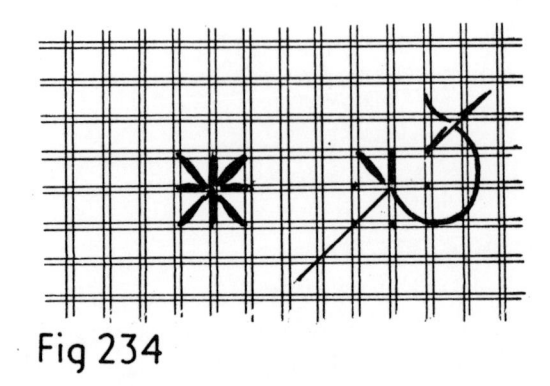

Fig 234

FRENCH SEAM
Place the two right sides of fabric together and machine or back-stitch ¼ in. (1 cm) from the raw edge. Trim turnings down and turn to wrong side. Machine ¼ in. (1 cm) from edge of fabric, Fig. 235.

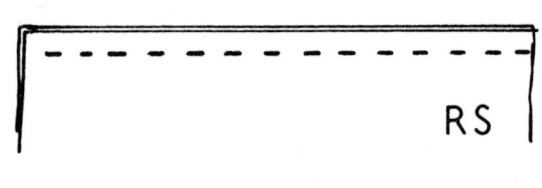

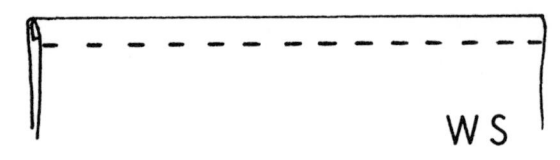

Fig 235

BIAS BINDING
Place the right side of binding (unfold one turning on bought binding) to the right side of fabric. Machine along the crease or back-stitch. Turn the binding over so that it shows equally on both sides, and hem into previous stitches, Fig. 236.

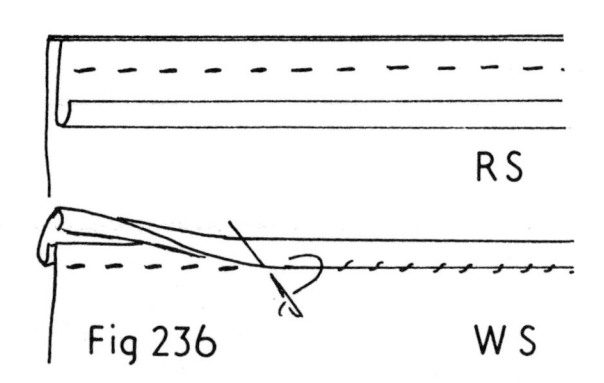

Fig 236

HEMMING

Turn under the raw edge and crease, and then turn over again to the depth required, usually about ¼ in. (1 cm) unless on a garment such as a skirt, when a deeper hem is used. This gives weight to the garment and it hangs better, Fig. 237.

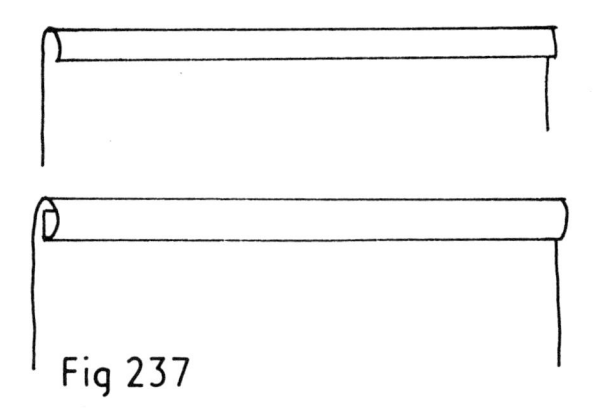

Fig 237

Books for reference

Embroidery Stitches, Barbara Snook (Batsford)
Primary Embroidery Stitches and Designs, A. V. White (Routledge & Kegan Paul)
Needlecraft for Juniors, A. V. White (Routledge & Kegan Paul)
New Manual of Sewing, A. V. White (E. J. Arnold)

Index

Apron, plain, 123; smocked, 120–1

Back stitch, 130
Beach bag, 125
Bias binding, 132
Binca canvas, working with, 45–54; hangings, 45; mat, 52–3; stitches, 46–7
Borders, 46–7
Buttons, covering with fabric, 15

Cat, tie-dyed, 70–4
Chain stitch, 131; detached, 131
Circle designs, 43–1; Curious Curvy Creature, 39–41; fish mobile, 34–5; toy fish, 36; Tudor rose pincushion, 36–7
Collage, Cute Little Miss, 19–23; flower panel, 12–13; texture and colour, 14, 24, 30; textured fish, 11–12
Cone figures, 7–9

Designs, circle, 34–41; triangle, 42–4; using maths for, 110–19
Dog, fabric-printed, 93–7

Embroidery, 98–109; Cute Jane, 105–9; Java canvas mat, 99; pencil man, 102–5; stitches, 46–7, 131–2; tissue-box cover, 100

Fabric, bonded and double jersey, 2; knitted, 2; woven, 1
Fabric printing, making blocks, 78–9; dog, 93–7; doll, 84–92; dyes, 79–80; puppet dress, 60
Fish collage, 11–12
Flat figures, 5–6
Flower collage plaque, 13

Gym-shoe bag, tie-dyed, 63–4

Hangings, Binca, 45–54
Hedgehog collage, 26–7
Hemming, 131

Insect collage, 27–30

Java canvas mat, 99; tissue-box cover, 100

Lion collage, 24–6

Matchstick figures, 6
Maths, flat, 110–19
Mobiles, 34–6
Motifs, 47–9

Needlecase, tie-dyed, 61–2

Over-blouse, 126–8
Oversewing, 131

Pencil man, embroidered, 102–4
Pincushion, tie-dyed, 60
Plaque, 18–19; how to cover with fabric, 110–11
Puppet, 60, 80–4

Reptile, tie-dyed, 74–7

Slip-over pinafore, 128–9
Smocking stitch, vandyke, 122; cable, 122
Snail, tie-dyed, 66–9
Stitches, back, 130; chain, 131; cross, 46; detached chain, 131; eye, 132; flower, 132; fly, 50; French seam, 132; long-eyed eye, 99; loop, 131; running, 130; vertical fly, 47; zigzag, 47

Three-dimensional patchwork, 31–3
Tie-and-dye, cat, 70–3; fish, 59; gym-shoe bag, 63–4; methods of tying, 56–7; needlecase, 61–2; pincushion, 60; puppet dress, 60; reptile, 74–7; snail, 66–8; using two dyes, 59
Triangle designs, 42–4

Yo-Yos, 15–18